THE DISABLED WILL

This book defends a comprehensive new vision of what addiction is and how people with addictions should be treated. The author argues that, in addition to physical and intellectual disabilities, there are volitional disabilities – disabilities of the will – and that addiction is best understood as a species of volitional disability.

This theory serves to illuminate long-standing philosophical and psychological perplexities about addiction and addictive motivation. It articulates a normative framework within which to understand prohibition, harm reduction, and other strategies that aim to address addiction. The argument of this book is that these should ultimately be evaluated in terms of reasonable accommodations for addicted people and that the priority of addiction policy should be the provision of such accommodations. What makes this book distinctive is that it understands addiction as a fundamentally political problem, an understanding that is suggested by standard legal approaches to addiction, but which has not received a sustained defense in the previous philosophical or psychological literature.

This text marks a significant advance in the theory of addiction, one which should reshape our understanding of addiction policy and its proper aims.

John T. Maier received his PhD in Philosophy from Princeton and his MSW from Simmons University. He is a psychotherapist in private practice in Cambridge, Massachusetts.

THE DISABLED WILL

A Theory of Addiction

John T. Maier

MAy 1, 2024

DEAR NEIL,

WHEN WE MET IN BUFFALO
YOU KINDLY GAVE ME A COPY
OF YOUR BOOK ON HARM, &
I WANTED TO RETURN THE FAVOR.
IT WAS GREAT TO MEET YOU, &
HOPE YOU ARE WELL,

John

Routledge
Taylor & Francis Group

NEW YORK AND LONDON

Designed cover image: ©Getty

First published 2024
by Routledge
605 Third Avenue, New York, NY 10158

and by Routledge
4 Park Square, Milton Park, Abingdon, Oxon, OX14 4RN

Routledge is an imprint of the Taylor & Francis Group, an informa business

© 2024 John T. Maier

ISBN: 978-1-032-53097-0 (hbk)
ISBN: 978-1-032-53096-3 (pbk)
ISBN: 978-1-003-41026-3 (ebk)

DOI: 10.4324/9781003410263

Typeset in Times New Roman
by MPS Limited, Dehradun

In memory of my parents

CONTENTS

ACKNOWLEDGMENTS

Earlier versions of this material have been presented to audiences at the University of California, Riverside; the Recovery Research Institute (Massachusetts General Hospital); the Philosophy and Psychiatry Talk Series (University of Granada); the Northern New England Philosophy Association; the Philosophical Bioethics Workshop (New York University); the Workshop on Mental Disorders and Modal Properties (Humboldt University); and the Romanell Center Bioethics Workshop (University at Buffalo). I would like to thank audiences at all those occasions for their insightful and useful comments.

Several people have been especially generous in providing discussion and written comments that have improved my understanding of these topics and have, I hope, made the book better than it would otherwise have been. I would especially like to thank Stephen Campbell, Jessica Flanigan, Robert Kelly, and T. Virgil Murthy. Kelly and Murthy have been consistently supportive of this project while pursuing their own work on addiction, and I encourage readers to consult each of their published and forthcoming publications.

Finally, over the years, I have had the privilege of learning about the experience of addiction from people whose names and stories are not for me to share. I would like to thank them all for their openness, honesty, and trust.

INTRODUCTION

This is a book about addiction. In the current cultural moment, we face a sizable catalog of books about addiction, from recovery memoirs to medical textbooks. It is reasonable to ask what purpose is served by adding one more title to this list.

The question is sharpened by reflecting on some of the current facts about addiction. In 2021, over 100,000 people died of drug-related overdoses in the United States, as compared to about 20,000 people per year only 20 years earlier (Spencer *et al.*, 2022). Considering this fivefold expansion of deaths by drug overdose, as well as the profound consequences of drug and alcohol use that are apparent in any American city, a book on addiction might be expected to somehow justify itself. How, exactly, does it speak to these dark facts?

This is not to say that there is no answer to be given to this kind of question. Books have played an outside role in our collective responses to addiction. One of the most prominent interventions for addiction in the last century, Alcoholics Anonymous, was in large part organized around the distribution and study of a single book, namely the very book, *Alcoholics Anonymous*, from which the movement took its name. But any book might be expected to, at least, give some kind of justification to its claim on our attention.

The account offered by this book is simple. I offer an account of what addiction is. This account is deeply rooted in the law and moral thought, but it is scarcely recognized in most contemporary discussions about addiction. Accordingly, most endeavors to address addiction in medicine and public policy labor under a misconception about the very nature of addiction itself.

DOI: 10.4324/9781003410263-1

It is no wonder that these efforts, despite best intentions, often go awry. For they do not even begin with a clear understanding of what addiction is.

What then is addiction? Addiction is a disability. I will go into some detail about how I understand the core idea of disability, but the basic idea is that we should think of addiction roughly as we think of blindness or deafness. These are distinctive aspects of some persons in our society, typically a minority of persons. These are not defects or features such that a person is worse off just in virtue of having them. Instead, they are simply different ways of being. So too is addiction, on the present view, a different way of being.

This is not to deny that people with addictions face profoundly bad outcomes, such as the epidemic of overdoses cited earlier. But, on the disability approach, these facts admit of a different kind of explanation. They are not products of addiction itself. Instead, they are products in large part of the discrimination and exploitation to which people with addictions are subject. Here too the case is analogous to that of other, more familiar, disabilities. To be blind is a disadvantage because society tends to discriminate in favor of those who are sighted and against those who are blind. Similarly, to be addicted is a disadvantage because society tends to discriminate in favor of the non-addicted and against those who are addicted. Disadvantage is on this view a product of discrimination, not of an inherent aspect of the person who is disabled.

The disability model gives us a way of thinking about addiction that is a genuine alternative to the often pathologizing models that have loomed large in medicine as well as in the popular imagination. Addiction is not a disease, let alone a chronic brain disease. It is not even a disorder, at least insofar as that term is normally understood. Addiction is not a response to an underlying mental health condition or trauma history, at least not necessarily so. Addiction is simply a different way of being – more specifically, I will argue, a different way of willing – that is, in itself, no worse than any other.

If this is correct, then the main focus of addiction policy should not be the treatment, or still less the 'cure,' of addiction. Rather, it should focus on removing the barriers and exploitative devices that are, on the present view, the true source of the harms associated with addiction. This is something that is already done by many public health approaches to addiction, but it extends, I will argue, well beyond the ken of public health. Properly reckoning with addiction requires us to rethink the very foundations of justice itself.

To return to the question with which we began, the aim of this book is therefore twofold. First, as I have already noted, this book offers an account of what addiction fundamentally is, an account that rejects the very presuppositions that guide many leading medical and political approaches to addiction. Second, just as importantly, this book does not only sketch a theory or analysis of addiction but rather it also proposes and defends quite practical and far-reaching interventions in our responses to addiction. While a book cannot ensure the implementation of these measures – that is something that must ultimately done through political means – this book aims to at least put them on the contemporary agenda, and to explain precisely why they should be there.

The view that addiction is a disability is scarcely discussed in the extensive philosophical and psychological literature on addiction. To my knowledge, my 2021 article on this topic is the first to explicitly state and defend the thesis that addiction is a disability.[1] The current book is the first book-length treatment of this topic. In this sense, the disability view may be regarded as a novel one. But in another sense, however, this is mistaken. The disability view is one that, even if not always formulated in these terms, has been with us for some time.

This is true, first of all, in the law. In the United States, alcohol addiction and (subject to certain conditions) drug addiction are protected disabilities under the Americans with Disabilities Act (ADA) and have been since its passage in 1990. In some sense, the boundaries of the ADA and its protections are still being litigated, but the disability view – relatively undiscussed in much of the literature on addiction – has been black-letter law in the United States for a long time. In this sense, the disability view articulated here is simply a statement of something that has been legally valid for decades.

This is true also more broadly in the practical work that is being done on behalf of people with addictions. This includes the work of attorneys pursuing the implications of the ADA, but it extends well beyond that. Consider the 'harm reduction' movement in addiction treatment. I will argue in what follows that this movement is best understood in terms of accommodation for a disability. In this sense, the disability view makes explicit the theoretical grounds for a practice that has already been implicit in the practice of public health.

Finally, the disability view of addiction depends on work that has already been done on behalf of people with disabilities more generally. The last several decades have seen a revolution in our understanding of disability, which has gone from being seen as an inherent affliction to being seen, instead, as a locus of discrimination and oppression. This change has been made in part by academic work, but even more so by concerted and focused activism on behalf of people with disabilities. What was once seen as an individual misfortune is now seen, instead, as a form of disadvantage that is in large part a product of social conditions. This book urges us to see addiction in the same way. But in this sense, the disability view of addiction rests on a foundation of work done on behalf of disabled people generally.

In all these ways, the disability view of addiction is less novel than it may seem. The precise formulation of this view and the arguments that I will give for it are, I think, distinctive, as are the implications that I draw from them. But the general idea that addiction is some kind of disability is something that has long been implicit in law and public health. In this sense, the arguments of this book simply formulate at the level of theory something that is already underway at the level of practice.

The disability view, then, is a certain kind of model or theory of addiction, and the aim of this book is to explain that view and to draw out its practical implications. This view is not altogether novel, as I have just explained, but it will nonetheless strike many readers as surprising, and I will therefore provide arguments to think that it is correct.

In this sense, the disability view is one more entrant to the dialectical contest between various theories of addiction, and one way of thinking of this book is as an articulation of why it should win that contest, of why the disability view is true and other views of addiction are false. And it is that, at least to some extent. But there is another way in which the disability view is not simply a theory of this kind. This is due to the demands of what I will call deference.

One of the lessons of the disability rights movement is that disability is, in part, an identity. Part of what it is for members of some class to count as disabled is for themselves to take themselves to be disabled, and to advocate for themselves in virtue of that identity. This is one way in which disability is a status that is chosen rather than imposed. Similar considerations extend to the disability that is addiction. Whether addiction is a disability will depend at least in part on the question of whether people with addictions identify, in the end, as disabled.

Different people with addictions will answer this question differently. But for the disability view to be plausible it must be the case at least that, on reflection, some critical mass of people with addictions would endorse the disability view. If the vast majority of people with addictions roundly rejected the view that addiction is a disability, even after due consideration of what exactly is implied by this claim, that would tell against the disability view. This is the way in which advocacy of the disability view must defer, in the end, to the attitudes of those whom it purports to describe.

Views of addiction generally do not subject themselves to this demand. If someone argues that addiction is a chronic brain disease, then it is not crucial that people with addictions themselves accept this view. It might be easier to implement the recommendations of this view if it wins assent among people with addictions, but their confidence in the view does not bear on its truth. Similarly for other views to be canvassed in what follows. There is extensive debate over whether addiction is a certain kind of disorder, or whether it is a certain kind of rational response to suboptimal circumstances. The attitudes of addicted people toward these views are sometimes considered, but seldom are they considered as evidence for or against these views themselves.[2]

Things are different with the disability view. To be plausible, it must be endorsed by some critical mass of people with addictions, on reflection. There is some imprecision in what counts as a critical mass here, and also in why counts as reflection. Arguably, the conditions for a clear and thoughtful evaluation of the disability view, by people with addictions themselves, have not yet been met. The view is scarcely made explicit in public discourse around addiction, at least outside of explicitly legal discussions. It would not be surprising if most people with addictions react with skepticism when first encountering the disability view, if only because the view has not been given an adequate defense.

Another purpose of this book, then, is to provide such a defense, to make the disability view available for reflection – most of all, for reflection by people with addictions themselves. If, at the end of that reflection, people with addictions hold that disability is not an identity that they are inclined to embrace, then I think we should be willing to abandon the disability view in light of that fact. But it is far from clear that this would be the outcome of sustained reflection on the view. And, in any case, the conditions for a reflective evaluation of the disability view have simply not yet been met, though this book aims to bring us closer to meeting them.

Considerations of deference also make my own experience with addiction relevant. By the lights of the views defended here, people with lived experience of addiction have a special kind of epistemic status with respect to the disability view, in the sense that we should defer in a certain way to the views of people with lived experience. It is a complicated question how my own experience should bear on the evaluation of my view. My preference is to let the view speak for itself, while also disclosing my own history to those who think it is relevant. For this reason, I will postpone discussion of my history to the Conclusion.

That then is the purpose of the book, which is to lay out a disability view of addiction and to draw out its implications for policy, while at the same time acknowledging that the truth of the disability view is beholden, ultimately, to addicted people themselves.

The first several chapters develop the basic framework for a disability view of addiction. Chapter 1 reviews and criticizes the leading theories of addiction. All these theories are united in their presupposition that addiction is a feature such that a person is worse off simply in virtue of having that feature, and that addiction is in this sense a defect. I argue that we should reject defect views of addiction, and instead defend a view on which addiction is not a defect, as the disability view will do.

There are many forms that a disability view of addiction might take. Chapters 2 and 3 outline the particular form that I will favor. Chapter 2 explains the constitutive connection between addiction and the will, and in particular the state of intention. Against those who propose understanding addiction in terms of desire and belief, I argue that a tripartite conception of the mind, of the kind developed by Michael Bratman, is necessary to capture the psychological aspect of addiction. In Chapter 3 I introduce the further idea that the will, like the body or the intellect, may itself be disabled, and explain what it means for someone to have a specifically volitional disability.

Chapter 4 states the specific form of disability view that I favor. Addiction is a volitional disability. This disability has two aspects. First, a certain pattern of forming and revising one's intentions and policies in an atypical way, what I refer to as volitional diversity. Second, a social pattern of discrimination and exploitation against people whose volition is in this respect atypical. Addiction then has psychological grounds but is ultimately a social phenomenon, one that is in part constructed through patterns of discrimination and exploitation.

The key questions posed by addiction on the disability view, then, are ultimately social and political ones. Accordingly, the last few chapters turn to these social and political questions. Chapter 5 considers the strategy of 'harm reduction,' which has proven a vital kind of intervention for people with addictions. I argue that the practice of harm reduction is endorsed by the disability view, but that the disability view gives a different understanding of its theoretical foundations. In particular, harm reduction is best understood as an accommodation for people with addictions.

Chapter 6 turns to the question of whether certain addictive substances can be legitimately banned by the state. I argue that the disability view gives us a new argument for an affirmative answer to this question. Certain kinds of addictive substances and technologies can be thought of as 'anti-accommodations,' and the state can prohibit their manufacture to protect the rights of addicted people. In this sense, harm reduction and prohibition, which are sometimes thought of as opposed policies, are symmetrical. One provides accommodations for addicted people, while the other restricts anti-accommodations for addicted people.

The political implications of the disability view run still deeper. As several authors have observed, the category of disability poses an important challenge to certain conceptions of justice, especially the classical liberal vision of distributive justice articulated by John Rawls. A similar point applies to the disability view of addiction. In Chapter 7, I address the question of how, given the disability view, we ought to understand addiction within the framework of distributive justice. I argue that thinking through this question leads us to a notion that has figured prominently in recent work on addiction, namely the idea of recovery capital. In particular, the goods of distributive justice, at least when it comes to the disability that is addiction, may be identified with recovery capital.

This book then falls, broadly, into two parts. The first articulates a certain view or vision of what addiction is, while the second thinks through the practical implications of this vision. As noted earlier, the validity of this view is ultimately not to be decided within the book itself. It depends on whether it is accepted by addicted people themselves, and what this book does is to put a certain vision of addiction forward for their consideration. Finally, as I have said, the Conclusion turns to the question of disclosure, and specifically to the question of how my own experience, or for that matter anyone's experience, bears on the disability view and its evaluation.

Notes

1 The article is by Maier (2021). There have been a number of discussions, most of all in the law, that understand addiction as a disability. An important earlier discussion in the philosophical literature is Wasserman (2004). But to my knowledge my article is the first to state and defend the disability view as a viable philosophical account of addiction, as a genuine rival to, for example, the disease view of addiction.
2 What empirical work there is on the views of addicted people toward theories of addiction suggests that these views are, at a minimum, both subtle and heterogeneous. See Newton *et al.* (2009) for one such study.

Works Cited

Maier, J.T. (2021). Addiction Is a Disability, and It Matters. *Neuroethics, 14*(3), 467–477.

Newton, T.F., De La Garza, R., Kalechstein, A.D., Tziortzis, D., & Jacobsen, C.A. (2009). Theories of Addiction: Methamphetamine Users' Explanations for Continuing Drug Use and Relapse. *American Journal on Addictions, 18*(4), 294–300.

Spencer, M., Miniño, A., & Warner, M. (2022). *Drug Overdose Deaths in the United States, 2001–2021.* Centers for Disease Control.

Wasserman, D. (2004). Addiction and Disability: Moral and Policy Issues. *Substance Use & Misuse, 39*(3), 461–488.

1

WHY ADDICTION IS NOT A DEFECT

1.1 The Disease Model of Addiction

What is addiction? The argument of this book will be that addiction is in the first place a disability, and that recognition of this point should fundamentally reshape our attitudes and policies toward addiction at both the individual and the social level. It will be helpful to begin by considering some other ways of answering our initial question.

The dominant answer to the question of what addiction is – within medicine, politics, and the broader culture – is that addiction is a disease. There are various accounts of what kind of disease addiction is. But, on the most widely held account, addiction is a disease with two aspects.[1] First, it is held specifically to be a disease of the brain. Second, it is held to be a chronic (as opposed to acute) disease. We thus arrive at the view that addiction is a chronic brain disease. Other established examples of chronic brain disease include Alzheimer's disease, Parkinson's disease, and multiple sclerosis. On the dominant model, that is the genus of which addiction is a species.

The chronic brain disease model purports to explain features of addiction that are otherwise perplexing. Those attending to addicted people – be they physicians or family members – are often baffled by the way in which the addicted person engages, again and again, in harmful and at times self-destructive behavior, despite her vows and apparent resolution not to do so.[2] Why does the addicted person behave like this? The chronic brain disease model has an answer. The addicted person is driven to behave in this way because she has a chronic brain disease that compels her to act

DOI: 10.4324/9781003410263-2

as she does. Just as a person with Alzheimer's disease can fail cognitive tasks that once seemed effortless, so does a person with an addiction fail to abstain from use despite her best efforts. It is the disease, rather than the individual, that is calling the shots.

The disease model thus explains behaviors that otherwise can seem inexplicable. It also promises a more humane approach to addiction treatment and policy. There is a history of regarding addiction as a moral failing and treating addiction along with the behavior resulting from it within the criminal justice system. To the advocate of the disease model, this approach seems perverse. We would not hold individuals with brain diseases criminally responsible for their symptoms. Neither should we hold individuals with addiction criminally responsible for their use, which is itself a kind of symptom.

The disease model suggests an alternative home for addressing addiction. Instead of the criminal justice system, addiction should be addressed within the medical system – hospitals, detoxification facilities, and outpatient clinics. Instead of being managed by judges and the police, people with addictions should be treated by psychologists, social workers, and most of all physicians. After all, physicians are the final authorities on disease, and just as we would expect an individual with Parkinson's disease to be treated by a physician, so should we expect a person with an addiction to be treated in the same way.

The disease model therefore promised, and to some degree delivered, a conceptual revolution in our understanding of addiction. Behavior that seemed unintelligible was rendered easily explicable, and a treatment regimen focused on criminal responsibility was shifted toward one more focused on medical interventions. It has been foundational for many contemporary approaches to addiction.

For all of this, we can ask a couple of questions about the disease model of addiction. First, is it true? Second, whether it is literally true, is it a useful or fruitful way of understanding addiction – a sort of 'useful fiction' in addiction treatment? I will argue that the answer to both questions is quite clearly negative. Addiction is not a disease, and the fiction that it is a disease has had unfortunate effects on our understanding of addiction and the lives of people with addictions.

1.2 Addiction and the Brain

The disease model of addiction, on its standard development, has three aspects: it holds that addiction is a disease, that it is chronic, and that it is a disease specifically of the brain. Each of these three claims is subject to serious doubt.

Begin with the last of these, the idea that addiction is a disease of the brain. First, if taken literally, this claim is immediately suspect. When compared with paradigm diseases of the brain, such as Alzheimer's disease and Parkinson's disease, addiction does not appear to afflict the brain in the same direct way. It is not itself associated with profound cognitive or motor impairment.[3] Addicted people do not in general demonstrate deficits in neuropsychological functioning.[4] The idea that the brain of an addicted person is diseased, if taken literally, is inconsistent with these simple facts.

Furthermore, addiction appears to be profoundly sensitive to the environment in a way that paradigmatic brain diseases typically are not. Several famous experiments illustrate this fact. Experiments carried out by Bruce Alexander and colleagues consider the propensity of rats to self-administer morphine in an addictive way.[5] They find that this is much less likely when the rats are placed in a hospitable environment with lots of opportunities for play and mating (a 'rat park') than it is in the restricted cages where animal experimentation is usually carried out. This suggests, plausibly, that morphine addiction may be sensitive to the environment in which the morphine use takes place. Another well-known case suggests that American servicemen in Vietnam became addicted to heroin at high rates, but that addiction rates plummeted upon return to the United States (Robins, 1993). These results too suggest that addiction lies not simply in the brain of the addicted individual, but in the environment in which that individual finds herself.

Considerations like these have led some to retain the spirit of the disease model while relaxing the requirement that addiction be a disease specifically of the brain. Thus the official definition of the American Society for Addiction Medicine (ASAM) holds (Herron & Brennan, 2019):

Addiction is a treatable, chronic medical disease involving complex interactions among brain circuits, genetics, the environment, and an individual's life experiences.

This definition preserves the not implausible idea that the brain and its mechanisms are somehow embroiled in addiction, without requiring that addiction literally be a brain disease.

Nonetheless, the ASAM account still takes it to be true and indeed definitional of addiction that it be a disease, and specifically that it be a chronic disease. Let us next consider this claim.

1.3 Is Addiction Chronic?

Medicine divides conditions into those that are acute and those that are chronic. Acute conditions develop relatively quickly and last a relatively short time – typically no more than a few weeks. Addiction is not an acute condition, since it is generally gradual in its onset and persists for a long period. If we understand addiction as a medical condition, it is natural to think that, since addiction is not an acute condition, it must be a chronic one.

Is addiction chronic? In popular portrayals, it is often taken to be. Addiction is held to be a lifelong condition that can be reversed, if it can be reversed at all, by a dramatic medical or spiritual intervention. Left to her own devices, the addicted person will, at best, remain unchanged and, more likely, get gradually worse. This is just what we would expect from a chronic condition.

This is a compelling narrative. But it is not borne out by epidemiological data. As Gene Heyman (Heyman, 2009) and others have pointed out, this data does not support a story of the kind of stasis or decline that are typically involved in chronic conditions. On the contrary, most people who meet the criteria for addiction early in life do not meet the criteria later in life. This is not only, and not primarily, because these individuals accept medical treatment or voluntary abstinence. Instead, many reduce their use under the influences of financial pressures, or family and work responsibilities. In short, many people 'age out' of addiction.[6]

The dynamics of addiction over the lifespan are immensely complicated, and we will have reason to revisit them in what follows. And the dynamics of chronic conditions are themselves complicated. The point here, however, is simple: we see, in the data, widespread recovery from addiction that is spontaneous in the sense that it takes place without any medical or psychosocial intervention. Spontaneous recovery of this kind is simply not a known phenomenon for chronic diseases. If addiction is a chronic disease, it behaves fundamentally differently from any other one that we know.

At this point we are led to revisit the very foundations of the account that we have been giving. We have argued that addiction is not a brain disease. I have now argued, following Heyman, that it is not a chronic disease either. Nor, for that matter, is it plausibly an acute disease. If addiction is a disease, then it is radically unlike the paradigms provided by the advocates of the disease model, and indeed unlike any other disease we know. So why think that addiction is a disease at all?

1.4 Disease, Compulsion, and Choice

Once we have become skeptical of the idea that addiction is a brain disease, and of the idea that addiction is a chronic disease, we naturally become skeptical of the idea that it is a disease at all. What motivated this idea in the first place?

In early discussions of the disease model, the supposedly compulsive nature of addiction assumes a large role. Alan Leshner, a major proponent of the disease model, claims that 'compulsive drug seeking and use' is what characterizes the disease of addiction (Leshner, 1997, p. 46). As we noted at the outset, this claim is central to the purported explanatory power of the disease model. If addicted people are subject to a disease that leads them to act compulsively, then their sometimes perplexing behaviors and choices become explicable as compulsions caused by an underlying disease.

To consider this claim, it is helpful to ask what compulsion is. In philosophical discussions, an act is taken to be compulsive just in case the agent had no option but to perform the act. If I compulsively turned on the light, then I had no option but to turn off the light. If we take this literally, this requirement is seldom, if ever met. A person will typically have some option of doing otherwise. We can understand compulsion in a somewhat more relaxed way, however. On this understanding, an act is compulsive just in case the agent has a powerful impulse to perform the act, and it would have required a powerful incentive to lead the agent to act otherwise.

Is addictive behavior compulsive even in this more relaxed sense? Certainly, the idea that it is looms large in the popular representation of addiction. But, again, the empirical evidence tells a different story. Consider work on contingency management.[7] This is a method of addiction intervention whereby a person with an addiction is offered a certain amount of money (or cash equivalent, such as a gift card) to refrain from using her substance of choice. Contingency management turns out to be highly effective, with surprisingly small incentives. One study, for example, showed significant reductions in cocaine use for small cash prizes, averaging well under $100 per person over the course of the study (Petry et al., 2004).

Such studies suggest that addictive behavior is not compulsive in even the relaxed sense defined earlier. People with addictions can refrain from use in response to relatively small cash incentives. Nor is this simply a laboratory finding. The individual-level findings from work on contingency management dovetail precisely with the population-level findings adduced earlier. At the population level, we find that individuals 'age out' of addiction in response to the distinctive incentives posed by adult life. At the individual level, as just noted, we find that individuals are quite willing and able to refrain from use in exchange for simple financial incentives. Both findings converge on the thought that addictive behavior is not, contrary to both medical and popular understanding, compulsive behavior.

Where does this leave the disease model? We have rejected two pillars of the standard disease model: the idea that addiction is a brain disease and the idea that addiction is a chronic disease. We have now rejected a third: that the disease of addiction manifests primarily as a compulsion to use the substance to which one is addicted. Furthermore, our consideration of this last point has led us to recognize that addictive behavior is variable and sensitive to reasons, including quite small monetary incentives. This suggests that what we are witnessing in addiction is not the symptoms of a disease at all, but rather rational and self-directed behavior.[8]

We are led at this point to take seriously the idea that, first, the chronic brain disease model of addiction is untrue to the empirical facts about addiction and, second, the very idea that addiction is a disease rests on a shaky philosophical foundation. These observations make it plausible to conclude that addiction is not a disease at all.

1.5 A Useful Model?

It is sometimes said that all models are false, but some are useful. That is to say that models involve a degree of idealization away from reality (in virtue of which they are false), but that same idealization may make some of them useful for the purposes of prediction and explanation. At this point, an advocate of the disease model might acknowledge that addiction is not literally a disease (like Alzheimer's disease, diabetes, or measles). Nonetheless, an advocate might claim, the disease model has been, and will remain, a useful model of addiction.

To begin, I want to acknowledge that there is at least one sense in which the addiction model, whatever its claim to truth, has had profoundly beneficial effects. The disease model has been the theoretical framework for many research programs and specific interventions in addiction treatment, and these programs and interventions have in turn led to significant improvements in well-being – and in many cases, saved lives – for many individuals. If we are to judge a model by its fruits, then these benefits of the disease model deserve to be noted.

What is more, the disease model has been adopted by many addicted people themselves. The idea that addiction is a kind of disease is foundational to many recovery programs and has been internalized as a useful framework for many individuals attempting to comprehend and manage their addictions. This is another sense in which the disease model has been a profoundly beneficial one.

I do not want to deny these practical benefits of the disease model. I do want to deny that they tell in favor of the disease model being useful in the relevant sense. While they do show that there have been some practical benefits in believing and propounding the disease model, they do not show that the disease model is useful for explaining addiction.

Further, I want to argue that it is doubtful that the disease model is in fact useful for these purposes. The disease model does not simply idealize away from some details about addiction. Rather, it adopts a basic orientation toward addiction – what I will call the defect model – that is misguided in its most basic assumptions. The disease model is an instance of a more general kind of explanation of addiction, namely the defect model, and the defect model is fundamentally flawed. This is why the disease model is not merely false in its details, but false in its basic framework, and hence not a useful model of addiction at all.

Indeed, once we recognize the theoretical limitations of the disease model, we can see that its practical benefits are limited as well. While the disease model has had some salutary effects, it has also given us a pathologizing and in certain ways stigmatizing narrative about addiction and elevated that narrative to the status of an orthodoxy. So, in addition to being false, the disease model has been in many ways actively harmful, most of all to addicted people themselves.

1.6 Condition or Behavior?

If we reject the disease model, how do we move beyond it? One way is by reconceiving the locus of addiction. On the disease model, addiction is an underlying condition, which explains the behavior of the addicted person. In contemporary work, many have proposed instead that addiction should be identified with the behavior itself. This provides an alternative conception of addiction: instead of conceiving of it as an underlying condition, like a disease, we should instead understand it as a certain pattern of behavior.

In recent decades, there have been several attempts to do this. Many of them drop talk of addiction altogether. Some authors, for example, have redescribed addiction as 'substance abuse' – this term figured in many institutional contexts.[9] Still, others have found the language of 'abuse' pathologizing, and have preferred to describe it with the milder epithet of 'substance misuse.'

A distinct approach – linguistically distinct, though in many ways philosophically similar – has held that addiction is not a disease but a disorder, with the nature of the disorder left to be specified. This approach is arguably the dominant one in psychiatry today, insofar as it constitutes the framework of the Diagnostic and Statistical Manual of Mental Disorders (DSM-5), the standard diagnostic manual for mental health conditions (APA, 2013). In the DSM-5, the familiar category of addiction is replaced with a family of disorders: Alcohol Use Disorder, Cannabis Use Disorder, Gambling Disorder, and so forth.

These approaches take great care to soften the more medicalized language of the disease model and replace it with non-judgmental and person-centered language. They also make, relatedly, a kind of metaphysical shift in their perspective on addiction. Rather than classifying addiction in terms of a condition that results in certain behaviors, they classify addiction primarily in terms of the behavior itself.

These behavior-oriented accounts of addiction do constitute a genuine shift away from the disease model. Nonetheless, they share with it a core idea: the idea that addiction is, as I will put it, a defect. I will argue that whatever their other advantages, accounts that focus on abuse, misuse, or disorder do not advance beyond the limitations of the disease model. They share with the disease model the core idea that addiction is, fundamentally, a defect.

1.7 Addiction as a Defect

What is a defect? In the simplest case, it is a feature of a person such that she is worse off just in virtue of having that feature. Diseases are paradigms of this kind of defect. To have a disease such as measles will almost always be to have a defect. If I contract measles, I am worse off just in virtue of having measles. This is why we treat measles when we reasonably can and adopt vaccinations to prevent the onset of measles in the first place.

When we turn from the disease model to the more behavior-focused understanding of addition described earlier, this characterization of defects needs to be extended somewhat. Nonetheless, it can be naturally extended as follows: a defect is a feature of a person, or a habitual behavior of a person, in virtue of which she is worse off just in virtue of having that feature, or just in virtue of habitually behaving in that way.

Note the restriction that the feature or behavior must make the person worse off 'just in virtue' of that feature or behavior. What does this restriction say, and why do we impose it? To answer the first question, this restriction says that the feature or behavior should make the person worse off all on its own, and it should not depend on the environment. At first approximation, a defect is a feature or behavior that makes a person worse off in any environment whatsoever.

Consider then the second question. Why do we impose this restriction on our account of defects? Consider a feature such as being relatively short (relative to some contextually determined standard). This is not a defect. Nonetheless, in areas where the built environment is designed for people of a certain height, being shorter than that height will make one slightly worse off, since it will take additional effort to navigate the built environment. There is a harm here, but it is not a product of being short in itself, but rather of an environment that is constructed in a certain way. Or consider a behavior such as riding a bicycle. We would not take this to be a defect either. Nonetheless, in areas where the built environment is actively hostile to cyclists, riding a bicycle will often be associated with an elevated risk of injury and death. We nonetheless do not consider riding a bicycle a defect. The harm involved in riding a bicycle lies ultimately in the environment rather than in the act itself.

This consideration is, as it turns out, of fundamental importance to the account that follows. For I will shortly argue that addiction is not a defect but, in virtue of discriminatory and exploitative social and environmental circumstances, it does in fact tend to make a person worse off.

Let us review. We have considered, and rejected, the disease model of addiction. Many contemporary approaches to addiction dispense with the letter of the disease model and focus instead on the addicted person's 'abuse,' 'misuse,' or 'disorder.' Such views are sometimes presented as alternatives to the disease model. On the present view, however, these views are variations on the same theme. The theme is that addiction is fundamentally a defect. The disease model holds that addiction is a relatively simple defect, like measles. The alternative approaches just canvassed hold that it is a somewhat more sophisticated form of behavioral defect. But it is a defect all the same.

Reflection on this larger family of approaches raises some fundamental questions. Consider the very starting point of these approaches: is addiction, in fact, a defect? How would we decide that question? And what would an alternative to the defect model even be?

1.8 On Difference and Defect

To claim that an aspect of a person or her behavior is defective is to make two claims. First, she is in a certain respect distinctive or different. Second, she is worse off just in virtue of this difference. It will be helpful to begin by distinguishing these cases.

Is the addicted person different? In some sense, the answer to this question must be affirmative. We do in fact have the language and concept of addiction, and in some sense, we can distinguish people who are addicted from people who are not. This distinction may well be a vague one, but it is a distinction, nonetheless. In this minimal sense, we can grant, an addicted person is different from a person who is not addicted.

Once we think more sharply about this question, however, its answer becomes somewhat less obvious. There are at least two ways in which the addicted person might differ from the non-addicted person. Earlier, we distinguished between views that locate the defect in addiction in the person herself, such as the disease model, and those that locate the defect in her behavior. We can draw this same distinction again in the case of difference. One view is that the behavior of the addicted person and the non-addicted person is different, and another view is that there is some more basic and non-behavioral difference between these two of people.

What is relatively uncontroversial is that the addicted person differs from the non-addicted person in her behavior. To be addicted is to use a certain substance or engage in certain activity in certain ways (or at least to have done so in the past), and this is the sense in which the addicted person is different from the non-addicted person, almost by the very definition of that term.

What is controversial is whether the addicted person differs from the non-addicted person non-behaviorally or, we might say, constitutionally. On some views, there is a constitutional difference between an addicted person and a non-addicted person. The disease model is one such view: it holds that the addicted person differs from the non-addicted person in a basic respect, namely that the addicted person has a disease while the non-addicted person does not. It is not, however, the only such view: one class of people might differ constitutionally from another class of people in all kinds of ways, of which having a disease is only one.

Alternatively, one might hold that there is no interesting constitutional difference between addicted people and non-addicted people. An advocate of this view will acknowledge that there is a behavioral difference between addicted people and non-addicted people – that much, as we have said, seems to follow from the very concept of addiction. But she will insist that there is no constitutional difference between addicted people and non-addicted people. What it is to be addicted, on such a view, is simply to behave addictively.

One way of holding such a view is by adopting a view of the kind canvassed earlier, on which addiction is a disordered form of behavior, and claiming that this disorder is not grounded in any constitutional difference between the addicted person and the non-addictive person. But, again, this is not the only form such a view could take. One might also hold that there is a behavioral difference between the addicted person and the non-addicted person but deny that this difference is a defect. That is to say, one might deny that it is a behavior that makes the addicted person worse off, by any reasonable standard, just in virtue of the behavior itself.

The distinction between defect and difference opens several possibilities in the theory of addiction, only some of which have been developed. Let us step back and consider the possible views of addiction that one could now take.

1.9 A Taxonomy of Views

We have now raised a couple of fundamental questions about addiction that in turn induce a taxonomy of possible views about addiction.

First: is the difference between the addicted person and the non-addicted person simply a difference in their behavior, or is there a further constitutional difference between the two that explains the differences in their behavior?

Second: is the difference between the addicted person and the non-addicted person (be it constitutional or simply behavioral) a defect, in the sense that the addicted person is worse off just in virtue of this difference?

Different answers to these questions yield four possible views of addiction, only two of which we have canvassed thus far.

One view holds that addiction involves a constitutional difference between the addicted person and the non-addicted person and that this difference is a defect or worse-making feature. The disease model of addiction is one clear and prominent instance of such a view.

Another view holds that addiction does not involve a constitutional difference between the addicted person and the non-addicted person and that the difference between the addicted and the non-addicted person is primarily behavioral. It agrees, however, that this difference is a defect, such that the addicted person is worse off just in virtue of her behavior. This is one natural interpretation of the 'misuse' or 'disordered use' views that are standard in many areas of contemporary clinical practice.

These two kinds of views are both defect views. But our distinction between difference and defect introduces two other possible kinds of views, which deserve consideration.

The most minimal view of addiction holds that there is no constitutional difference between the addicted person and the non-addicted person and that the behavioral difference between the two is not a fundamental difference in kind. Addiction is just a distinctive, but not inherently worse, mode of behavior, and it is not grounded in any real difference between the addicted and the non-addicted person. This broadly deflationary view of addiction has been endorsed by several authors who have held that addiction is everything from a rational response to circumstances to a distinctive kind of lifestyle choice.

Finally, another view holds that there is a constitutional difference between the addicted person and the non-addicted person that grounds the behavioral difference between the two but denies that it is a defect or worse-making feature. The difference between the addicted and the non-addicted person is a real but non-evaluative difference between the two. It is a difference, but no more than a difference. This view has generally not been defended, or even considered, in work on addiction. But it is the kind of view, I will argue, that we ultimately ought to take.

Where we began with one view of addiction, the disease model, we now have a family of four possible views. I have argued against the disease model, but it simply represents one kind of view. We have not considered arguments against the view that addiction is a behavioral defect, nor against the deflationary view that addiction is a mere behavioral difference. How should we evaluate these views?

1.10 The Role of a Theory

To begin, we can ask what work a theory of addiction is supposed to do in the first place. We are generally able to recognize addiction, in the sense of distinguishing addicted people from non-addicted people, at least in most cases. A theory of addiction is not needed primarily for diagnosis. As I understand it, a theory of addiction has a more fundamental role to play. It is needed for explanation and justification, specifically to explain addictive behavior and to justify our treatment of addicted people. Let us take each of these in turn.

A theory of addiction can be expected to explain addictive behavior in the following sense. We have already observed that it is in some sense definitional of addiction that the addicted person and the non-addicted person behave differently. We have distinguished between views on which this behavior is a defect and one on which is it simply a different kind of behavior. But, whichever of these views one takes, one would hope that a theory of addiction would explain what it is about addiction such that the addicted person behaves as she does.

A theory of addiction can also be expected to justify our treatment of addicted people in the following sense. Most modern societies enact a range of policies with respect to addicted people. Some of these policies are punitive, such as sentencing guidelines for the use and sale of certain addictive substances. Others are protective, such as laws prohibiting certain forms of discrimination against addicted people. A theory of addiction can be brought to bear on such policies in a couple of ways. First, where such policies are legitimate, it can underwrite these policies, and explain why they are appropriate. Second, in cases where these policies are flawed, it can explain what is wrong with them, and guide the search for better ones.

Sometimes a theory of addiction makes specific claims that are factually false. I have argued that there is a good case that the disease model is such a theory. But often it will be more difficult to evaluate the case for or against a certain theory. This is especially so when we are considering broad strategies in the theory of addiction, as we are largely doing here.

When this is the case, it can be helpful to reflect on the work that a theory of addiction is supposed to do and ask whether a given theory can be reasonably expected to meet it.[10]

1.11 Explanation and Behavioral Defect

Let us consider again the view that addiction is a behavioral defect. On this view, the addicted person acts in a way such that she is worse off simply in virtue of acting that way. But her behavior is not driven by any underlying disease or other constitutional defect. It is simply a disorder of behavior. This behavior will involve, in the first place, using certain substances or engaging in certain activities in certain atypical ways. On this view, to be addicted just is to use or act addictively. There is no addiction 'above and beyond' the behavior itself.

This kind of picture of addiction can feel like a humane one. It claims that there is something wrong with the addicted person but does not attribute the wrongness to who she intrinsically is. It therefore feels like it can find a flaw in the addicted person while acknowledging the possibility of change, a change that need not come (as on the disease model) from a medical intervention, but can come simply from the addicted person herself, perhaps with the assistance of some education. It is not surprising that this picture lies behind much clinical work.

Yet this theory faces a simple question. It is the question of explanation that we have asked for a theory of addiction to answer. Why, on this picture, does the addicted person act as she does?

The theory we are considering has great difficulty answering this question. On the one hand, it cannot explain the addicted person's behavior in terms of some underlying defect, like a disease. For it is definitional of this view that there is no such constitutional defect involved in addiction. Yet, since it takes the behavior in question is in some way defective or disordered, it still demands some kind of explanation. By the lights of this theory, the addicted person is acting in a way that by its very nature makes her worse off, yet there is no underlying defect in virtue of which she is behaving that way. This account renders inexplicable the very behavior that a theory of addiction is supposed to explain.

The problem posed here is, in a way, an ancient one. Many philosophers have wondered how an agent can act in a way that makes her worse off even when she appears to have no defect of knowledge or cognition. This is sometimes called the problem of *clear-eyed akrasia*, and it is central to the theory of agency.[11] If we accept that addictive behavior is defective, then the case of addiction makes this problem especially acute. And one need not turn to philosophy for this problem to have force. The behavior of addicted people can often seem perplexing to those who care for them, and indeed sometimes to addicted people themselves. The failure of this model to explain behavior that it takes to be defective is not an incidental shortcoming, but a flaw in the very foundations of the model.

The behavioral defect view can look like an advance on the disease model, but it is in an unstable position. Either it must trace the addicted person's behavior to some underlying defect, in which case the behavior is explained, or it must withdraw the claim that the behavior is defective. If it takes this latter strategy, the behavior in question still must be explained, but it can be assimilated to behavior more generally and explained in terms of general strategies of action explanation.

We have already rejected the former strategy, at least the standard development of that strategy in the disease model. But the latter strategy remains open. What would it mean to retain the thought that addiction is merely a behavioral difference, but to deny that this behavior involves a behavioral defect? Several authors have developed thoughtful answers to this question.

1.12 Addiction as Rational Behavior

On a standard picture, most behavior advances an agent's preferences or goals, in light of what that agent knows or believes. Someone wants an ice cream, believes there is ice cream at the grocery store, and so goes to the grocery store. For behavior to be rational, on a minimal conception of rationality, is simply for it to advance an agent's preferences, by the lights of her beliefs, in this sense. Going to the grocery store will therefore count as rational in the case described. On this picture, most human behavior is rational in this minimal sense, and its obvious diversity is due to the fact that agents differ widely in what they believe, and still more widely in what they want.

The simplest development of the view we are now considering – a view on which the addicted person behaves distinctively, but on which her behavior is not inherently defective – appeals to this broad notion of rationality. If behavior is rational in this broad sense, then it is thereby, almost by definition, not defective. The framework of preference and beliefs affords resources by which one can explain the distinctive patterns in the behavior of addicted people without attributing these to anything in the constitution of addicted people themselves.

It is therefore not surprising that many authors have advanced precisely this kind of view of addiction. There are several ways in which it has been developed.

A relatively early development of this view was proposed by the philosopher Herbert Fingarette in his book *Heavy Drinking* (Fingarette, 1989).

Fingarette's view was that the use of large amounts of alcohol, which would be dubbed alcoholism or 'alcohol use disorder' in most medical contexts, is typically not a disorder at all. Rather, 'heavy drinking' is a certain kind of pattern of behavior that people take up in the course of life, for a variety of reasons. Certain forms of alcohol use have been pathologized, but it is our tendency to pathologize aberrant behavior, rather than any underlying aspect of the behavior itself, that is the source of the idea that there is any behavioral defect here at all.

We might naturally extend Fingarette's understanding of alcohol use to an account of addiction generally. Let us say that some people have a strong preference for the use of certain substances or engagement in certain activities. They thereby do what they can to maximize their use of those substances or engagement in those activities, even when doing so conflicts with the pursuit of other, more conventionally pursued, goods. This will lead to choices that are frowned upon in many contexts, but then so too are many socially atypical behaviors. This behavior is nonetheless rational, in the broad sense of rationality sketched earlier.

Fingarette's view, though rarely endorsed by contemporary authors, does suggest a model for understanding addiction as rational behavior. It is, therefore, a useful entry point to more contemporary, and more widely held, ways of developing this idea.

One development has become especially prominent in many psychological discussions, both among addiction professionals and among addicted people themselves. On this understanding, addiction is best thought of as 'self-medication' (Khantzian, 1997). The addicted person experiences difficulties in mental or physical health that demand treatment, such as chronic pain, trauma, depression, or anxiety. She therefore uses certain substances (or engages in certain activities) to treat those difficulties. Thus, an addictive substance such as alcohol, cocaine, or nicotine will serve as a form of self-administered medication for a genuine symptom or condition that the addicted person is attempting, in her own way, to manage.

This is an account on which addiction is counted as rational insofar as it is one on which addictive behavior may be naturally understood as a pursuit of one's preferences relative to one's beliefs. The addicted person wishes to treat a mental or physical health condition and has beliefs about the best way to do so. These beliefs may be false, but that does not imply that she is irrational, but merely that she is mistaken about the best form of treatment. The addicted person is in some sense misguided, but her behavior is, relative to her beliefs, rational.

This model has been much more widely adopted than the kind of rational behavior model suggested by Fingarette. This is for at least two reasons.

First, it retains the thought that there is, after all, some kind of defect involved in addiction. This will typically be the physical or mental condition that the addicted person's substance use or behavior aims to medicate. The defect will not be the source or cause of the addicted person's behavior, as it is on the disease model. Instead, it will be the object of her behavior, or that to which her behavior is a response. So there is, after all, a defect involved in addiction, just not in the place where the disease model puts it. The self-medication model therefore preserves our thought that there is something defective in the addicted person, and this makes it familiar and thus acceptable as a model of addiction.[12]

Second, the self-medication view preserves the thought that addiction is an essentially medical phenomenon, one that is best managed within the medical system. On the disease model, this is because addiction is a disease, and disease is something best treated by physicians and other medical professionals. On the self-medication model, the story is somewhat more complicated. On this model, the addicted person has effectively usurped the role of the medical professional. She is doing, poorly, the same thing that the medical professional can do somewhat better. The role of medical intervention, on this model, will not be to treat addiction but to replace it: to find some better way of treating the condition that the addicted person has been treating with behavior or substance use. The self-medication model, therefore, also preserves the centrality of medical practice to the understanding and management of addiction.

These are not the only models on which addiction is understood as a species of rational behavior.[13] Nonetheless, they constitute two simple models of what it would mean to deny that addiction involves a constitutional defect and to deny that addictive behavior is inherently defective. On both models, addictive behavior is rational and intelligible. This understanding perspective on addictive behavior is part of what makes them so appealing. Nonetheless, I will now argue, it is also what opens them to the same kind of problem about explanation that was already raised against the behavioral defect model.

1.13 Explanation Again

On the behavioral defect model, the addicted person engages in behavior that inherently makes her worse off even though she does not have any underlying defect (like a disease) that explains her behavior. The challenge for that view was to explain why she does so. On the rational behavior model, the addicted person does not engage in such behavior, so the model does not face exactly that challenge. But it does face a similar challenge.

The challenge is as follows. Let us grant that the addicted person's behavior is not inherently defective. Nonetheless, as a matter of empirical fact, the addicted person does engage in behavior that leads to devastating outcomes, both for herself and for those she cares about, and often does so knowingly and repeatedly. The problem is to explain how that behavior is compatible with the supposition that addictive behavior is always rational.

To take one example of what needs to be explained, the use of opioids is known to lead to potentially fatal overdoses. Individuals are not always maximally rational in calculating harms, especially when those harms lie far in the future. But overdose is a real and proximate risk, which many opioid users knowingly confront. This is a datum that any theory of addiction needs to explain.

The disease model readily explains such behavior: it is compulsive behavior due to a disease. So too can the behavioral defect model: this is precisely the kind of defective behavior that is characteristic of addiction. But what will the rational behavior model say? Consider a model on which addiction is understood as a certain mode of living. It is perhaps intelligible how someone rationally prefers a life in which a large part of one's time is given over to the acquisition and use of sedating or relaxing substances. Certain romanticized accounts of opium use (de Quincey, 1821/2013) seem to suggest such a life. It is harder to understand, however, how one might rationally choose a life in which a known and proximate risk of a fatal overdose is constantly present. It is perhaps not inconceivable that someone could choose such a way of life, but the fact that such a life seems to be chosen by so many individuals on such a large and increasing scale begins to push against the limits of what is rationally intelligible.[14]

Consider then the self-medication model. Again, it is plausible that someone might use opiates to medicate chronic pain (which is, after all, the primary function of opiates) or mental health conditions. It is also plausible that someone might use such a medication excessively and might overdose as a result (as in fact is a known risk of many over-the-counter pain medications). What is less plausible is that someone might continue to self-medicate by using a substance that is known to her to have a high risk of potentially fatal overdose. Again, the phenomenon of overdose, especially on the scale at which we currently see it, seems to suggest a mechanism other than rational behavior.

The rational behavior model does explain a lot of facts about substance use. Consider alcohol use. Many people use alcohol as part of a lifestyle that involves occasional socialization and relaxation, where the disinhibiting effects of moderate alcohol use have a role to play. Many people also self-medicate mental and physical health conditions, arguably less effectively, through the use of modest amounts of alcohol.[15] The same is true of many prohibited drugs. The neuroscientist Carl Hart has recently argued, compellingly, that many users of drugs such as cannabis and cocaine use them as a component of a rationally designed life, where these drugs are used for recreation and community, as well as for self-medication (Hart, 2021). As a general model of substance use (as well as of behaviors such as gambling and video game playing), the rational behavior model has significant plausibility.

The objection, however, is that the rational behavior model fails to account for precisely those cases where the concept of addiction feels most necessary. These are those cases where a person's substance use or behavior is so clearly self-destructive that it appears to outrun the bounds of rationality altogether. Even if most of an addicted person's behavior can be accommodated under a heading such as self-medication, there remain some aspects of addiction that appear recalcitrant to this kind of explanation.

Let us review what these arguments from explanation have shown. We initially considered the view that addiction is a behavioral defect that is not grounded in any underlying constitutional defect. The objection to this view was that it could not explain why the addicted person acts as she does. We then considered the view that addiction is a species of rational behavior. This view does explain much substance use and behavior classed as addictive. It fails, however, to explain cases of severe self-harm – such as repeated overdoses in the case of opiates – that are characteristic of addiction. The rational behavior model can explain a lot, but it seems to leave paradigm cases of addictive behavior unexplained.

It is tempting here to fall back on a constitutional defect model of addiction. If addicted people had a constitutional defect that compelled them to behave in certain irrational ways, that would count as an explanation of their behavior of the kind being demanded. I have already argued, however, against the most prominent form of this model, namely the disease model of addiction. I want to begin to sketch out a different model, to suggest how it addresses the problem of explanation, and how it yields the foundation for a theory of addiction more generally.

1.14 Addiction as Difference

The taxonomy we introduced earlier yielded four different possible models of addiction, only three of which we have considered. The last is the following. There is indeed a constitutional difference between addicted people and non-addicted people, contrary to the behavioral defect or the rational behavior model. This difference, however, is not a defect, not something in virtue of which addicted people are inherently worse off, contrary to the disease model. It is merely a difference.

There are different ways to develop this kind of model, but the best version of this model, I think, holds that addiction is a disability. Furthermore, reflection on more familiar kinds of disability sheds light on how we can articulate a genuinely explanatory theory of addiction that does not require us to hold that an addicted person has any kind of defect.

Consider blindness. A blind person's sensory system works differently from that of sighted people. Since most people are not blind, social spaces and the built environment tend to be designed in a way that favors sighted people. Furthermore, blind people are subject to systemic discrimination in employment, housing, and other basic activities and goods. Accordingly, a blind person faces a range of obstacles, in most contemporary societies, that a sighted person does not face. In this sense, to be blind is often to be disadvantaged.

It does not follow, however, and is not true, that to be blind is to be defective. That view of blindness has long been dominant in popular and medical conceptions. But in recent decades disability advocates have convinced many of us of the basic error in that view.[16] It is not true that someone who is blind is inherently worse off, just in virtue of being blind. This is not to deny that blind people are often disadvantaged. But, in the case of blindness, we have learned to find the locus of this disadvantage in social structures rather than in blindness itself. Blindness, considered in itself, is a mere difference.[17]

In saying that addiction is a disability, I am saying that we ought to understand addiction in the same way. Addicted people are not inherently worse off, just in virtue of being addicted. In itself, addiction is a mere difference. Addicted people are disadvantaged, and indeed addiction is associated with profoundly negative and often tragic life outcomes. But these outcomes are not due simply to addiction itself. Rather, they are due to the complex interaction between the difference that constitutes addiction and the forces of institutional and individual discrimination to which addicted people are typically subject.

This view can be difficult, for some, to even consider. While many acknowledge the stigma and prejudice that addicted people experience, it can be tempting to insist that those harms are, as it were, simply added on to the underlying harm of addiction itself. This is how entrenched in our thinking the defect model of addiction can be. It is similarly difficult for many people to consider the possibility that blindness is not a defect. Yet many of us have come to accept that it is not. A similar conceptual shift still needs to be made in the case of addiction, and one aim of this book is to help to make it.

That said, at this point in the argument I am not yet defending the truth of the disability view. I am simply defending its possibility and its coherence.

This is important to do because, as noted at the outset, the disability view of addiction is scarcely even considered, let alone adopted, in most contemporary work on addiction.

The disability view also completes, as noted earlier, the taxonomy of views we have been considering. The disability view rejects the idea that addiction constitutionally involves a disease or other defect – indeed, it is explicitly opposed to that view. It also rejects the idea that addictive behavior is inherently defective. In this way, the disability model rejects the defect model of addiction, on either of these two developments.

Its relationship to the rational behavior model is somewhat more complicated. The advocate of the disability model does not deny that much addictive behavior can be understood as a species of rational behavior, either in terms of a way of life, self-medication, or some broader range of ends. Yet it rejects the idea that this is a complete explanation of addiction. The disability model holds that there is a basic and non-behavioral difference between addicted people and non-addicted people and that the failure to acknowledge this is one reason why the rational behavior model, for all its strengths, is inadequate as an account of addiction.

Thus, there is an alternative to both defect models and to the rational behavior view of addiction. This is the view that addiction is a constitutional difference. The disability view is a plausible development of this kind of view, one that finds antecedents in previous work on other disabilities, such as blindness.

This account, however, immediately raises at least two sets of questions. First, what is the difference in addiction? If it is not a disease, what is it? And why does the advocate of the disability view insist that, unlike something like a disease, it is not a defect, but merely a difference?

Second, if addiction is merely a difference, what accounts for the profound harms to which people with addictions are subject? As noted earlier, some of these are plausibly attributed to discrimination and stigma, but many of them appear to be 'self-inflicted.' What, for example, leads people to use opiates in such a way that results in repeated overdoses? How could a difference that leads to such outcomes not count as a defect?

These are fundamental questions, and the account of addiction that I will now develop aims to answer them.

Notes

1 The disease model has a long history, dating at least to the 18th-century American physician Benjamin Rush, and it figures foundationally in the texts of Alcoholics Anonymous and its related groups. A classic statement of the contemporary version of this view, on which addiction is a chronic brain disease of the kind described in the text, is Leshner (1997).

2 Here and in what follows I will use 'person-centered' language such as 'addicted people' or 'people with addictions,' as opposed to terms such as 'addict' or 'alcoholic.' On my view, these latter terms are accompanied by such an overlay of stigma and bias that they are not appropriate to use in clinical or academic works such as this one. There is another point of view, however, on which these terms are actively embraced by the very people whom they have long been used to stigmatize. On this point of view, the avoidance of these terms in favor of more clinical language is itself problematic. The issues here are complicated, and intertwined with the very questions of stigma and identity that will be central to this book. For present purposes, I only mean to make clear how I will be speaking, and why I am speaking that way, while recognizing with some degree of humility that this way of speaking may not be, in the last analysis, the best one.

3 The prolonged use of certain substances, such as alcohol, can be associated with profound cognitive impairment. But in such cases the impairment is plausibly an effect of addiction rather than a cause or correlate of addiction itself.

4 One interesting study (Rounsaville et al., 1982) published before the widespread adoption of the disease model, contrasts the neuropsychological functioning of three groups: a group of people with opiate addiction, a group of people with epilepsy (a clear case of a brain disease), and a group of 'normal' controls. It finds no significant differences between people with opiate addictions and the controls on any neuropsychological testing.

5 See Gage and Sumnall (2019) for a review of these experiments as well as some cautionary notes on their proper interpretation.

6 See Heyman (2009, pp. 65–88) for a comprehensive survey of these findings. To take just one example, one survey finds that, among people with a history of addiction, 75 percent have no symptoms of addiction by age 37, and only 30 percent have ever mentioned their addiction to a physician (Heyman, 2009, p. 70).

7 See Prendergast et al. (2006) for an overview and meta-analysis of this work.

8 It is an interesting question whether there are in fact any compulsions at all, or whether the very idea is a fiction. I am agnostic on this question. Some clinically atypical behaviors, such as trichotillomania (hair-pulling disorder) appear to be better candidates for the kind of irresistible tendencies that Leshner and others attribute to people with addictions. So, the conclusion here is that if there are compulsions, as there well may be, then addiction is not among them. I am grateful to Stephen Campbell for raising this question.

9 It figures, for example, in the name of the US federal agency responsible for much addiction-related funding, the Substance Abuse and Mental Health Services Agency (SAMHSA).

10 There is a further demand that the theory that I will defend, on which addiction is a disability, must meet. I will argue that the disability view implies a certain kind of deference: the view is true only if a substantial number of the people whom it is supposed to describe accept it as a good description. Since this is a demand that is in a certain way internal to the disability view, and is not a criterion that other views are obliged to meet, it is one that I set aside in the present discussion.

11 See Davidson (1980, Essay 2). It is important to mark here the distinction that (Holton, 1999) draws between akrasia and weakness of will. The question at issue in the text, and in Davidson's essay, is akrasia. In contrast, I will argue that the mechanisms of addiction are much closer to what Holton calls 'weakness of will' – though, for reasons to be developed later, I reject both Holton's account and the very label of 'weakness' itself.

12 In an important unpublished discussion of these topics (Murthy, ms.), T. Virgil Murthy identifies and criticizes precisely this aspect of the self-medication model.

13 Some notable versions of this broad family of views are Heyman (2009), Pickard (2012), and economic approaches such as Becker and Murphy (1988).

14 The scale of the opioid epidemic is vast. While it is often associated with the United States, and indeed with certain regions of the United States, it is a worldwide and ongoing phenomenon. See Robert *et al.* (2023) for one recent estimation of its global extent.

15 The empirical literature suggests that people do indeed attempt to self-medicate certain conditions, notably nervousness and anxiety, with alcohol, though it is unclear whether this strategy is in fact an effective one. See for example Swendsen *et al.* (2000) and Carrigan and Randall (2003)

16 For one overview of this intellectual and political movement and its profound effects, see Fleischer and Zames (2001)

17 This is a long-standing view in the disability community, but one important recent statement of such a view in the philosophical literature is Barnes (2016).

Works Cited

American Psychiatric Association. (2013). *Diagnostic and Statistical Manual of Mental Disorders (DSM-5)*. American Psychiatric Publications.

Barnes, E. (2016). *The Minority Body: A Theory of Disability*. Oxford University Press.

Becker, G.S., & Murphy, K.M. (1988). A Theory of Rational Addiction. *Journal of Political Economy*, *96*(4), 675–700.

Carrigan, M.H., & Randall, C.L. (2003). Self-Medication in Social Phobia: A Review of the Alcohol Literature. *Addictive Behaviors*, *28*(2), 269–284.

Davidson, D. (1980). *Essays on Actions and Events*. Oxford University Press.

de Quincey, T. (1821/2013). *Confessions of an English Opium Eater*. Oxford University Press.

Fingarette, H. (1989). *Heavy Drinking: The Myth of Alcoholism as Disease*. University of California Press.

Fleischer, D.Z., & Zames, F. (2001). *The Disability Rights Movement: From Charity to Confrontation*. Temple University Press.

Gage, S.H., & Sumnall, H.R. (2019). Rat Park: How a Rat Paradise Changed the Narrative of Addiction. *Addiction*, *114*, 917–922.

Hart, C. (2021). *Drug Use for Grown-Ups: Chasing Liberty in the Land of Fear*. Penguin.

Herron, A., & Brennan, T.K. (2019). *The ASAM Essentials of Addiction Medicine*. Lippincott Williams & Wilkins.

Heyman, G.M. (2009). *Addiction: A Disorder of Choice*. Harvard University Press.

Holton, R. (1999). Intention and Weakness of Will. *The Journal of Philosophy*, *96*(5), 241–262.

Khantzian E.J. (1997) The Self-Medication Hypothesis of Substance Use Disorders: A Reconsideration and Recent Applications. *Harvard Review of Psychiatry*, *4*(5), 231– 244.

Leshner, A.I. (1997). Addiction Is a Brain Disease, and It Matters. *Science*, *278*(5335), 45–47.

Murthy, T.V. (ms.). What Is It Like to Be an Addict? The Perceptual Model of Substance Use Disorder. Unpublished ms.

Petry, N.M., Tedford, J., Austin, M., Nich, C., Carroll, K.M., & Rounsaville, B.J. (2004). Prize Reinforcement Contingency Management for Treating Cocaine Users: How Low Can We Go, and with Whom? *Addiction*, *99*(3), 349–360.

Pickard, H. (2012). The Purpose in Chronic Addiction. *AJOB Neuroscience*, *3*(2), 40–49.

Prendergast, M., Podus, D., Finney, J., Greenwell, L., & Roll, J. (2006). Contingency Management for Treatment of Substance Use Disorders: A Meta-Analysis. *Addiction*, *101*(11), 1546–1560.

Robert, M., Jouanjus, E., Khouri, C., Fouilhé Sam-Laï, N., & Revol, B. (2023). The Opioid Epidemic: A Worldwide Exploratory Study Using the WHO Pharmacovigilance Database. *Addiction*, *118*(4), 771–775.

Robins, L.N. (1993). Vietnam Veterans' Rapid Recovery from Heroin Addiction: A Fluke or Normal Expectation? *Addiction*, *88*(8), 1041–1054.

Rounsaville, B.J., Jones, C., Novelly, R.A., & Kleber, H. (1982). Neuropsychological Functioning in Opiate Addicts. *The Journal of Nervous and Mental Disease*, *170*(4), 209–216.

Swendsen, J.D., Tennen, H., Carney, M.A., Affleck, G., Willard, A., & Hromi, A. (2000). Mood and Alcohol Consumption: An Experience Sampling Test of the Self-Medication Hypothesis. *Journal of Abnormal Psychology*, *109*, 198–204.

2

ADDICTION AND THE WILL

2.1 The Psychological Basis of Addiction

In the previous chapter, we considered various theories of addiction. Most of these were what I called defect models of addiction: they involved the claim that the addicted person differed in some way from the non-addicted person and that the addicted person is worse off just in virtue of this difference. I suggested an alternative model of addiction, on which there is a difference between the addicted and the non-addicted person, but on which it is a 'mere difference.' Specifically, I advocated the view that addiction is a disability.

That debate – between a defect model and a mere difference model – is a debate about the evaluative valence of the features that demarcate addiction. There is, however, another fundamental question to be asked about the nature of these features. What kind of features, exactly, are those in virtue of which someone counts as an addicted person? In the previous chapter we also considered the question of whether it was the addicted person's behavior or some constitutional feature of the addicted person herself that distinguished addiction, and I argued that it was some feature of the addicted person herself. But we can then ask: what kinds of features, exactly, are these? That is the question that will be our focus in this chapter.

It is instructive here to consider, again, the disease model. As we discussed in the previous chapter, this is a view on which (at least on its standard development) the features that distinguish the addicted person are specifically neurological ones: the addicted person is subject to a brain disease, just as is (for example) someone with epilepsy. In the previous

DOI: 10.4324/9781003410263-3

chapter, I argued that it is implausible to think that addiction, even if it were a disease, is specifically a disease of the brain.

Rejecting a strictly neurological definition for addiction does not mean, however, that we need to exile addiction from the head altogether. Many contemporary writers would be reluctant to understand addiction in neurological terms. But they would nonetheless be sympathetic to the idea that addiction is best understood in psychological terms. That is, the features that distinguish the addicted person from the non-addicted person are fundamentally features of the addicted person's psychology.

The psychological conception of addiction is widespread in academic work.[1] It is also part of our ordinary concept of addiction. When people speak of having 'an addictive personality,' we know roughly what they mean. They seem to mean, at first approximation, that they have certain psychological tendencies that – abstracting from the features of any given substance or activity – are characteristic of addiction. This is implicitly to understand addiction in the first place in terms of the psychological structures or dispositions that characterize it.

I agree that we should give a psychological characterization of addiction. But I will argue that previous attempts at characterization go wrong in at least two ways. First, as discussed in the previous chapter, they have tended to get the valence of these differences wrong. What they have understood as psychological defects are in fact mere psychological differences. Second, they have often put the psychological differences in the wrong place. In particular, previous accounts have understood addiction in terms of psychological states such as belief (or perception, or judgment) and desire (or urges, or preferences). But that is not the psychological locus of addiction. Instead, as I will argue, the difference that characterizes addiction is fundamentally a difference in the will.

In short, I agree with those who have given a psychological characterization of addiction, but disagree with most characterizations that have given, both in terms of their evaluative valence (typically negative) and their psychological elements (typically, beliefs and desires). Instead, an account of addiction should be evaluatively neutral and should take the will as its primary element. This chapter will begin to outline such an account.

This account will require us to adopt a distinctive view of the mind, on which it is fundamentally tripartite in nature, consisting not only of beliefs and desires but also of intentions. This view is a natural one, and its philosophical pedigree is ancient.[2] Furthermore, it has been rigorously developed and defended in contemporary philosophy, notably in the work of Michael Bratman (Bratman, 1987), which I will return to later. Nonetheless, this tripartite view of the mind is opposed to a view that remains popular in philosophy and orthodox in much of the social sciences, on which the mind is bipartite, consisting just of beliefs and desires. Let us begin, then, by considering the bipartite view and how some have attempted to accommodate addiction within such a framework.

2.2 The Belief-Desire Model

One way of thinking of the mind is as having two distinct but complementary modes of engaging with the world. On the one hand, it endeavors to represent the world just as it is, as accurately as possible. On the other, it wishes to change the world, to make it conform to how the agent would like the world to be.[3]

One way of regimenting this conception of the mind is by distinguishing two kinds of mental states: beliefs and desires. Both represent a way the world could be. Belief represents how the agent takes the world to be. Desire represents how the agent would like it to be. For example, an agent might believe that she is located in Boise, but might desire that she is located in Bali (or conversely).[4]

Belief and desire are described in different ways, and sometimes the differences are merely verbal. Other times they are more substantive. In particular, the language of belief and desire is sometimes replaced, especially in economics and other social sciences, with the language of credence and preference. Credence and preference are gradable notions, in the sense that they can be compared on a scale, and are quantitative notions, in the sense that the scale can be accurately described in numeric terms. These aspects of credence and preference raise special considerations, especially when we attempt to model addiction within such a framework, but the discussion that follows will focus primarily on the more general notions of belief and desire.

It is plausible that there are such things as beliefs, and as desires. What is distinctive to the belief-desire model is the thought that these two states are exhaustive, and thus that other, superficially distinct, psychological phenomena must be somehow reduced to a basis of belief and desire. Of special interest to us in what follows is how we are supposed to understand agency and volition in terms of the belief-desire model.

Begin with agency. Donald Davidson (Davidson, 1980, Essay 1) proposes that action itself may be analyzed in terms of belief and desire, in the sense that what it is for an event to be an action is for it to be caused in the right way by a certain kind of belief and a certain kind of desire. This is a view on which the belief-desire model is written into the nature of agency in its very foundations.

Consider then volition. What, on the belief-desire model, is an intention to perform a certain act? Davidson (Davidson, 1980, Essay 5) holds that it is, roughly, a belief that it is desirable that one performs the act. David Velleman and others hold that it is a belief that one will perform the act (Velleman, 1989). However precisely this account is developed, the idea is that intention itself, and the faculty of the will more generally, does not figure as a fundamental constituent in the belief-desire model of agency and volition.

I think this approach fails to do justice to our ordinary conception of the mind, on which states like intention have a fundamental role to play. More specifically, this approach fails to accommodate certain basic facts about addiction. For addiction is, I will argue, an aspect of the will. Furthermore, this volitional conception of addiction has considerable intuitive support. Nonetheless, under the influence of the belief-desire model, the tendency in philosophy as well as the social sciences has been to understand addiction in terms of some particular kind of desire, some particular kind of belief, or some combination thereof. Let us begin by considering such accounts.

2.3 Addiction and Desire

Part of the popular conception of the addicted person is as someone overcome by certain urges or desires, ones which either bypass her agency altogether or which are so powerful that they take priority in all, or almost all, of her endeavors. We might then take addiction to be definitionally connected to the presence of a certain kind of desire.

Something like this view is usefully articulated in an essay by the philosopher R. Jay Wallace, who takes himself to be articulating something like the 'popular understanding' of addiction (Wallace, 1999). Wallace suggests that, on this understanding, the addicted person is characterized by her susceptibility to what Wallace calls 'A-desires.' These desires, Wallace suggests, are distinguished by several distinctive properties.

First, A-desires are 'resilient': they persist for long periods of time, in ways apparently unconnected with the agent's own concerns. In addition, A-desires are 'intense', often constituting cravings – a term that figures prominently in many desire-based conceptions of addiction. A-desires are additionally linked in relatively direct ways with pleasure and pain, both the pleasure of their satisfaction and the pain of their non-satisfaction. Finally, Wallace suggests, these desires seem to have a 'physiological basis', in the sense of being grounded in some underlying process in the person whose desires they are. This is an elegant picture of how the presence of a certain kind of mental state – namely, A-desires of the kind Wallace describes – could be constitutive of addiction.

Another aspect of the A-desire picture is that A-desires are psychological defects. Indeed, Wallace is explicit on this point. The very presence of these desires constitutes a defect, on Wallace's view: 'a condition that impairs our ability to act well, without necessarily depriving us of the capacity to think clearly and rationally about what we are to do' (Wallace, 1999, p. 629). In virtue of their resilience, Wallace suggests, these desires are such that an agent subject to them may 'succeed in deliberating correctly about what they ought to do, but will nevertheless be impeded in their capacity to translate their deliberated verdicts into action' (Wallace, 1999, pp. 629–630).

In this sense, on the picture suggested by Wallace, addiction is constituted by a kind of desire that is a defect, such that someone is worse off simply in virtue of having that desire. This desire-based model of addiction is in this way a certain kind of implementation of the defect model. One may, however, also develop a desire-based model in a more purely descriptive way.

As I understand it, the picture of addiction advanced by the philosopher Gary Watson has this structure.[5] For Watson, 'to become addicted is to acquire an appetite' (Watson, 1999, p. 76). Such an appetite, Watson writes, is a 'felt need, a source of pleasure and pain, that has a periodic motivational force that is independent of one's capacity for critical judgment' (Watson, 1999, p. 76). It is this essentially motivational and judgment-independent aspect of an appetite in virtue of which this view counts as a desire-based account.

An appetite, however, is not a defect. We typically conceive of the natural appetites of a being – such as hunger and thirst – as aspects of that being that are neither good nor bad in themselves, and which if anything tend to her long-term benefit. Acquired appetites may not tend to an agent's long-term benefit, but neither do they tend toward her long-term harm. They are simply appetites, which in themselves are evaluatively neutral.

Here then is one way in which the belief-desire model might accommodate addiction. There are certain desires (or impulses, or appetites) that are constitutive of addiction. On one kind of view, these desires are defects, such that the person who has them is worse off just in virtue of having them. This is the kind of view that is suggested by Wallace. On another kind of view, these desires are evaluatively neutral, such that having these desires does not in itself make one worse off, though they may well have negative consequences in certain kinds of environment. This is the kind of view that is suggested by Watson. Either view is one on which it is the presence of certain desires, or desire-like states, that distinguishes the addicted person from the person who is not addicted.

2.4 Addiction and Belief

A different approach takes the addicted person to be distinguished not by the nature of her desires but by the nature of her beliefs. What it is to be addicted is to have beliefs of a certain kind about the substance or activity to which one is addicted, beliefs that may be distinctive in their contents or their cognitive dynamics – for instance, these beliefs might be disposed to persist even in the face of countervailing evidence.

This kind of approach is seldom made explicit in the philosophical literature, but it underwrites a large swath of clinical practice.[6] For example, one of the best-established interventions for substance use disorders is Cognitive Behavioral Therapy (CBT) (McHugh *et al.*, 2010). Among other things, CBT aims at eliciting and revising the 'core beliefs' that animate a person's addictive behavior. A fundamental presumption of this kind of intervention is that it is precisely an agent's beliefs that are at the core of her addictive behavior, such that belief revision may be reasonably hoped to be a meaningful intervention in the treatment of addiction.

In addition to guiding clinical practice, a cognitive understanding of addiction underwrites much public health practice. One response to widespread tobacco addiction, for example, has been the introduction of public health campaigns that emphasize the negative effects of tobacco. One understanding of the hypothesis underwriting such campaigns is that tobacco addiction is at least partly grounded in certain beliefs, beliefs which such campaigns aim to alter.

The cognitive models suggested by these interventions are, in my terms here, defect models. That is, they presume that the belief that underwrites addiction is fundamentally a flawed one, either because it is based on insufficient evidence or because it persists even in the face of evidence against it. This is not however a mandatory aspect of such models. One might instead hold that addicted people are distinguished by their beliefs, but deny that these beliefs are worse-making features.

This kind of approach has been developed in recent work by the philosopher T. Virgil Murthy. Murthy advocates what she calls a 'perceptual model' of addiction, on which a substance use disorder (for some substance S) is characterized by a certain set of 'perceptions, beliefs, and emotions regarding S' (Murthy, ms., p. 16) These might include, for example, the belief that it is in some sense necessary for one to consume S. Crucially, on Murthy's view, these beliefs are not inherently defective, though they will often be regarded by others as irrational. They are simply the beliefs that characterize addiction, without thereby constituting defects or yielding a defect model of addiction.

Murthy herself describes her view as one on which addiction is a disability. It is therefore important, again, to distinguish two questions. The first question is whether addiction is to be understood on a defect model or not. The second is how we should understand the psychological basis of addiction. Like the desire-based account, the belief-based account can be developed in either way. Much clinical work seems to assume that addiction is grounded in defective beliefs. Murthy's view, in contrast, holds that the beliefs that are constitutive of addiction are merely different, and not defective. Both approaches understand addiction as a fundamentally cognitive phenomenon, but their understandings of the valence of these cognitive features of addiction are quite different.

2.5 Addiction and Maximization

As we have said, the belief-desire model of the mind is widely held. If we understand the mind in this way, then there are at least two psychological states that could ground addiction, namely beliefs or desires. There is also a third possibility, which is that addiction is grounded in both belief and desire, without being reducible to either one of them considered singly.

This is a natural understanding of the approach to addiction that is suggested by work in the social sciences, and especially economics. One aim of a certain kind of economic thought is to understand a wide array of human behavior in terms of an agent's utility maximization, where this, in turn, is understood as the satisfaction of her preferences (corresponding to desires) relative to her credences (corresponding to beliefs).

This framework, which I will refer to simply as maximization, applies naturally to much rational economic activity, such as buying groceries or negotiating wages. It is harder for some to see how a phenomenon such as addiction might be captured within such a framework. But this is precisely what the economists Gary Becker and Kevin Murphy did in an influential paper on addiction (Becker & Murphy, 1988). Their core idea is that addiction involves strong dependencies of current preferences on past use, such that using a substance heavily yesterday will strongly increase one's preference for using it today. They develop this basic insight into a formal model which, they argue, predicts several features of addiction, such as the usefulness of 'cold turkey' strategies for ending addictive use.

From the present point of view, what is interesting is how the maximization model understands addiction wholly in terms of a distinctive pattern of preferences and credences. That is to say that addiction is understood in terms of a certain psychological basis, a psychological basis which in turn is exhausted by beliefs and desires (or credences and preferences). It is also worth emphasizing the valence of this account. The belief-based and desire-based accounts of addiction were traditionally developed as defect models, which could also be developed in more purely descriptive ways. The maximization model, in contrast, is explicitly descriptive from the outset. Much of the point of this model is to understand behavior that is often understood as defective as just another variety of maximization. Becker and Murphy are explicit in taking the rationality of addiction to be precisely what they are aiming to describe.[7]

We might in principle develop an account on which addiction is instead grounded in a defective pattern of beliefs and desires. This possibility, however, is difficult to accommodate on standard maximization frameworks. For it is the spirit of maximization accounts to impose only very weak requirements on an agent's credences and preferences – for example, to require that her preferences be transitive, in the sense that if an agent prefers outcome A to outcome B, and prefers outcome B to outcome C, that she prefers outcome A to outcome C. One might in principle argue that addictive motivation might fail even one of these thin requirements of rationality. But a more common view is that an addicted person's credences and preferences are rational in this thin and formal sense and that any defect in her psychology lies instead in the source of the credences and preferences themselves.

To review, the belief-desire model of the mind has informed much empirical and philosophical work on addiction, and it yields several different accounts of the psychological bases of addiction. Addiction might be distinguished by a certain kind of belief or perception, by a certain kind of desire or appetite, or by a certain kind of pattern among a person's beliefs and desires (or credences and preferences). Each of these in turn might be understood as a psychological defect, something that inherently makes its bearer worse off, or as a mere psychological difference.

There is much to be learned from any one of these six forms of psychological models of addiction, but in the following, I want to draw out some considerations – initially informally, and then in a more systematic way – for finding all of them inadequate. For what is curious about these models is that they omit any mention of the psychological features that seem most distinctive of addiction.

2.6 Addiction and the Will

When we describe addictive behavior, we often use the language of choice and volition. Addiction is said to involve making choices that can seem, to the non-addicted person, perplexing. It is said to involve a lack of control over one's behavior. Or, to use a phrase to which we will return, the addicted person is said to be 'weak-willed.'

The idea that addiction involves some kind of failure of the will is also reflected in the *DSM-5* criteria for substance use disorders. The first of these criteria is using a substance 'in larger amounts or over a longer period than was intended.' The second appeals to 'unsuccessful efforts to cut down or control' one's use (APA, 2013, p. 490).[8] Thus the clinical conception of addiction, like our popular understanding of addiction, reflects the idea that addiction somehow essentially involves the will, what the will of the addicted person can do, and also what it apparently cannot do.

These observations about addiction, however, are difficult to accommodate within the belief-desire model. For a person to have a distinctive pattern of intentions, or for her to fail to control certain aspects of her behavior, is not in the first place for her to have certain beliefs or desires. This is an immediate challenge to the belief-desire model as an account of addiction, whether or not that account is a defect model or purely descriptive.

Some philosophers have rejected the thought that intentions are indeed distinct from beliefs and desires. As noted earlier, David Velleman (Velleman, 1989) and others have defended the view that intention is a specific kind of belief. If some such thesis were true, then addiction might be accounted for, in a roundabout way, in terms of beliefs.

But most advocates of belief-desire models of addiction have not necessarily been endorsing these forms of reduction. Instead, they have been assuming that the belief-desire model is the only rigorous account of psychology on offer. But this is not so. There is an alternative, and it is, I will argue, a much more natural framework for understanding the psychological basis of addiction.

2.7 The Tripartite Model of Mind

The belief-desire model is a two-part framework for understanding the mind: the mind consists of belief and desire (or credence and preference), and all else reduces to this. A natural alternative to this, in light of the foregoing, is a tripartite model of mind. On this view, the mind consists of three kinds of states: beliefs, desires, and volitions, where this last term is a generic term for various states of the will.

The most prominent and well-developed articulation of a tripartite theory in contemporary philosophy is developed by Michael Bratman, in Bratman (1987) and subsequent work. For Bratman, the core volition is an intention to act, specifically a future-directed intention to act. A future-directed intention to act is, at first pass, a plan to act in that way at that time. This plan may foreclose certain alternatives. For instance, if one intends to have dinner in New York tomorrow, that forecloses being in Boston tomorrow night. It also leaves some alternatives open or undecided. For instance, one may intend to have dinner in New York tomorrow without yet settling at which restaurant one will have dinner. We are, Bratman suggests, planning agents, and future-directed intentions are a core expression of this aspect of our agency.

In addition to future-directed intentions (henceforth simply 'intentions'), Bratman emphasizes the significance of a distinct kind of volition, namely policies. A policy is, at first pass, a kind of generalized intention, one which governs a range of actions. I might, for instance, have a policy of getting up at 7 a.m. every morning. This is not an intention to get up at that time on any given morning, but rather a volition that governs an entire indefinite range of mornings. Like an intention, a policy has the function of excluding certain courses of action, while leaving others undecided. Like an intention, it may be thought of as imposing practical structure on an otherwise undecided future.

Taken together, intentions and policies are the core volitions in Bratman's account.[9] They will also be the core volitions in the account of addiction that I will develop in what follows. I think we should leave open the idea that there are different conceptions of the will and that the account of addiction developed here might be developed within different frameworks. Nonetheless, there are several reasons for approaching the will in terms of Bratman's planning model.

The first is methodological. As we have seen, the belief-desire model is appealing in part because it offers a rigorous framework within which concepts such as addiction may be framed, which may seem to make the phenomenon of addiction more tractable. It is sometimes thought that appeals to the will are comparatively unsystematic. The planning model articulated by Bratman constitutes a corrective to this kind of skepticism, insofar as it allows us to make claims about the will within a clear and systematic framework.

Second, this is a view that allows us to accommodate differences in volition. One of the notable aspects of agents is the variety that their practical lives may take. Some people form detailed long-range plans and stick to them, come what may. Others guide themselves by the lights of a few simple policies and short-term plans and leave things open otherwise. We want a framework to accommodate this variety, or what I will call volitional diversity. As I will argue in the next section, the planning framework allows us to do this in a natural way.

Third, while it accommodates volitional diversity, this view still allows us to mark a distinction between difference and defect. For Bratman, while there are many acceptable forms that volitional structures may take, there are also some volitional patterns that are irrational, regardless of one's aims. Notably, if one fails to intend the necessary means to one's intended acts, one is thereby irrational. If a volitional tendency invariably involves that kind of practical irrationality, we can reasonably hold that it is a volitional defect, as opposed to a mere volitional difference.

It is intuitive to think that a descriptively adequate account of addiction will appeal to volition. The planning model developed by Bratman allows us to do this within a clear framework, one which permits us to pose and evaluate questions and hypotheses about volition in a rigorous way. This framework accommodates volitional diversity, while at the same time allowing us to mark the distinction between difference and defect. Let us consider how to think about volition and addiction within this framework.[10]

2.8 Volitional Difference

Agents differ in their volitions. One agent may intend to have a hamburger for lunch, while another may have a policy against eating meat. This basic kind of volitional diversity is familiar. It is also fundamental for any account of how agents can successfully coordinate with one another. To take one example, John Rawls understands distributive justice in terms of primary goods, and primary goods in terms are defined as what agents will need for any life plan they might have (Rawls, 1971). In this sense, recognition of the variety of life plans – and volitional diversity more generally – is foundational for Rawls's theory of distributive justice.[11]

What are the sources of volitional difference? There are several. First of all, agents may simply have different desires and beliefs. One agent wants an ice cream and believes there is ice cream at the supermarket, and so forms an intention to go to the supermarket. Another does not want an ice cream, and so does not form that intention. Still another does want an ice cream, but believes (perhaps falsely) that there is ice cream at the coffee shop, and so forms an intention to go to the ice cream shop. An agent's volitions depend in part on her beliefs and desires and, since agents differ in their beliefs and desires, they differ in their intentions as well. This is one source of volitional difference.

It is not, however, the only source of volitional difference. For agents may differ in their volitions even when they have the same desires and beliefs. A simple illustration of this is given by cases where an agent faces a choice between two equivalent options. For example, it may be that two routes to work take the same amount of time and have the same amount of traffic. Two agents might well have the same desire (to get to work) and the same belief (the routes are equivalent) and yet one agent might intend to take the first of the routes, and the second might intend to take the other. There is nothing to decide between the two routes, so each agent just chooses one of them. So, this is another source of volitional difference.

As Bratman points out (Bratman, 1987), these cases are not unusual. Modern life in general presents us with a host of basically equivalent options: the many possible routes to work, the hundreds of cans of soup at the supermarket, the identical socks in one's sock drawer. Navigating such a world is often a matter of forming choices in the face of such equivalencies. Thus, even for maximally informed agents who are alike in their preferences, the world inevitably induces a degree of volitional difference.[12]

Although they are prevalent, these cases are not necessarily the most common, and not the most significant, source of volitional difference. Another source is posed by incommensurable options. When two options are incommensurable, the issue is not that they are equivalent, but that they are incomparable. Consider a choice between two moral options: staying home to care for an ailing child, or dedicating oneself to political advocacy for an important cause. There are profound and measurable differences between these choices. One may weigh up the costs and benefits of such a decision, and that ultimately might guide one's choices. But arguably these calculations do not wholly decide the matter. One must make a choice, and it may well be that either choice is permissible relative to one's beliefs and desires. Accordingly, different agents will choose differently, even when they have the same desires and beliefs in all salient respects. So, incommensurability represents yet another source of volitional difference.

We have now identified at least three sources of volitional difference: differences in agents' beliefs and desires, the presence of equivalent options, and the presence of incommensurable options. The first of these sources is psychological, while the latter two arise from aspects of the world itself. These latter two sources of difference are especially significant – in light of the belief-desire model – because they show that an agent's volitions are underdetermined by her beliefs and desires. Two agents may have the very same beliefs and desires and yet have different volitions – for instance, when they make different choices in the case of equivalent or incommensurable options. In this sense, there is volitional difference above and beyond differences in beliefs and desires.

2.9 Volitional Diversity

In addition to volitional differences that have their source in beliefs and desires, and volitional differences that have their source in equivalent or incommensurable options, there are also volitional differences that have their source in the will itself – that is, in the faculty that is responsible for the formation and maintenance of volitions. This is a particularly significant source of volitional difference, which I will refer to as volitional diversity.

To approach the topic of volitional diversity, it is helpful to consider the topic of intention reconsideration. Agents form intentions in the light of certain circumstances, and these circumstances may change. For instance,

I may plan lunch with a friend tomorrow, when the weather forecast predicts probable sun. By the following morning, the weather forecast predicts probable rain. This may bear on my decision in various ways. For example, the walk to the restaurant is less appealing in the rain, which may be a reason to postpone the lunch, other things being equal. Something like this is almost always the case with our future-directed intentions, as the world is in flux and will almost always change, however slightly, in ways that we do not always foresee. How shall we revise our intentions in light of these facts?

In answering this question, we seem to face a dilemma. On the one hand, if we are always ready to revise our intentions, then there will be no end to the demands for revision. As just noted, there is almost always some unforeseen change in the facts that might bear on one's decision, and so a policy of constant openness to revision will, in effect, be a policy of constant revision. No decision will be truly settled, in a way that we ourselves and other people can rely on – which is one purpose of forming intentions in the first place. Intentions that are open to revisions on any grounds seem to be as good as no intentions at all.

On the other hand, if we are never ready to revise our intentions, our problems are just as bad. An agent who commits to her intentions come what may will find herself engaged in acts that are, by her own lights, pointless. Someone who keeps her intention to have lunch even if it is raining, the restaurant is closed, and her friend cancels is not a paradigm of practical rationality. Rather, she too is someone who seems to have lost touch with the very considerations that lead us to form intentions in the first place. Intentions that are never open to revisions on any grounds at all may be even worse than no intentions at all, as they may actively steer an agent toward acts that she has no interest in performing.

Bratman suggests that we respond to this kind of dilemma by articulating reasonable standards of reconsideration.[13] A reasonable agent will reconsider her intention under some circumstances, but not under any circumstances. Crucially, there is not a unique standard of reconsideration. Some agents will be prone to reconsideration (while still not reconsidering under all circumstances). Others will be more reluctant to reconsideration (while still reconsidering under some circumstances). There is a range of acceptable tendencies toward reconsideration of one's intentions.

Similar remarks apply to the reconsideration of one's policies. Someone may have a policy, for example, of never eating dessert with lunch. She might face a couple of questions with respect to that policy. One is whether it makes sense to consider an exception to that policy, for example, for a piece of birthday cake. Another is whether it makes sense to reconsider that policy wholesale, for example, in light of a new lunch companion who does enjoy having dessert with lunch. Some agents will be quite open to reconsidering their policies, while others will tend to stick to their policies unless there are very strong grounds for reconsideration. Either is legitimate; here too there is a range of acceptable tendencies.

These ranges are a source of volitional diversity. Two agents may be alike in their beliefs and desires, and also in the worlds that they inhabit, and yet may end up with different volitional states, even setting aside the differences due to equivalent or incommensurable options. For example, two agents might each intend (separately) to go to the park tomorrow, and the expected temperature for tomorrow might drop overnight. The first agent, prone to reconsideration, might revise her intention and intend to go to the museum instead. The second agent, reluctant to reconsideration, might stick to her intention and intend to go to the park. These agents are alike in what they want and believe, they face commensurable and inequivalent options, neither one is irrational, and yet they end up in different places. That is one consequence of volitional diversity.

Once we recognize the existence of volitional diversity, we can begin to acknowledge its scope and its impact. Much of life consists of forming plans and policies for the future and then navigating changing circumstances by the lights of these plans and policies. The question of how much one maintains one's plans, and how much one responds to changes in the world, will often determine the shape of the life that one ends up living. So volitional diversity is a major source of difference not only in volitions but also in lives themselves.

One useful way of thinking about volitional diversity is by analogy with neurodiversity. Consider autism spectrum disorder (ASD). Individuals with ASD have often been understood, within psychology and psychiatry, as having some kind of neurological or cognitive shortcoming, relative to supposedly normal persons who do not have such a shortcoming. Against this tendency, persons with ASD have advanced the view that they are simply different, not in any way deficient, in their neurological or cognitive functioning or style. The cognitive style characteristic of ASD may be less common than 'normal' varieties of cognitive functioning, but it is not inherently worse. It is simply different. This is the perspective defended and advanced, originally by the scholar and activist Judy Singer, as 'neurodiversity' (Milton, 2020).

Volitional diversity may be thought of as a cousin of neurodiversity. The animating idea of neurodiversity is that there is a range of neuro-cognitive styles and that those that are less common – for example, those involved in ASD – are often pathologized. But this pathologizing is a mistake: there are simply a range of neuro-cognitive styles, none inherently worse (or better) than any other. Similarly, I want to say, for volition. There are a range of volitional tendencies, and those that are less common are sometimes pathologized – we will see, in the next section, one form that this kind of pathologizing may take. But this too is a mistake: there are simply a range of volitional styles, none inherently worse (or better) than any other. This is what it means to acknowledge volitional diversity.

2.10 On 'Weakness of Will'

To appreciate the nature of volitional diversity, and the stigma that it can sometimes attract, it will be helpful to consider a case in some detail.

Consider an agent who is very inclined to revise her intentions and policies. It is not that her intentions and policies are always open to revision, for any reason – a case that we considered earlier – but simply that she tends to revise her intentions and policies much more frequently than the average person. Such a volitional tendency will impose costs, such as the time spent in reconsideration and the challenges of interpersonal coordination. These costs may be compensated for by other benefits, or they may not be. Nonetheless, this volitional style is not inherently worse or better than any other. That is the perspective urged by volitional diversity.

It is instructive to contrast this perspective with the philosopher Richard Holton's influential work on 'weakness of will' (Holton, 1999). Holton points out that there is a long-standing philosophical literature on akrasia or 'acting against one's better judgment': this is the phenomenon whereby an agent judges that she ought to do A but does not do A, and indeed performs some other act instead. Thus, I might judge that I ought to eat broccoli with my dinner but not eat broccoli with my dinner and eat some potato chips with my dinner instead. Here I am judging that I should do one thing, but acting contrary to my judgment, a conflict that can be, at least on certain theories of motivation, puzzling.

Holton points out that contemporary philosophers often dub this phenomenon 'weakness of will.' But, as Holton points out, that feels like a misnomer. After all, akrasia does not appear to involve the will at all, at least not directly. Rather, it is a cognitive phenomenon, whereby one's beliefs (about what is good or appropriate) are in conflict with what one does. If one held the belief-desire model, then perhaps one might try to assimilate 'weakness of will' to this kind of basically cognitive phenomenon.[14] But if one has a more expansive view of the mind, one which genuinely makes room for the will and volitional states, then one need not do this.

Instead, Holton recommends, as I have, the kind of tripartite model of the mind described by Bratman. Whatever 'weakness of will' is supposed to be, it is presumably a feature of the will, understood again as the faculty responsible for forming and maintaining volitions. Holton notes, plausibly, that a person described as 'weak-willed' will generally follow the kind of intention-revision policy described earlier: she will be inclined to revise her intentions in situations where most people would not revise their intentions. Indeed, Holton suggests defining 'weakness of will' in exactly this way. At first approximation, Holton proposes, 'a person is weak-willed if she revises her intentions too readily.'[15]

From the perspective of volitional diversity, there is something correct, but also something questionable, in Holton's proposal. On the one hand, he is correct to observe that the phenomenon that gets described as 'weakness of will' is in the first place a volitional one, and not cognitive. He is also correct to suggest that this phenomenon is correctly described in terms of tendencies toward intention revision.

What is more questionable is the negative normative valence that Holton adds to this phenomenon. For Holton, 'weakness of will' is not merely a statistically atypical tendency to revise one's intentions. Instead, it is also an object of criticism, namely that the agent is 'too ready' to revise her intentions. Holton maintains that this critical aspect is needed to capture the essentially negative aspect of an attribution of 'weakness of will.' In particular, Holton takes it to be a virtue of his account that it underwrites the 'stigma' that is attached to weakness of will (Holton, 1999, pp. 253–254).

But it is important to be precise about the source of the negative valence of 'weakness of will.' One possibility is that this negative valence is appropriate: 'weakness of will' represents a specific kind of failure of practical rationality, which is appropriately criticized and stigmatized. This is Holton's view. Another possibility, however, is that this negative valence has its genesis in something altogether external to the theory of rationality. There is a tendency for statistically typical people to form negative judgments about statistically atypical people, and to suppose that these judgments are underwritten by some genuine evaluative difference. For instance – to return to the autism spectrum and the question of neurodiversity – there is a tendency for people with statistically typical neuro-cognitive styles to assume that persons with statistically atypical neuro-cognitive styles are in some sense worse off than people with typical styles. But one lesson of the neurodiversity perspective is that this is a mistake. While there is a difference here, the idea that one of these alternatives is worse than the other is a projection of the prejudices of the statistical majority rather than of any underlying evaluative facts.

From the perspective of volitional diversity, we should say something similar about the phenomenon of 'weakness of will.' Some agents are indeed more prone than others to revise their intentions. This is a genuine and important source of volitional difference, above and beyond other psychological and non-psychological differences between agents. But this is simply a difference: someone is not inherently worse off in virtue of having this volitional tendency. In certain circumstances – especially, as we will see, circumstances that are specifically designed to exploit this tendency – a person with a tendency toward revision of her intentions may end up with atypically bad outcomes. But this is not an inherent feature of this volitional tendency, which is, in itself, neither good nor bad.

From this perspective, the negative aspect of Holton's account is not justified by his description of the phenomenon. Neither is the term 'weak-willed.' I have been intentionally putting this word in quotation marks throughout this discussion, and there is a reason for this. We do, as Holton observes, have an ordinary concept of 'weakness of will,' and the label 'weak-willed' aims to represent this concept. It turns out that this conception is an admixture of a descriptive and a normative element. The lesson to be drawn from this is not that we want to follow the ordinary concept and describe the will in a negative way. Instead, we want our theory of the will to be properly descriptive – as Bratman's account is, and as the volitional diversity perspective is – and in this respect to move beyond the ordinary concept, which blends a descriptive account with certain inherited prejudices about atypical volitional tendencies.

As we should treat this ordinary concept cautiously, so too should we treat the term 'weak-willed' itself with caution. This term is so much a part of ordinary language that we apply it, without hesitation, to ourselves and others. If I do not keep my diet, I call myself 'weak-willed.' If a student does not set aside enough time to finish her paper, she is 'weak-willed.' And so forth. This phrase, and the idea behind it, is so much a part of our everyday speech that we seldom reflect on it.

But we should reflect on it. This term is, at best, an insult.[16] It expresses the judgment that there is something wrong with certain patterns of intention revision. This judgment is unwarranted, and certainly should not be smuggled into purportedly descriptive language. Terms like 'weak-willed' have the unfortunate effect of taking certain prejudices and making them seem as if they are part of the very fabric of agency. This way of speaking and thinking is then reified within sophisticated philosophical accounts, such as Holton's. All of this rests on a mistake.

I will therefore not be using the term 'weak-willed,' or proving a philosophical account of 'weakness of will.' On the approach defended here, there is no such thing to account for. This is not because agents do not ever display a tendency to revise their intentions – some certainly do – but because the presupposition that there is something inherently wrong with this tendency is simply not met. In what follows, I will be insistent on describing volitional differences and diversity descriptively. If there are any evaluative judgments to be made about these differences, these will be made explicit.

2.11 What Is a Volitional Defect?

In the foregoing, I have emphasized the significance of volitions and their independence from beliefs and desires. I have described multiple sources of volitional difference: how agents may have different intentions and policies, even relative to the same beliefs, desires, and circumstances. I have emphasized in particular the significance of volitional diversity, how agents' different volitional tendencies – for instance, a tendency to revise one's intentions more frequently than is typical – may be a systematic source of volitional difference.

In all of this, I have stressed that these are entirely descriptive categories. So far as has been said, there is nothing inherently bad, or good, about any one of these volitional differences. Or, if there is some evaluative valence to these differences, that is something that must be argued for, and not simply assumed. I have criticized the concept and label of 'weakness of will' on precisely the grounds that it assumes, without justifying, such differences.

We can still ask, however: are there any volitional differences such that a person is worse off just in virtue of having those differences? To adopt the language of the previous chapter, are there any volitional defects? If there is simply no such thing as a volitional defect, then we can immediately conclude that all volitional differences are merely descriptive. If on the other hand, there are volitional defects, then we can ask the further question of whether some given volitional difference is a defect, and how we would decide this question.

To get a handle on this question, it is helpful to compare volitions to beliefs and desires. Are there any beliefs, or patterns of belief, that are defective, such that a person is worse off, from the point of view of belief, just in virtue of having them?[17] Plausibly, there are.[18] Consider, for example, the following pattern of beliefs. Someone believes a proposition p, believes that p implies some proposition q, and yet does not believe the proposition q. This is plausibly a genuine defect in belief: someone is worse off, from the point of view of belief, just in virtue of having this pattern of beliefs.

Consider then desire. It is customary to think that the idea of a defective desire is misguided – desires are in themselves, one might think, neither good nor bad. But here too we can understand patterns of desire as defective, at least when these are represented as preferences. One clear example is given by violations of the requirement of transitivity discussed earlier. Consider an agent who prefers some outcome A to some outcome B, who prefers some outcome B to some outcome C, and who also prefers outcome C to outcome A. Well-known arguments show that such an agent can be offered a series of propositions such that she will be sure to lose money in response to that series of propositions (Pettigrew, 2020). In this way, this pattern of desires is a plausible example of a defect in desire. That is, these are desires such that one is worse off simply in virtue of having them.

We can now ask: are there defects in volition, in the same way that there are defects in belief and desire? Plausibly, in this case, too, the answer to this question is that there are. One much-discussed variety of volitional defect is what is sometimes called 'means-end incoherence.' Let us say that an agent intends to perform an act A, believes some act B is a necessary means to A, and yet does not intend to do B. Whatever the world is like, such an agent is worse off, from the point of view of volition, simply in virtue of having that combination of intentions and beliefs.[19] In this respect, there may be volitional defects, just as there are defects in belief and desire.[20]

The framework of intentions and policies suggests further grounds for volitional defects. Consider, for example, someone who has a policy of performing act A when in circumstances C yet who consistently, when in circumstances C, does not intend to A. Whatever her policies and intentions, such an agent is in some sense in a kind of volitional conflict, such that there is some defect in her volitions just in virtue of those volitions themselves, and their relationship to one another.

There is, then, such a thing as volitional defect. Means-end incoherence is one clear example, and the planning framework plausibly yields some additional kinds of examples. Yet there are limits to volitional defect. Not just every atypical volition is a defect, and not every pattern of volitions that makes an agent worse off, in her actual circumstances, will count as a volitional defect. At first pass, volitional states need to at least exhibit some kind of inconsistency or incoherence to count as defective.

We have not been given any reason to think that the phenomena that I have identified as volitional diversity typically involve a defect. In particular, the tendency to readily revise one's intentions, more readily than most people do, does not appear to involve any incoherence or inconsistency. Instead, it appears to simply be one volitional pattern among many, different but not in any respect worse. This is a further reason to reject the label of 'weak-willed.' It would be a harmful insult even if it did describe an actual volitional defect. The fact it appears to be based on no evaluative facts at all makes it doubly objectionable.[21]

Volitional defect therefore represents a real but circumscribed phenomenon. Whenever we encounter some form of volitional diversity, there can be a natural inclination to understand it as a kind of defect. This is particularly so when it is a relatively unusual tendency or one that tends to lead to bad outcomes in the actual circumstances, or, especially, both. But the foregoing discussion is meant to keep us mindful that – with volition as with much else – what seems defective may simply be unfamiliar.

2.12 The Volitional Basis of Addiction

With that understanding of volition in place, we can now return to the topic of addiction. What is the psychological basis of addiction? Fundamentally, I want to propose, the psychological basis of addiction is volition. Addiction typically involves volitional difference, but it most fundamentally and essentially involves a distinctive kind of volitional diversity.

Begin with volitional differences between the addicted person and the non-addicted person. A person addicted to some activity A (where A may be the use of some given substance) will typically form intentions to A on a regular basis, often in circumstances where a person who is not addicted will not form the intention to A. She may well form policies of doing A, which again may hold in circumstances where a person who is not addicted would typically not do A. These volitional differences will mirror and often underwrite, the behavioral differences between the addicted and the non-addicted person. What we often see, in addiction, is a pattern of volition and behavior that is reliably – and, from the point of view of a non-addicted person, atypically – directed toward doing A.

This is an important volitional difference, but it is not to be identified, I want to suggest, with addiction itself. Someone may regularly intend to use a substance, and regularly act on her intentions, without thereby being addicted to using that substance. This is the point that heavy use does not in itself suffice for addiction, a point acknowledged even by most accounts that understand addiction as what I have called a behavioral defect.

What then is the psychological element that is distinctive to addiction? If someone endorses an account of addiction on which desire or belief (or their combination) is central, one might locate the salient difference in desires or belief. If, however, we take seriously the independence of volition, we have another way in which to distinguish the addicted person from the non-addicted person. The difference between the addicted person and the non-addicted person lies not merely in their volitions and policies, but in their tendencies with respect to those policies. Addiction is not a mere matter of volitional difference (as is, for example, the distinction between typical and heavy use) but a genuine matter of volitional diversity.

What kind of volitional diversity? At first approximation, addiction to some activity A (where, again, this may be the use of a certain substance) involves an atypical tendency to form intentions and policies to A, and to revise policies against doing A. The atypicality in question here is, again, statistical. If the A-directed volitions of a given population form something like a normal distribution, the tendencies of a person addicted to A will occupy a far tail of that distribution. Indeed, that atypicality is partly constitutive of what it is to be addicted.

This picture of the volitional character of addiction resembles an account that we have just considered, namely Holton's account of 'weakness of will.' What is the relationship between these two accounts? It is roughly accurate to say that anyone who satisfies this condition for addiction will also satisfy Holton's account. That is, at first approximation, someone is addicted to A only if she is 'weak-willed' with respect to A. There are, however, two crucial clarifications to be amended to this claim.

First, as was already emphasized in our earlier discussion, the label 'weak-willed' has a pejorative aspect that is no part of the present account of addiction. Again, it is the volitional phenomenon identified by Holton, and not the negative valence involved in his characterization, that we should want to pursue.

Second, this kind of volitional diversity is necessary, but not sufficient, for addiction. There are additional conditions on addiction, beyond this core of volitional diversity, which must go into a full account of what addiction is. These conditions, which are essentially non-psychological in nature, are ones we will explore in what follows.

With those qualifications in place, we can accept that addiction essentially involves a kind of volitional diversity, which is roughly that identified by Holton under the label 'weakness of will.' Once we have discarded that label and the kind of thinking about the will that lies behind it, we face another, more constructive task. How should we think about volitional diversity, if we are not to understand it in a stigmatizing way? How do we understand its place both in individual psychology and in social organizations that need to accommodate psychological diversity in all of its forms? How, finally, do we understand the specific kind of volitional diversity that is partly constitutive of addiction? To answer these questions, I suggest, we need to develop our minimal notion of volitional diversity into an expansive notion of volitional disability. That is the task of the next chapter.

Notes

1 See Svanberg (2018) for an introductory overview of this kind of work.
2 Plato, notably, endorses a kind of tripartite theory; see Singpurwalla (2010).
3 This is Elizabeth Anscombe's distinction in 'direction of fit' (Anscombe, 1957).
4 There is a considerable philosophical literature on how exactly these kinds of representations are to be understood; see Lewis (1979) for one influential proposal.

5 Another important account that may fall in this family is the 'liberal' account of addiction defended in Foddy and Savulescu (2010), which takes desire to be central to addiction while explicitly endorsing a minimal and descriptive model of addiction, one that sees continuity between addiction on the one hand and ordinary strong desires on the other.

6 A notable exception in the philosophical literature is Neil Levy's work on understanding addiction as a disorder of belief in Levy (2014).

7 As I noted in Chapter 1, one way of understanding Becker and Murphy's project is as a particular implementation of the idea that addiction is best understood as a rational response to a suboptimal predicament – a predicament created, on their view, by past consumption itself.

8 The DSM-5 is a broadly behavioral account of addiction of the sort that we, in Chapter 1, rejected. Nonetheless, it is telling that the DSM-5 appeals to psychology to fix the reference of the kinds of behaviors that purportedly distinguish addiction, and that these psychological references include volitional ones. Furthermore, it bears repeating that the DSM-5 does not give a general account of substance use disorders, but rather criteria for diagnosing a range of particular substance use disorders. The quoted remark is taken from the criteria for alcohol use disorder, but similar phrases occur in the criteria for other substance use disorders as well.

9 An important third element is self-governing policies, which are policies of treating specific considerations as reasons (Bratman, 2000). It is only the first two elements, namely intentions and first-order policies to act in certain ways, that will figure in the account of addiction that I will develop here.

10 A number of other writers have thought to explore the question of addiction from within a broadly Bratman-based framework; one notable proposal in this direction is that of Richard Holton (Holton, 1999), which I will consider in some detail later

11 The theory of distributive justice and the nature of primary goods will turn out to be fundamental to the development of the disability view of addiction, and we will return to these topics at length in Chapter 7.

12 This is the phenomenon that gives rise to what Barry Schwartz calls a 'paradox of choice': a plurality of choices gives rise to feelings of anxiety and regret (Schwartz, 2004). In fact, the empirical support for this alleged paradox is somewhat mixed (Scheibehenne *et al.*, 2010). The present point turns only on the existence of this phenomenon, and is neutral on its value or disvalue.

13 The account of reconsideration is an integral part of the theory of rational agency developed in Bratman (1987); see especially Chapter 5.

14 This is the kind of strategy that Donald Davidson, for example, endorses in his treatment of 'weakness of will' (Davidson, 1980, Essay 2).

15 (Holton, 1999, p. 247). Holton goes on to slightly refine this initial proposal: an agent is weak-willed only if the intentions she revises too readily are 'contrary-inclination defeating' (Holton, 1999, p. 257), where an intention is contrary-intention defeating just when it is in some sense meant to resist desires to the contrary. I will leave this refinement implicit in what follows, as does Holton. In later work (Holton, 2009), Holton introduces some further clarifications to this initial account, and develops his own account of some of the mechanisms of addiction, which is quite different from the kind of account to be defended in what follows.

16 At worst, it is a slur. For one account of the distinction between slurs and insults, see Orlando & Saab (2020). I am grateful to Lauren Ashwell for discussion on this point.

17 The qualification, 'from the point of view of belief,' is meant to exclude those cases that are in some sense external to the aim of belief itself. In a world where people who believe that roses are not red are rewarded with untold riches, the belief that roses are red is in some sense a defective one, but this is plausibly not the kind of defect we are concerned with here. For a helpful exploration of the aim of belief, see Wedgwood (2002).

18 While the example in the text is a kind of formal defect in belief, it is also possible that beliefs admit of a more substantive kind of defect. In particular, beliefs may be true or false, and a false belief is plausibly a defective one. This marks at least one asymmetry between belief, on the one hand, and desire and intention, on the other, since belief is answerable to the world in a distinctive kind of way. Thanks to Robert Kelly for helpful comments on this point.

19 The qualifier here is meant to capture the same point made earlier with respect to belief – that while we can imagine circumstances in which this combination of attitudes is rewarded, this combination of attitudes is somehow defective with reference to the aim or purpose of volition itself.

20 It is an interesting question exactly how alike these defects are to one another. The almost logical nature of means-end incoherence has led some to return to the thought that volition is to be assimilated to belief after all (Setiya, 2007). Bratman resists this line of reasoning for reasons given in Bratman (2009).

21 Even when we turn to aspects of the will that seem plausibly to involve a defect, such as means-end incoherence, the stigma involved in a term like 'weak-willed' is inappropriate. Means-end incoherence is described, at worst, as 'irrationality,' a mild epithet if it is an epithet at all. Our linguistic practices suggest that we tend to be fairly mild and understanding in our descriptions of the will and its variations.

Works Cited

American Psychiatric Association. (2013). *Diagnostic and Statistical Manual of Mental Disorders (DSM-5)*. American Psychiatric Publications.

Anscombe, G.E.M. (1957). *Intention*. Blackwell.

Becker, G.S., & Murphy, K.M. (1988). A Theory of Rational Addiction. *Journal of Political Economy*, *96*(4), 675–700.

Bratman, M. (1987). *Intention, Plans, and Practical Reason*. Harvard University Press.

Bratman, M. (2009). Intention, Belief, Practical, Theoretical. In S. Robertson (Ed.), *Spheres of Reason*. Oxford University Press.

Bratman, M. (2000). Reflection, Planning, and Temporally Extended Agency. *The Philosophical Review*, *109*(1), 35–61.

Davidson, D. (1980). *Essays on Actions and Events*. Oxford University Press.

Foddy, B., & Savulescu, J. (2010). A Liberal Account of Addiction. *Philosophy, Psychiatry, & Psychology*, *17*(1), 1–22.

Holton, R. (1999). Intention and Weakness of Will. *The Journal of Philosophy*, *96*(5), 241–262.

Holton, R. (2009). *Willing, Wanting, Waiting*. Oxford University Press.

Levy, N. (2014). Addiction as a Disorder of Belief. *Biology & Philosophy*, *29*(3), 337–355.

Lewis, D. (1979). Attitudes de Dicto and de Se. *Philosophical Review*, *88*(4), 513–543.

McHugh, R.K., Hearon, B.A., & Otto, M.W. (2010). Cognitive Behavioral Therapy for Substance Use Disorders. *Psychiatric Clinics*, *33*(3), 511–525.

Milton, D. (Ed.). (2020). *The Neurodiversity Reader*. Pavilion Publishing.

Murthy, T.V. (ms.). What Is It Like to Be an Addict? The Perceptual Model of Substance Use Disorder. Unpublished ms.

Orlando, E., & Saab, A. (2020). Slurs, Stereotypes and Insults. *Acta Analytica*, *35*(4), 599–621.

Pettigrew, R. (2020). Dutch Book Arguments. *Elements in Decision Theory and Philosophy*. Cambridge University Press.

Rawls, J. (1971). *A Theory of Justice*. Belknap Press.

Scheibehenne, B., Greifeneder, R., & Todd, P.M. (2010). Can There Ever Be Too Many Options? A Meta-Analytic Review of Choice Overload. *Journal of Consumer Research*, *37*(3), 409–425.

Schwartz, B. (2004). *The Paradox of Choice*. Harper Perennial.

Setiya, K. (2007). Cognitivism about Instrumental Reason. *Ethics*, *117*(4), 649–673.

Singpurwalla, R. (2010). The Tripartite Theory of Motivation in Plato's Republic. *Philosophy Compass*, *5*(11), 880–892.

Svanberg, J. (2018). *The Psychology of Addiction*. Routledge.

Velleman, D. (1989). *Practical Reflection*. Princeton University Press.

Wallace, R.J. (1999). Addiction as Defect of the Will: Some Philosophical Reflections. *Law and Philosophy*, *18*(6), 621.

Watson, G. (1999). Disordered Appetites: Addiction, Compulsion, and Dependence. In Elster, J. (Ed.), *Addiction: Entries and Exits*. Oxford University Press.

Wedgwood, R. (2002). The Aim of Belief. *Philosophical Perspectives*, *16*, 267–297.

3

VOLITIONAL DISABILITY

3.1 The Disability Perspective

In Chapter 1, I argued against views of addiction on which addiction is considered a defect, a feature of a person such that she is worse off just in virtue of having that property. More specifically, I argued against views on which addiction is a defect of the agent herself (such as the disease model of addiction), those on which addiction is a defect in the agent's behavior (such as the behavioral disorder model), and those on which addiction involves a rational response to some underlying defect (such as the self-medication model). I proposed that we consider instead a view on which addiction is not a defect but is instead a real but evaluatively neutral difference between the addicted and the non-addicted person.

In Chapter 2, I considered the forms that this kind of difference might take. I introduced a tripartite picture of the mind on which the mind consists fundamentally of beliefs, desires, and volitions, none of which can be reduced to any of the others. I argued that the most plausible psychological basis for addiction is volition. In particular, I suggested that addiction is associated with a kind of volitional diversity, specifically a tendency to form and revise one's intentions in a certain sort of way. This is a tendency that has been associated with the epithet 'weak-willed' though, as I argued, we should reject that term and its evaluative implications. The volitional diversity involved in addiction is a difference, but not a defect.

In this respect, the account of addiction and the will developed in Chapter 2 begins to make good on the promissory note issued in Chapter 1. That is, Chapter 2 articulates the psychological grounds for a view on

DOI: 10.4324/9781003410263-4

which addiction is a real, but non-defective, difference. But this is only the beginning of an account of addiction. Addiction is not merely a psychological phenomenon. It can inform the entire scope of a person's life plans and self-conception. And it takes place within a social and political context. We want our account of addiction to be as expansive as the phenomenon that it purports to describe, and an account of addiction that attends only to individual psychology does not yet do that.

In this chapter, I propose to expand the foregoing account of addiction in just that way. The key idea will be that of disability. Work on disability represents one of the most significant developments in normative thought that has taken place in recent decades. A disability perspective has already informed, implicitly, much of the foregoing discussion. In particular, the idea that differences among agents should not be conceived of as defects, despite a tendency in our thinking to do just that, has been a theme running through the entire discussion thus far. This is a line of thinking that has its grounds in the theory of disability, and in turning to the topic of disability we can make that dependence explicit.

The introduction of disability, however, also raises several new issues. There is not just one theory of disability, and there is an ongoing debate about the best way to understand disability. The approach here will aim to be as ecumenical as possible. The picture of disability that I will be drawing on owes much, in its broad contours, to the 'social model' of disability.[1] Specifically, I will proceed with a picture of disability on which it involves two broad factors. First, a difference in the disabled person (an 'impairment,' though like many I find this label to be a problematic one).[2] Second, an environment and society that is structured in ways inhospitable to the disabled person (this is the 'social' aspect of the social model). But more than any particular model of disability, I want to draw on three broad themes about disability, which jointly constitute what I understand as a certain kind of perspective on disability. These themes are endorsed and were often first advocated by the proponents of the disability model, but they are shared also by disability theorists who disavow that model and its presuppositions.[3]

The first theme has already been prominent in our earlier discussion of addiction. This is that the difference involved in disability is not itself a defect. To be deaf, for example, is to have a different manner of processing perceptual inputs, but not to have one that is defective. As a kind of corollary to that observation, deafness is not necessarily something that needs to be treated or fixed – for example, through the implantation of cochlear implants.[4] This perspective rejects the 'medical model' of disability, on which disability is a condition that demands treatment or cure.

The second theme has also been suggested in our earlier discussion. This is that the adverse outcomes associated with disability are typically to be attributed to the environment in which the disabled person finds herself. For example, deaf people are known to have poor health outcomes relative to the general population, and this is due not to any inherent aspect of deafness but rather to the fact that deaf people have difficulty accessing a health system that is designed for hearing people and that discriminates against people who are deaf (Kuenburg et al., 2016). Thus the disability perspective is oriented toward the environment, and in particular to the impact of systematic discrimination, when giving explanations of the outcomes related to disability.

The third theme in the disability perspective builds on these two earlier ones. This is that, when we turn from describing disability to actually making changes that benefit people with disabilities, we want to focus on legal and political institutions. While there is a role for medical and other clinical interventions in serving people with disabilities, the primary focus of disability policy should be ensuring that differences between people are acknowledged and, when it is needed, provided with reasonable accommodations. While the first theme holds that disability is not primarily a medical issue, and the second theme holds that it is not primarily an individual-level one, the third theme explicitly recognizes that disability is, in the first place, a legal and political concern.

The main purpose of this book is to explain what it means to take a disability perspective on addiction, and the theoretical and practical implications of doing so. This chapter begins that explanation by offering an account of the particular kind of disability that is involved in addiction, namely volitional disability. To understand what volitional disability is, it will be helpful to begin with other, more familiar, varieties of disability.

3.2 Kinds of Disability

Many philosophical discussions of disability generally focus on physical disability.[5] Physical disabilities are disabilities that essentially involve some difference in the physical constitution of the disabled person, such as deafness, blindness, or paraplegia. Often when people think about disability, it is physical disabilities that they have in mind. This can be a barrier to accepting the view that addiction is a disability, for there appear to be notable asymmetries between physical disability on the one hand and addiction on the other.

Most obviously, addiction does not essentially involve any difference in the physical constitution of the addicted person – though many people with addictions will also have or acquire physical disabilities, and conversely.[6] If addiction is a disability, it is not a disability of the body itself. As a corollary, addiction tends to not be visible in the way that many (though not all) physical disabilities are. This hidden aspect of addiction is another reason why the possibility of addiction being a disability can often be neglected.

In addition to this asymmetry in the grounds of disability, there is also a difference in the kinds of responses that physical disability and addiction demand. Physical disability demands, among other things, a certain form of physical accommodations: these are alterations to the built environment that make it more navigable to the disabled person. Wheelchair ramps and Braille labels are two prominent such accommodations. Yet addiction does not appear, superficially, to demand these particular kinds of alterations to the built environment.

In short, the most commonly discussed variety of disability is physical disability. Physical disability involves a difference in physical constitution, often (but not always) visible, and demands, among other things, specific kinds of physical accommodations. Addiction, by contrast, does not essentially involve any physical difference, nor any visible difference, and does not appear to demand distinctive kinds of accommodations. If we are looking for a model for understanding addiction as a disability, it makes sense to look elsewhere.

One thought is that addiction might instead be assimilated to the family of disabilities that are called 'developmental disabilities.' Developmental disabilities involve distinctive differences in a person's learning, behavior, or language use. They are so-called because they typically arise in the course of the developmental period. Common examples include autism spectrum disorder and ADHD (attention-deficit hyperactivity disorder). Unlike physical disabilities, developmental disabilities do not essentially involve any change or difference in a person's physical constitution. And, unlike many physical disabilities, developmental disabilities need not be readily visible to an outside observer. Finally, while developmental disabilities do demand accommodations, especially in educational contexts, they do not typically demand the specific forms of accommodations that are appropriate for physical disabilities. In all of these respects, developmental disability seems like a more appropriate model for addiction than physical disability.[7]

But is addiction a developmental disability? There are a couple of challenges to the proposal that it is. First, addiction is much more heterogeneous in its chronology. While developmental disabilities often emerge in childhood and persist thereafter, addiction is known to begin and especially to remit at a wide spectrum of ages along the lifespan (Heyman, 2013). In most cases, the diagnosis of substance use disorder is made in early adulthood, unlike conditions such as ADHD where studies indicate a vast majority of individuals exhibit significant symptoms in childhood.[8] In short, addiction tends to emerge later in the lifespan and to have a quite broad range of ages of onset when it does emerge, which makes it hard to assimilate to developmental disabilities.

We might get around this point by expanding our concept of developmental disability, and perhaps by revising our language for it, but another challenge looms. This is that addiction, unlike autism spectrum disorder and ADHD, is not primarily cognitive in its presentation. Rather, its primary indicators are certain patterns of choice and behavior. As I argued in the previous chapter, addiction appears to be associated with certain distinctive modes of volition, which makes it unlike the most familiar cases of developmental disability.[9]

We might expand our notion of developmental disability to accommodate this point, but a more plausible and less arbitrary route is to recognize that there may simply be another kind of disability at issue in addiction and to try to articulate what that kind of disability is.

The kind of disability involved in addiction is neither physical nor developmental. Instead, it is, as I have indicated, volitional. The disability involved in addiction is a disability of the will. What is a volitional disability? The account of the will and its varieties developed in the last chapter provide us with materials to begin to answer that question.

3.3 From Volitional Diversity to Volitional Disability

In the previous chapter, I distinguished between volitional difference and volitional diversity. Volitional difference is any case where two agents have different intentions and policies. Many cases of volitional difference will be grounded in differences in other psychological differences, specifically differences in belief and desire. But there are interesting cases where agents may have volitional differences without any other psychological differences. For example, as we discussed in the previous chapter, there are cases where an agent must choose between two equivalent or incommensurable options, and where her beliefs and desires therefore underdetermine what choice she will make.

Volitional diversity is a further phenomenon, which depends neither on differences in belief and desire nor on features of the external situation. It arises from the fact that the very manner in which agents maintain or revise their plans and policies, in response to shifting information, may take a variety of forms, none of them better or worse than any other.

A core form of volitional diversity is the case where an agent is atypically prone to form intentions and policies to perform an act A, and atypically prone to revising her policies against doing A. Such an agent will, under almost all circumstances, have a pattern of doing A significantly more frequently than a typical agent might. This behavioral difference is not grounded in the agent's beliefs or desires, or in external facts. Rather, it is grounded, in a certain way, in the will itself.

In the previous chapter, I noted that this is the phenomenon that that is sometimes referred to as 'weakness of will,' and hence that 'weakness of will' may be understood as a kind of volitional diversity. Here I want to defend a further claim about this kind of volitional diversity: it amounts, not merely to volitional diversity, but to a form of volitional disability.

To assess this claim, or any claim about volitional disability, we need to answer two foundational questions. First, under what conditions does someone count as having a volitional disability? Second, still more generally, when does anyone count as having a disability at all?

Let us begin with the second, more general, question. I do not propose to offer a general theory of disability, in the sense of articulating necessary and sufficient conditions for someone's having a disability. I am skeptical that there is such a theory to be given. But, as I have already noted, I am working in a broad sense within a 'social model' of disability. On this conception of disability, disability involves both an internal aspect and an external, environmental aspect. From this point of view, if we are concerned with locating the considerations by which a 'mere difference' becomes a genuine disability, it is natural to find those considerations in the environment in which the disabled person finds herself.

There are many such considerations, but advocates of the social model as well as subsequent writers have identified one as being especially significant: the fact of widespread and often systematic discrimination against the difference in question. Why does the perceptual difference involved in deafness constitute a disability? In part because that difference is discriminated against, by people who do not have this difference, in systematic ways. So, in response to our second question, about the nature of disability generally, an essential part of the answer is the fact that a disability is something that is systematically discriminated against. In a manner of speaking, that discrimination is part of what makes it a disability in the first place.

Return now to the first question. Under what circumstances does someone count as having a volitional disability? The foregoing discussion suggests that at least two pieces must be in place. She must have volitional tendencies that constitute volitional diversity – that is, atypical patterns of forming and revising intentions and policies, ones which outrun simple differences in desire and belief. In addition, those volitional tendencies must be the subject of discrimination in the society in which she finds herself. At first approximation, volitional disability may be understood as volitional diversity that is subject to discrimination.

This is not a complete analysis of what it is to have a volitional disability, let alone of what it is to have a disability generally.[10] There are several complications to volitional disability, some of which will be addressed in what follows. Nonetheless, this account gives a kind of picture of volitional disability that allows us to identify its general contours, to identify instances of its type, and to distinguish it from earlier accounts of volitional disability. The next section explores each of these features of the account.

3.4 Understanding Volitional Disability

What is volitional disability, on the present account? I have suggested that it is volitional diversity that is subject to discrimination. But what exactly does this claim amount to?

It is easiest to begin with what this account emphatically does not say. On the account of volitional disability suggested here, volitional disability does not involve any volitional defect. In the previous chapter, we explicitly defined volitional defect and gave core examples of it, such as means-end incoherence. Volitional diversity, and so volitional disability, is simply a different phenomenon.[11] Insofar as there is a negative aspect to volitional disability, it comes not from anything internal to the agent's will but rather from the social reactions – namely, discrimination and exploitation – against her volitional style.

Volitional disability has features that distinguish it from other core forms of disability. Unlike physical disability, it is not typically visible or connected in any distinctive way to an agent's physical constitution. Unlike developmental disabilities, it does not typically arise in the context of development and is not associated with any distinctive forms of information processing. Volitional disability, we may say, is on the present account an invisible and post-developmental form of disability, which constitutes a distinct class of disability.[12]

What are the members of this class? That is, on the present account of volitional disability, what is an actual example of volitional disability? We have already discussed one plausible candidate in the previous chapter. This is the volitional tendency that involves a tendency to form intentions and policies to do an act A and to revise one's policies against doing A. To make the case that this form of volitional diversity amounts to a volitional disability, we need to argue that this volitional tendency is the subject of discrimination and stigma. That argument has, to some extent, already been made. Indeed, the very fact that this tendency is commonly referred to as 'weakness of will' is prima facie evidence of that stigma. Further arguments for this key claim will be developed in what follows.

There are likely other members of this class as well. Consider a persistent tendency to not form intentions at all, even in circumstances where most people would form some intention or other. Such a volitional state is not to be identified with a lack of desire or belief, but rather a regular non-formation of intentions or policies despite the presence of desires or beliefs that typically suffice to ground volitions. This is a kind of volitional diversity. It is also, arguably, a stigmatized one. It is something like the tendency that was described, by medieval philosophers, as *acedia*, and which was understood by them as a kind of volitional vice (Daly, 2007). This kind of refusal of volition can be similarly stigmatized in contemporary culture, even though, as I have suggested, it is simply one form the will may take, not inherently worse than any other.[13]

I will return later to the varieties of volitional disability. But it is certainly the volitional tendency referred to as 'weakness of will' that is the most prominent, and also the most stigmatized. This is no small part because of its association with addiction. I suggested in the previous chapter that there is a tight connection between addiction and this form of volitional diversity. I have now argued that this form of volitional diversity constitutes, due in part to the forces of discrimination and stigma, a volitional disability. Putting these claims together, we arrive at a central contention of this book: that addiction is a disability, specifically a volitional disability. That claim too is one that we will return to, and indeed its full elaboration will be the task of the next chapter. Before coming to that, I want to consider in more detail the features of volitional disability itself.

3.5 Volitional Disability and Outcomes

One aspect of disabilities that cannot be neglected is that they are associated with suboptimal outcomes. As noted earlier, deafness appears to be associated with obstacles in accessing health care (Kuenburg *et al.*, 2016) and is associated with economic and educational challenges as well (Welsh, 2019). It has even been conjectured that hearing impairment is associated with lower life expectancy, though recent research has called that association into question (West & Lynch, 2020). Whatever the precise nature of these correlations, they are widespread and long-standing. This suggests that the explanation for such correlations will have to be an appropriately deep one.

One idea, often simply assumed, proceeds from a certain picture of what disability is. Disability, it is assumed, is a certain kind of defect. People who are disabled will therefore encounter a wide variety of suboptimal outcomes, in virtue of their disability. Indeed, part of the evidence for the claim that disability is a defect is supposedly the very fact that it is so strongly associated with those outcomes.

In the case of deafness, many of us have come to accept that this explanation misconstrues the relationship between deafness and disadvantage. It is not that deafness, in itself, is a defect and hence the cause of suboptimal outcomes. Rather, deafness is systematically discriminated against, and this discrimination is the actual source of suboptimal outcomes. Sometimes the mechanism by which this discrimination works is relatively clear, as in the discrimination against the deaf embedded in many educational systems. Often it is more insidious and widespread, like the discrimination that deaf people encounter in accessing basic health care. In either case, it is our attitudes toward deafness, rather than deafness itself, that are the real origins of disadvantage.

Volitional disability, too, is associated with suboptimal outcomes. People who are atypically inclined to form intentions to A, and to revise policies against A, often experience outcomes much worse than those who do not have these tendencies. This is especially so when A is an activity that is itself correlated with suboptimal outcomes, such as gambling, drinking alcohol, or eating high-calorie food. Here it can seem natural to offer the very explanation we rejected in the case of physical disability. According to this explanation, the volitional disability in question is a defect. It therefore leads people to regularly engage in activities such as gambling or alcohol use, which in turn leads to suboptimal outcomes. Indeed, the very fact that the tendency leads to these outcomes is evidence that it is a defect.

Nonetheless, I want to suggest, we should understand the relationship between volitional disability and disadvantage in the same way we do the relationship between physical disability and disadvantage. Volitional disability is not, as I have already suggested, a defect. Volitional disability is indeed correlated with suboptimal outcomes. But these outcomes are in large part an effect of social forces.

One of these forces is discrimination. Like physical disability, volitional disability is systematically discriminated against and stigmatized. Another, however, is the distinct but related influence of exploitation.[14] Volitional disabilities, which affect the faculty of decision itself, are especially vulnerable to social mechanisms that are specifically designed to exploit people with the disabilities in question. This exploitation can be extreme in its effects and may make the idea that volitional disability is a defect seem almost inevitable. But here again, this is a mistake: the suboptimal and at times devastating outcomes associated with volitional disability are not the product of volitional disabilities itself, but of a social and economic system comprehensively designed to exploit those disabilities.

3.6 Discrimination and Exploitation

To begin, consider the discrimination to which people with volitional disabilities are subject. Some of this discrimination is simple individual-level bias. People with volitional disabilities are often regarded, in their interactions with other people, as in certain respects objectionable. When Holton argues that people with 'weakness of will' are stigmatized and that his account is meant to vindicate this stigma, this is the sort of phenomenon he has in mind.[15]

Other forces of discrimination are more structural. In principle, any system that is designed to determine whether or not individuals form or revise intentions in a distinctive way may realize discrimination against people with volitional disabilities. Arguably the most significant form of discrimination against people with volitional disabilities is discrimination that is explicitly directed at people with addictions, which we will consider in detail later.

So, one source of suboptimal outcomes for people with volitional disabilities is discrimination against those people – that is, negative judgments and the willful denial of opportunities. However, another major source of suboptimal outcomes for people with volitional disabilities is the exploitation of those people – that is, the creation of institutions or markets that are designed to extract as much as possible from people with volitional disabilities. This kind of process is especially common, and especially insidious, for the kind of volitional disabilities involved in addiction.

How does this work? Consider a volitional disability with respect to gambling. Let us say that someone has a tendency to form intentions to gamble – specifically, to take risky bets with a high probability of loss – and to revise her intentions against gambling. Such a person will tend to lose money over time, which may or may not be compensated by the enjoyment and anticipation of placing bets. This is a familiar kind of volitional tendency, which is witnessed in a wide range of social contexts.

Consider, however, a society where individuals are aware that some other people have this tendency, and are legally allowed to offer bets. Such individuals will have incentives to make these bets as accessible and salient as possible, while at the same time making the odds on these bets as unfavorable as possible.[16] In such a world, the bad outcomes associated with this tendency will be far worse than they would be in a world where no one intentionally aimed to exploit such volitional disabilities.

As it happens, we live in such a world, and increasingly so: consider, in the United States, video poker, 'scratch tickets,' and online sports gambling. Such products make the poor outcomes associated with gambling much more readily attainable than they would otherwise be. Nor is this the only such case. Goods such as cigarettes and hard alcohol may each be thought of as technologies for the exploitation of volitional disabilities.

So, we should acknowledge that people with volitional disabilities do experience suboptimal outcomes, relative to people who do not have volitional disabilities. This can make it tempting to conclude that volitional disabilities involve a defect. But this does not follow. Much of the disadvantage associated with volitional disability is due, not to any underlying defect, but rather to the discrimination and exploitation directed at people with volitional disabilities.

Here one might ask: why isn't the susceptibility to discrimination, and particularly to exploitation, itself evidence of a defect? That is, if people with the sort of intentions with respect to gambling described earlier can so easily be exploited into financial losses, is that itself evidence that they have a volitional defect? But these questions disregard the crucial question about the source or origin of the harms in question. For it is crucial that the source of the harm in cases of discrimination and exploitation, the wrong-making feature, is something external to the addicted person herself.

This is not merely a point about what is labeled as a 'defect.' It is a practical point about the possible locus of change. If someone has a defect – for example, a disease – then the best way to improve the outcomes that she confronts will be to treat the person herself. If someone faces bad outcomes because she is susceptible to exploitation, then there is another way to intervene, namely to change the forces and circumstances that may lead to her exploitation. This point is vital because it points us toward how we might actually address the bad outcomes to which people with volitional disabilities are subject. That is an issue that will be taken up at length in the discussion to follow.

3.7 Disability and Harmful Acts

I have been arguing that volitional disability is not a defect. It is associated with suboptimal outcomes, but these are the product of something external to the volitional disability, namely discrimination and exploitation, rather than of the volitional disability itself. But there is a further argument for the claim that volitional disability is a defect that is important to answer.

This is what I will call the argument from harmful acts. Consider the act of smoking a cigarette. By any reasonable standard, this is an act that is harmful to a person: tobacco is a well-known carcinogen, and smoking a cigarette involves, at a minimum, burning and inhaling that carcinogen. When one smokes a cigarette, there is a clear medical sense in which one does some harm to oneself.

Now consider a volitional tendency to form intentions and policies to smoke, and to revise policies against smoking. This will normally count as a volitional disability. Is this a defect – that is, is one worse off simply in virtue of having that volitional disability? I have argued that it is not. This volitional tendency is, in itself, neither good nor bad.

Yet there appears to be a simple argument that this is wrong. Smoking a cigarette is, we have said, bad. And a volitional tendency of the kind just described makes it more likely, other things being equal, that one will smoke a cigarette. Let us grant that the very existence of cigarettes and their associated harms is, as I have argued, a product of discrimination and exploitation. Nonetheless, according to this argument, a tendency that makes one more likely to do something that will harm oneself seems to be, by its very nature, a defect. So volitional disabilities, at least when they are directed at intrinsically harmful acts, are defects after all.

Here, however, we must take some care. Begin with desires. Agents typically have all sorts of desires for acts or states of affairs that will make them worse off. Thus, someone may desire to smoke a cigarette, ride a motorcycle without a helmet, or for that matter wager their life savings on a single game of roulette. Someone who has such desires is in some sense worse off since these desires render her ever so slightly likely to engage in one of these acts. Yet desires for suboptimal outcomes are not defects but are rather a familiar and indeed typical aspect of human psychology.[17]

Matters do not change significantly when we consider volitions. An intention to ride a motorcycle without a helmet, or a policy of doing so, will make one more likely to ride a motorcycle without a helmet. And that is an act that may well lead to harm to oneself. But these volitions are not in themselves defects. We may attempt to talk someone out of these intentions. But we do not conclude that her will is defective, just in virtue of having these volitions.

It is an interesting and relevant question why exactly volitions that are likely to lead to harm are not considered defects of the will. At first pass, our answer to this question is likely to be a broadly procedural one: these volitions are arrived at through a process of reflection and deliberation that is not in of itself defective. In short, it is the sources rather than the effects of a volition that are relevant to this assessment, and even volitions that may well lead to harm may nonetheless be perfectly sound in their sources.[18]

We can now return to the objection made earlier. For some volitional disabilities, the mere fact that the person has that volitional disability will make that person more likely to encounter suboptimal outcomes because it makes the person more likely to engage in potentially harmful acts. Does it follow that the volitional disability is a defect? It does not, for two reasons.

First, as argued in the previous section, the ultimate source of the harm is not the behavior itself, but forces of discrimination and exploitation that are themselves malleable. Second, even if we hold fixed the forces of discrimination and exploitation, as does the argument from harmful acts, the mere fact that someone tends to perform acts that are bad for her is not itself evidence of a defect. Much human behavior is directed at ends that are in some sense suboptimal, and in this sense, the person with a volitional disability is no more defective in her aims than anyone else. What is distinctive about her predicament is that she is the subject of widespread discrimination and exploitation. It is these that should be the focus of our attention.

3.8 Kinds of Volitional Disability

As there are many kinds of physical and developmental disabilities, so there are many kinds of volitional disability. I have already discussed at least a couple of these in the foregoing. It will be helpful to taxonomize these varieties and discuss their relationships to psychological phenomena on which we have an independent grasp.

The kind of volitional disability that I have focused on the most is the one that involves an atypical tendency to form intentions and policies to A, and to revise policies against not doing A. As I have said, this is the tendency that gets labeled, pejoratively, as 'weakness of will.' It is a tendency that also has a strong constitutive connection to the phenomenon of addiction, as I have already suggested and which I will develop more explicitly in what follows.

Another kind of volitional disability that I have discussed earlier is the disinclination to form intentions at all, even in the presence of typical desires. This is a phenomenon that I have described with the medieval label of acedia. This tendency is stigmatized in various ways and is often characterized as a vice, either as laziness or 'sloth' or, in certain contexts, as cowardice. Again, the point of view urged here is that this is simply a form that the will may take, not inherently worse or better than any other, and that the stigma encountered by those whose willing does take this form is the product of a discriminatory environment, rather than any defect in the will itself.

The tendency of acedia is sometimes described, in psychiatric contexts, as avolition. Avolition, sometimes characterized in terms of the failure to initiate activity, is often taken to be a symptom of schizophrenia spectrum disorders, among other conditions.[19] Here we must take great care in separating the descriptive from the evaluative element of such a symptom. What may be true is that acedia or avolition is correlated with certain mental health diagnoses, and in that respect may be understood as a symptom of them. What we should reject is the thought that there is anything inherently defective or in need of 'treatment' in avolition.[20] This is a distinction that we will revisit in depth when we turn, in the subsequent discussion, to the diagnosis and treatment of addiction.

These are just two examples. It seems to me likely that there are many more. The idea of volitional disability sits at the intersection of two ideas that are not always popular, and which are rarely understood in tandem. The first is that the will is a faculty in its own right, not to be reduced to other psychological elements. The second is that disability is to be understood as difference and that the negative valence associated with disability arises from the powerful and often implicit forces of discrimination and stigma. When we hold both of these ideas, aspects of the mind that are usually understood as defects turn out to simply be aspects of the will that have been misunderstood. As this is true of acedia and 'weakness of will,' so is this true of many other tendencies of the will that have been, in previous discussions, wrongly pathologized.[21]

3.9 Addiction and Disability

The tendency that will be our focus in what follows is addiction. In the previous chapter, I argued that addiction is characterized by a certain kind of volitional diversity, namely 'weakness of will.' In this chapter, I have argued that this form of volitional diversity is in fact a volitional disability. As I noted earlier, this is a short step to the central argument of this book, namely that addiction is a disability. The next chapter will elaborate on this conception of addiction. Let us close this chapter, however, by considering how these argumentative pieces hang together, and by clarifying what exactly the relationship is between addiction and disability, on the present account.

Begin with stigma. I have emphasized, in the foregoing, how 'weakness of will' is stigmatized, and how this is part of what makes it a volitional disability. Addiction is itself, of course, widely stigmatized, in remarkably open and unapologetic ways. One study suggests that 54% of people believe that people with drug addictions can be legitimately denied housing and that 90% of people would be unwilling to have a person with drug addiction marry into their family (Barry *et al.*, 2014). Such beliefs, as in the case of 'weakness of will,' are echoed in pejorative language. Indeed, while the term 'addict' is often embraced by individuals with addictions, and is used even in some of the academic literature on addiction, it remains a pejorative in many linguistic contexts.[22]

Stigma is, as I understand it, a kind of individual-level discrimination, where negative attitudes are held and expressed by individuals. The individual-level discrimination involved in stigma is transformed into widespread and often institutionalized discrimination. The legal forms that this stigma can take, and the resources that addicted people might have to respond to it, will be discussed in detail in what follows.

A similar phenomenon is at work when we consider exploitation. Earlier I discussed the exploitation to which people with volitional disabilities are subject. As I indicated, it is addiction that is especially prone to this kind of exploitation. The regular and 'frictionless' delivery of substances such as nicotine and alcohol, as well as experiences such as gambling, is one of the hallmarks of contemporary markets. On the present view, this is exploitation of addiction, and it is simply an extension, albeit a radical one, of the exploitation to which people with volitional disabilities of all kinds are already subject.

With those observations in place, we can return to the relationship between addiction and the volitional tendencies that are, I hold, characteristic of addiction. I have argued that addiction implies volitional diversity, in the sense that anyone who has an addiction with respect to some substance or activity has atypical volitional tendencies with respect to that substance or activity. Specifically, if A is the activity or use of the substance in question, they have an atypical tendency to form intentions and policies to A and to revise policies against doing A. But we can also ask: what more is there to addiction? Is addiction simply a volitional tendency of that kind, or are there further conditions on addiction?

I want to suggest that the answer to this question is fully given by our earlier account of discrimination and exploitation. That is, addiction is, from the psychological point of view, nothing more than a volitional tendency of the kind described. What makes a certain volitional tendency an addiction is the discrimination and exploitation to which it is subject. In short, addiction is a volitional disability: that is, a volitional tendency that is discriminated against and exploited in certain distinctive ways.

We therefore have a kind of hierarchy of difference and discrimination that is useful to review. At the ground level, we have volitional difference, which is a mere difference in intentions and policies, and volitional diversity, which is a higher-order difference in a person's tendencies of volition formation and revision. These ground-level differences are entirely descriptive: they mark off the variety of forms that the will may take. At a higher level, we introduce the notion of disability. Here, external and environmental factors convert volitional diversity into volitional disability: volitional disability is volitional diversity that is discriminated against and exploited in a certain way. Addiction is then identified as one kind, arguably the most prominent kind, of volitional disability. This narrative of construction is metaphorical; typically, these 'levels' of addiction will happen, as it were, all at once.

On this picture, addiction is a disability, specifically a volitional disability. When a certain kind of volitional diversity is discriminated against and exploited in certain ways, it amounts to an addiction. That is simply what addiction is. This is the central thesis of this book, and I have now explained its content. Specifically, I have explained what exactly it means for addiction to be a disability, and what kind of disability it is.

This is what I will disability model of addiction. With the disability model in place, we can revisit some fundamental questions in philosophy and psychology of addiction. What is the difference, if there is one, between addiction and heavy or excessive use? Can certain aberrant behavioral tendencies (such as video game playing) amount to addictions? Why do people with addictions persist in their use, despite consequences that they know to be harmful? Under what conditions do people with addictions recover from their addictions, and what is 'recovery' anyway? The next chapter begins to address how the disability model answers these and other questions.

Notes

1 The term was introduced by Mike Oliver; see Oliver (2013) for an important overview of the idea of the social model and its subsequent reception.
2 The term 'impairment' is central to classical statements of the social model; for responses to at least some of the concerns that have been raised against it, see Oliver (2005).
3 Barnes (2016) is an important recent example of a work that endorses these claims about the broadly social nature of disability while rejecting a number of the key tenets of the 'social model' as it is standardly understood.
4 Cochlear implants, small electric devices that enable hearing in some deaf people, are an ongoing subject of controversy within the deaf community precisely due to their supposed aim of 'fixing' or 'curing' deafness; see Sparrow (2005) for one sympathetic exploration of these criticisms.
5 This, for example, is the explicit focus of Barnes (2016).
6 For one recent treatment of the overlap between addiction and physical disabilities, see Reif et al. (2023).
7 Though she does not frame it as a disability, the proposal that addiction is to be understood in terms of disordered learning is central to the argument of Maia Szalavitz's treatment of addiction in Szalavitz (2016).
8 On the age of onset for substance use disorders, see McGorry et al. (2011); on the age of onset of ADHD, see Kieling et al. (2010).
9 It bears noting that ADHD, especially in its hyperactive type, is distinguished, like addiction, by involving certain patterns of behavior (APA, 2013, pp. 59–66). However, this need not indicate that addiction is a developmental disability. It may instead indicate that, once we introduce the category of volitional disability, some conditions understood as developmental disabilities may be better understood as volitional disabilities, or disabilities of the will.

10 Later I will add that exploitation, in addition to discrimination, has a crucial role to play in the constitution of addiction in particular.

11 Someone with a volitional disability may of course also exhibit some kind of volitional defect, such as means-end incoherence, just as anyone might. The point here is that volitional disability does not in itself involve any kind of volitional defect.

12 While these forms of disability are distinct, they are also related. What relates them? As I have already indicated, I do not offer. general analysis of disability that explains why all these particular kinds of disability are disabilities. But we can make general observations about what connects them. The guiding idea of the approach taken here is that these various disabilities are distinct in their etiologies and internal structures but alike in the kinds of discrimination and stigma to which they are subject.

13 This form of volition is closely related to what contemporary psychiatry describes as avolition, which is taken to be a core symptom of schizophrenia spectrum disorders (Foussias & Remington, 2010), and which I will discuss at greater length later. For a literary exploration of the experience of acedia, and what a medical treatment for it might look like, see Kunkel (2005).

14 There is a significant philosophical literature on exploitation, some but not all of which draws on the central role of exploitation in Marx's account of the relationship between capital and labor. See Zwolinski *et al.* (2022) for a helpful introduction to some of these issues.

15 Writes Holton: 'There is considerable stigma attached to being weak willed. I think that the account offered here correctly the times that it is deserved' (Holton, 1999, p. 253).

16 For an incisive and devastating account of how these kinds of considerations have been applied and leveraged within increasingly sophisticated 'gambling machines,' see Schüll (2014)

17 One might ask: why are these not defects? We might extend the notion of a defect so that any psychological state of an agent that raises the probability of a suboptimal outcome for that agent will count as a defect. But since most of what we desire is not in fact what is optimal for us (due in part, but arguably not solely, to our ignorance), this expansive notion of defect is too broad to be workable: almost every desire and volition that an agent has will count as a defect.

18 We do not need to reject the possibility that some volitions might count as defective just in virtue of their contents. Perhaps intentions to take one's own life might be ipso facto defective, as has been argued by Kant among others (Cholbi, 2000). In the typical case, however, the mere fact that execution of an intention will make that agent worse off does not imply that the intention itself is defective.

19 A reluctance to initiate action is typically classed among the 'negative symptoms' of schizophrenia, commonly contrasted with 'positive symptoms' such as hallucinations and delusions.

20 It is a further question whether a schizophrenia spectrum disorder is properly thought of as a defect, such that one is inherently worse off simply in virtue of having it. This is something of an axiom in most clinical discussions, but it is not altogether obvious. One reason for doubt is that some aspects of schizophrenia spectrum disorders may be understood as volitional disabilities, in the way described in the text. Another is that there are deep symmetries between schizophrenia spectrum disorders and autism spectrum disorders (de Lacy & King, 2013), and the latter are plausibly understood as involving psychological differences, rather than psychological defects.

21 Consider, for example, some of the behavioral tendencies deemed disorders in the DSM-5, such as 'fetishistic disorder,' which involves 'recurrent and intense sexual arousal from either the use of nonliving objects or a highly specific focus on non-genital body parts' (APA, 2013, p. 700). The spirit of the present approach is to consider the possibility that these are volitional disabilities, arising from natural forms of variation in the human will, and that any distress associated with them is due to discrimination and stigma, rather than to any inherently wrong-making feature in such habits or tendencies.
22 As noted in Chapter 1, this is one reason why I avoid this term (and cognate terms such as 'alcoholic') in favor of person-centered language such as 'individuals with addictions.'

Works Cited

American Psychiatric Association. (2013). *Diagnostic and Statistical Manual of Mental Disorders (DSM-5)*. American Psychiatric Publications.

Barnes, E. (2016). *The Minority Body: A Theory of Disability*. Oxford University Press.

Barry, C.L., McGinty, E.E., Pescosolido, B., & Goldman, H.H. (2014). Stigma, Discrimination, Treatment Effectiveness and Policy Support: Comparing Public Views about Drug Addiction with Mental Illness. *Psychiatric Services*, *65*(10), 1269–1272.

Cholbi, M.J. (2000). Kant and the Irrationality of Suicide. *History of Philosophy Quarterly*, *17*(2), 159–176.

Daly, R.W. (2007). Before Depression: The Medieval Vice of Acedia. *Psychiatry*, *70*(1), 30–51.

de Lacy, N., & King, B.H. (2013). Revisiting the Relationship between Autism and Schizophrenia: Toward an Integrated Neurobiology. *Annual Review of Clinical Psychology*, *9*(1), 555–587.

Foussias, G., & Remington, G. (2010). Negative Symptoms in Schizophrenia: Avolition and Occam's Razor. *Schizophrenia Bulletin*, *36*(2), 359–369.

Heyman, G.M. (2013). Addiction and Choice: Theory and New Data. *Frontiers in Psychiatry*, *4*, 31.

Holton, R. (1999). Intention and Weakness of Will. *The Journal of Philosophy*, *96*(5), 241–262.

Kieling, C., Kieling, R.R., Rohde, L.A., Frick, P.J., Moffitt, T., Nigg, J.T., Tannock, R., & Castellanos, F.X. (2010). The Age at Onset of Attention Deficit Hyperactivity Disorder. *The American Journal of Psychiatry*, *167*(1), 14–16.

Kuenburg, A., Fellinger, P., & Fellinger, J. (2016). Health Care Access among Deaf People. *The Journal of Deaf Studies and Deaf Education*, *21*(1), 1–10.

Kunkel, B. (2005). *Indecision: A Novel*. Random House.

McGorry, P.D., Purcell, R., Goldstone, S., & Amminger, G.P. (2011). Age of Onset and Timing of Treatment for Mental and Substance Use Disorders: Implications for Preventive Intervention Strategies and Models of Care. *Current Opinion in Psychiatry*, *24*(4), 301.

Oliver, M. (2005). Defining Impairment and Disability: Issues at Stake. In Emens & Stein (Eds.), *Disability and Equality Law*. Routledge.

Oliver, M. (2013). The Social Model of Disability: Thirty Years On. *Disability & Society*, *28*(7), 1024–1026.

Reif, S., Lee, M.T., & Ledingham, E. (2023). The Intersection of Disability with Substance Use and Addiction. In D. McQueen (Ed.), *Oxford Research Encyclopedia of Global Public Health*. Oxford University Press.

Schüll, N.D. (2014). *Addiction by Design: Machine Gambling in Las Vegas*. Princeton University Press.

Sparrow, R. (2005). Defending Deaf Culture: The Case of Cochlear Implants. *Journal of Political Philosophy*, *13*(2), 135–152.

Szalavitz, M. (2016). *Unbroken Brain: A Revolutionary New Way of Understanding Addiction*. St. Martin's.

Welsh, W. (2019). The Economic Impact of Deafness. *JADARA*, *24*(3), 72–80.

West, J.S., & Lynch, S.M. (2020). Demographic and Socioeconomic Disparities in Life Expectancy with Hearing Impairment in the United States. *The Journals of Gerontology Series B*, *76*(5), 944–955.

Zwolinski, M., Ferguson, B., & Wertheimer, A. (2022). Exploitation. In E.N. Zalta & U. Nodelman (Eds.), *The Stanford Encyclopedia of Philosophy*. Metaphysics Research Lab, Stanford University.

4

ADDICTION AS VOLITIONAL DISABILITY

4.1 The Disability Model

The previous chapter articulated a conception of volitional disability and explained how addiction can be understood as a particular kind of volitional disability, defined in part by underlying volitional diversity and in part by external forces of discrimination and exploitation. This is *the disability model* of addiction.

The disability model can be contrasted with other models of addiction that we have already considered. Like the disease model, it holds that there is a feature of addicted people in virtue of which they are inherently different from non-addicted people. Unlike the disease model, however, it does not understand this difference as a pathology. Rather, it understands it as an evaluatively neutral feature of the will.[1]

The disability model also contrasts with the disordered use model of addiction. The disability model recognizes that addiction may often involve use that leads to adverse outcomes. But it does not take these outcomes to be definitional of addiction. Instead, it understands them as outputs of certain volitional tendencies, on the one hand, and a discriminatory and exploitative social environment, on the other.

As I said at the outset, these other models of addiction are defect models of addiction. They hold that there is something inherently wrong with the addicted person, either with her constitution or her behavior. The disability model, in contrast, denies that addiction is a defect. It acknowledges that addiction is often associated with adverse outcomes. But it explains these in terms of the complex interaction between volitional tendencies which are

DOI: 10.4324/9781003410263-5

evaluatively neutral and a social environment that is often designed to discriminate against and exploit addiction.

Finally, the disability model can be contrasted with self-medication models and other kinds of 'rational behavior' models of addiction. As I suggested in Chapter 1, these models tend to covertly involve versions of a defect model, where the defect is the underlying condition that is medicated or otherwise managed by addiction. In addition, simple models of rational behavior have difficulty explaining the tragic outcomes to which addicted people are subject. The disability model, as I have said, is able to explain them in terms of a particular conjunction of atypical volitional patterns and exploitative social conditions.

We therefore have, in the disability model, a genuine and coherent alternative to previous models of addiction. We can now ask whether the disability model can deliver answers to some of the long-standing questions in the psychology and philosophy of addiction and whether these answers are plausible. I will argue that it can indeed do this and that the disability model is a comprehensive and compelling approach to the theory of addiction.

4.2 Addiction and Use

Some central problems in the theory of addiction are problems of demarcation. Among these is the question of how to distinguish addiction to a substance from simple use of that substance.[2] Use, even heavy use, appears to be neither sufficient nor necessary for addiction. Someone may use some substance – alcohol, say – heavily, and yet not be addicted to alcohol. Conversely, someone may be addicted to alcohol and not use alcohol heavily, at least not at the present moment. What then is the relationship between addiction and use?

On certain models of addiction, this connection is a relatively tight one. Notably, on the disordered use model, addiction is simply a certain kind of use, so substance use may be thought of as subsuming the kind of use that constitutes addiction. Other models of addiction, which think of addiction as an underlying feature of a person, understand the relationship between addiction and use in a more indirect way.

The disability model is a model of the latter kind. To be addicted to a substance is to have a certain kind of volitional tendency with regard to the use of that substance. In particular, one will be inclined to form intentions and policies to use that substance and to revise policies against such use. This kind of volitional state will tend, other things being equal, to lead to actually using that substance. This is why addiction will often be strongly associated with use.

But things will not always be equal. For one thing, addiction may be, and typically is, coupled with other volitional tendencies. Someone may be addicted to alcohol and at the same time ambitious for career advancement, and so may confine her drinking to certain proscribed times or locations. A volitional tendency toward alcohol use is quite compatible with other conflicting tendencies that serve to constrain or redirect that tendency. A second kind of case is where someone, recognizing her volitional tendencies, decides to abstain from use altogether. This is an especially important case for thinking about what 'recovery' from addiction might look like on the disability model, and we will consider it in more detail shortly.

Conversely, there may be use of a substance, indeed even excessive and harmful use, that does not constitute addiction. Again, there are at least two ways in which this might occur. The most common is where a person's use is simply not reflective of any underlying volitional tendency. For example, college students may drink alcohol in large amounts, often with terrible consequences, and yet their volitions with respect to alcohol may be typical. In this case, excessive drinking is a response to certain social structures and incentives rather than to a feature of the will. In such cases, there is use, often harmful use, that does not constitute addiction.

A second kind of case arises from the fact that, on the disability model, addiction is constituted, in part, by an experience of discrimination and exploitation. If there is a tendency to use a certain substance, one which is underwritten by an atypical tendency of the will, which is simply not discriminated against, then it will not, on the present account, amount to an addiction. Arguably the use of tobacco had something like this status in certain cultures, and at certain times – regarded by some people the way we now regard stamp-collecting or birdwatching, as a slightly unusual habit.[3] These then would constitute another case of use without addiction.

In this respect, the disability model aligns with those models that draw a relatively sharp distinction between addiction on the one hand and use, even heavy and harmful use, on the other. Like the disease model, the disability model understands the behavior of the addicted person as a manifestation of an underlying condition rather than as constitutive of the addiction itself. But there is a crucial difference. The disease model sees the behavior as a symptom, the condition as a medical one, and the manifestation of addiction as something that is, in some sense, unresponsive to the addicted person's will. But on the disability model, the distance between addiction and use is a product precisely of the will, and the way in which each of us may act contrary to our volitional tendencies, even when those tendencies are atypical and pronounced.

The gap between addiction and use, and the understanding of that gap proposed by the disability model, is especially significant in a case introduced briefly earlier, namely abstinence. Here the disability model is, I think, especially well-positioned to understand the distinctive dynamics of addiction.

4.3 Abstinence

If addiction were a disordered pattern of use, as the use disorder model has it, then we would expect the goal of addiction treatment to be the attainment and maintenance of an ordered pattern of use. But this in general is not the aim of much addiction treatment. Instead, both physicians and non-professional recovery communities tend to recommend complete abstinence from a given substance, even when moderate use of that substance is considered typical. For example, if one is addicted to alcohol, it is recommended that one abstain altogether from the use of alcohol. There has been a tendency among advocates of 'harm reduction' – which we will discuss in much greater detail in what follows – to soften this recommendation and to treat a reduction of use as a more realistic treatment goal. Nonetheless, abstinence constitutes something of a regulative ideal in the management of addiction.

Why is this? Why is abstinence a goal in the treatment of addiction, and one so strongly embraced by many people with addictions themselves? I noted earlier that this is a puzzling question for the disordered use model. It is puzzling also for the self-medication model and other views that take addictive behavior to be in some sense rational. If a person is using a substance to treat some underlying psychological condition, then there is no principled reason why total abstinence from the use of that substance is a desirable goal. On the contrary, it would seem that one would reduce, but not eliminate, the use of a substance that is serving a useful purpose.[4]

The disability model, on the other hand, gives a clear account of abstinence, both its origin and its purpose. On the disability model, addiction is in the first place a feature of the will, and the will is distinguished in the first place by binary choices and exceptionless policies. That is, volition is binary in the sense that there are not degrees of intention, in the way that there may be degrees of belief or desire. Similarly, policies will typically recommend always performing an action in a certain circumstance rather than weighing considerations for or against that action. Their simple and exceptionless nature is one of the things that makes volitions so useful for practical reason, as they fix clear signposts for navigating a variable world.

Sometimes addiction is thought of as falling afoul of these kinds of clear guidelines. There are prohibitions – be they social or personal – against the excessive consumption of certain substances, but the addicted person, driven by excessive desire, violates these prohibitions and consumes excessively anyway. On the disability model, however, this is the wrong way of thinking about addiction. Addiction does not bypass the will but is rather a tendency of the will itself. To have an addiction is to tend to form certain sorts of volitions under a range of circumstances, and not at all to violate volitions in response to one's desires.

Accordingly, addiction may be marked, on the disability model, by a measure of habituality.[5] This aspect of addiction can seem puzzling on certain conceptions of addiction, but it is readily intelligible on the disability model. It reflects the fact that addiction is a specifically volitional disability and that this does not mean that the will of the addicted person is not 'weak' or otherwise defective, but rather that it takes a certain distinctive form.

Return now to abstinence. Consider someone who has an atypical tendency to form intentions and policies to A, and to revise policies against doing A, where A is the use of some substance. Someone may well recognize that she has these volitional tendencies, and may further recognize that these tendencies lead to poor outcomes, given the actual environment in which she lives and the actual discriminatory forces to which she is subject. Recognizing these facts, she may make one of several choices.

First, she might simply endorse her volitional tendencies and accept the poor outcomes that she expects to come with them. This is a choice that is in fact taken by many people with addictions. Second, she might attempt to change her volitional tendencies. For example, she might try to reason her way toward being less inclined to form volitions to A. This is an approach encouraged by many cognitive therapies for the treatment of addiction, which locate addiction in deep but changeable patterns of thought and behavior (McHugh *et al.*, 2010). Third, she might form policies that restrict her use in certain ways. This strategy is attractive, although it faces a clear problem: the volitional tendencies at issue are tendencies to, among other things, revise one's policies, so someone who knows she has these tendencies can rationally foresee that she will be likely to revise any policies against use that she sets for herself.

There is another choice. One might simply not admit A into the realm of volition at all. That is, one might structure one's deliberations so that A is never considered as an option at all. This is not to form a policy with regard to doing A, not even to form a policy that one will never A under any circumstances whatsoever. As we have already seen, the volitional tendencies involved in addiction are precisely tendencies to revise any such policies. Rather, this kind of deliberative attitude should be understood simply as a refusal to form A-directed volitions at all.

It is crucial, on this picture, that we do not think of addiction solely on the model of belief and desire. When they are put into a formal framework, such models typically require that an agent must have, at least in principle, a credence and a utility for any proposition whatsoever.[6] But the model of volition makes no such requirement. One may simply refrain from the project of having volitions about a certain action at all.

This, I am suggesting, is how we ought to understand abstinence. Abstinence should not be understood on the model of a policy or a resolution to refrain from use for a certain, perhaps indefinite, period. Rather, it should be understood as a deliberate refusal to form certain kinds of volitions. So understood, it is a natural response – not the only possible response, but one legitimate response – to the recognition that one has an addiction. That is, if one recognizes that one has certain volitional tendencies with respect to a certain activity (where this may, again, be the use of a substance), and recognizes that those tendencies will lead to poor outcomes in one's actual circumstances, one may reasonably refrain from engaging in the project of volition, with respect to that activity, altogether.

As I have said, the disability model, which emphasizes the essentially volitional aspect of addiction, is a natural home for this picture of abstinence. Since abstinence is such a notable feature of both addiction treatment recommendations, and the practice of addiction recovery, this is another count in favor of the disability model. It bears emphasizing that the disability model does not mandate, or even necessarily recommend, abstinence. It simply explains why it is one intelligible response to the fact of addiction. We will return to this topic, and to the subtle question of recovery itself, in greater detail in what follows.

There is a final question to be considered about abstinence, which is connected to the theme of the previous section. Can someone who is deliberately abstinent from a substance, perhaps for a long period, still be addicted to that substance? On many models of addiction, it is difficult to understand how this could be the case. On the disordered use model, for example, someone who has purposely refrained from use for a long period is no longer using that substance and so they are not disorderly using that substance, almost by definition. Similarly, if we understand the disease model literally, it is plausible that someone who shows no symptoms of addiction for years or decades is therefore simply no longer someone who has the disease.

These are intuitive answers, but they seem to fall afoul of two points: the reports of people with addictions, on the one hand, and the known facts about the development of addiction over the life cycle, on the other. As to the first point, many people with a history of addiction identify as 'addicts' even long after they have refrained from using the substance in question for a long stretch of time. This is in part because 'addict' may function as a kind of historical identity, that one does not relinquish simply because one's orientation to one's addiction has changed.[7] It is also because reflection on the fact that one is addicted may be action-guiding: it may, for example, lead one to refrain from using even small amounts of the substance in question because doing so may lead to a return to 'active' addiction.

This brings us to the second point. There is robust data indicating that 'relapse' is a real phenomenon in the dynamics of addiction.[8] In its simplest form, a person uses a substance addictively for a period of time, completely refrains from use for an extended period of time (which may well be years or decades), and then returns immediately to addictive use when they resume use again. The simplest model of this kind of behavior is that addiction is a condition that persists even when one does not use a substance in question, such that one may immediately resume addictive use after a long period of abstinence. It is more difficult to understand this behavior on models, which include the disordered use and perhaps also the disease model, on which addiction does not persist in long periods of abstinence.

The disability model, on the other hand, can naturally accommodate the thought that addiction persists during periods of abstinence. Since addiction is grounded in a certain kind of atypical volitional tendency, and there is no reason to think that atypical volitional tendencies revert to typical ones over time, the presumption on the disability model is that someone who is addicted to a substance will continue to be addicted to a substance, whether one, in fact, uses that substance. This presumption may be defeated, but if it is not defeated then a person's addiction will remain. This is in a way a reflection of the non-evaluative nature of the disability model: since the model does not understand addiction as any kind of deviation from 'normal' or 'healthy' functioning, it also does not presume that someone who is not using a substance will somehow return or revert to a state of non-addiction. Being addicted is simply an aspect of who one is, and it does not change of its own accord.

In addition to recognizing the phenomenon of relapse, the disability model also acknowledges the first point, that addiction is, in part, an identity. On the understanding of many people with addictions, whether one is addicted depends not only on one's current or recent behavior but also on how one understands one's past behavior. The disability model recognizes this aspect of addiction and explains it as a feature of disability generally. Whether one is disabled depends in part on whether one identifies as disabled, and this is as true for addiction as it is for any other disability. This is not to say that people are infallible about their own addictions, but rather that someone's addicted status depends in part on her own self-understanding. This is one way in which the disability model is, as I have said, deferential to the perspective of the addicted persons.

Accordingly, the disability model can make sense of the phenomenon of being both addicted and abstinent, potentially for lengthy periods. It can therefore accommodate the reports of individuals in some recovery communities, as well as the phenomenon of relapse to addiction after long periods of abstinence. This then is further evidence of the explanatory power of the disability model.

4.4 The Boundaries of Addiction

Addiction is a relationship to an act, typically but not always the act of using a certain substance. In the previous two sections, we asked what kind of relationship that must be. Some models of addiction require that this relationship be quite a close one. On the disability model, it is more indirect. Heavy use and even disordered use do not suffice for addiction, and one may be addicted without necessarily using in a heavy or disordered way. Indeed, on the disability model, one may be abstinent for years or decades and nonetheless still have an addiction.

We can also ask what kind of act this must be. We have thus far been considering cases where the act is the use of a substance, paradigmatically a substance such as alcohol or an opiate. But we can ask whether one might have an addiction to other substances: might someone be addicted to coffee, for example? We can additionally ask whether addiction may extend to activities that do not involve the use of substances and, if so, how far. It is plausible that someone may be addicted, for example, to gambling. Might someone be addicted to sex, or to viewing pornography? Could someone be addicted to playing video games? These questions can seem frivolous, but what motivates them is something quite serious: excessive video game use, for example, can have pronounced and widespread effects on a significant proportion of children and adolescents (Gentile, 2009). This makes it even more urgent to deliver a principled answer to these questions about demarcation.

Some models of addiction are inclusive on such questions and indeed are designed to be so. The disordered use model – as it is developed in the *DSM-5* and so in much contemporary psychiatric practice – purposively does not introduce a general category of addiction from which particular substances or activities may be included or excluded. Instead, it gives a list of disorders: Alcohol Use Disorder, Gambling Disorder, and so forth. The list is, in principle, indefinitely extensible. Any substance or activity that may be deemed disordered may be added to this list, which specifies the form of a disorder but leaves its specific content open.

To take another example, the self-medication model of addiction may be extended to a variety of substances and acts. Alcohol and opiates may be used to self-medicate, but so too may gambling, video games, or even exercise. The self-medication model understands addiction in terms of its object or aim, and a variety of substances or activities may serve the very same aim. Therefore, the self-medication model, like the use disorder model, yields an ecumenical picture of addiction.

The advent of such models has arguably supported the broader view of addiction that has generally taken hold in popular thinking about addiction. Addiction is understood as a broad phenomenon, to which many people are in some way subject, not confined to the specifics of alcohol addiction or opiate addiction. A limited understanding of the scope of addiction is a product of an outmoded view that gives too much attention to the specific mechanisms of addiction, and not enough to its broader psychological role.

The disability model takes an equivocal view of these developments. On the one hand, the tendency to take seriously conditions such as video game addiction is a salutary one. As noted earlier, these conditions often lead to poor outcomes, in part because they are subject to extensive discrimination and exploitation. Indeed, the somewhat cavalier tone in which such addictions are sometimes discussed is itself evidence of a discriminatory attitude toward them. Any tendency that will lead to an increased understanding of such conditions is to be, at least for that reason, welcomed.

On the other hand, an expansive understanding of addiction can lead to minimizing the impact of addiction, in the following way. On the simplest development of an expansive view of addiction, anything whatsoever might be a potential object of addiction: alcohol and opiates may be, but so too may sweets or jogging. Such a model can tend to conflate addiction with something like heavy use, as opposed to the quite specific volitional dynamics proposed by the disability model.[9]

Furthermore, while the disability model does not impose any fixed conditions on what kinds of substances or activities one may be addicted to, it does impose real albeit vague boundaries on the category of addiction, so that not just anything may count as an addiction. On the disability model, a volitional tendency is an addiction only if it is subject to discrimination and exploitation. Many of the volitional tendencies that are sometimes classed, with some seriousness, as addiction, simply fail to meet this test.

It is sometimes suggested, for example, that 'workaholism' is an addiction or an addiction-like tendency, which plays the same functional role for some people as alcoholism or opiate addiction plays for others. On the disability model, this is simply wrong. It may well be that a tendency to excessive work is driven by a form of volitional diversity, indeed that it may sometimes even be driven by the same kind of volitional diversity as a paradigm addiction: that is, such a person might tend to form intentions and policies to work and to revise policies against working. But this does not make such a tendency an addiction, for such a tendency is not in general the object of discrimination – if anything it is, at least in certain contexts, valorized. Those who are inclined to class this tendency as an addiction are perhaps attempting to undo this valorization – perhaps under the belief that excessive work is overly praised in modern market economies – and to attach to this tendency the same opprobrium that is attached to addictions. But on the disability model, this is a mistake. What needs instead to be recognized is that the tendency to form intentions to work is, in itself, neither good nor bad. It is simply one form that the will may take, one that, as it happens, is rewarded in many contemporary social arrangements.

On the disability model, then, it may make sense to expand the bounds of addiction, but not without limit. The bounds of addiction are set ultimately by the forces of discrimination and exploitation. One may not be addicted to anything whatsoever. This is not because of any internal limitations on the will, but because of the boundaries imposed by social attitudes: only some things are actually the objects of discrimination and exploitation, and it is these that constitute the possible objects of addiction.

4.5 The Puzzle of Addictive Motivation

These questions about the nature and scope of addiction are open and ongoing. But even when we restrict ourselves to core cases of addiction, there are longstanding and indeed ancient questions to be asked. Consider someone, for example, who regularly uses alcohol, who is atypically inclined to form intentions to use alcohol and to revise policies against using alcohol, and whose alcohol use has severely impaired her professional and personal life. On any reasonable account of addiction, this person counts as addicted to alcohol. Yet there are still puzzles about this kind of case. Indeed, such a simple case raises these questions especially acutely.

The core puzzle is what I will call the puzzle of addictive motivation. The puzzle is roughly this. By and large, people tend to do what they believe to be in their self-interest. There are a whole variety of exceptions to this principle, notably the way in which people frequently sacrifice their own well-being for that of their family members, their fellow citizens, or, occasionally, for distant strangers. People do not, however, tend to knowingly act in ways that they foresee will lead to actual harm to themselves. Or, when they do, such behavior calls out for explanation.[10]

The addicted person, of the kind just described, does appear to act in something like this way. What then explains her behavior? This is the puzzle of addictive motivation, and theories of addiction may be divided according to the answers that they give to it. The disease model explains such behavior as a kind of compulsion, such that the addicted person literally has no option but to do what she does. The self-medication model and other forms of rational behavior models tend to understand it in terms of the underlying defect that the addicted person is trying to treat. And the disordered use model, as we have seen, has difficulty even answering the question.

How then does the disability model answer? To begin, it emphasizes the importance of uncoupling a person's beliefs and desires from her volitions. If people always acted to maximize the satisfaction of their desires, and if the satisfaction of one's desires were what made someone's life go well, then it would perhaps be puzzling how anyone could fail to act to make her life go well, except through some kind of ignorance. But the picture of the will that animates the disability model rejects at least the first of these premises. Agents often act in ways that do not maximize the satisfaction of their desires.

This shows up in the simplest cases of volition. Consider someone who has a policy of going for a run every day. It may well be that on some rainy morning, the person would strongly prefer not running to running. Nonetheless, following her policy, she may go for a run anyway. This might be because she has some stronger desire – say a desire for fitness or for self-discipline – operating in the background and that it is this desire that trumps her desire to not run. But no such story need be in place to render her behavior intelligible and, indeed, familiar. People frequently act contrary to their desires and follow their policies instead.

As a policy may persist even when it does not best satisfy one's desires, so may a volitional tendency persist even when it does not best satisfy one's desires. One may recognize that one has certain tendencies to form intentions to run, to travel, or to read that outrun one's desires, and which are atypical compared to most people's volitions with respect to these activities. One may even recognize that one would be better off if one did not have these tendencies. One may nonetheless rationally retain these volitional tendencies and let them guide one's actions and one's broader plans and policies.

I am sketching here a certain picture of practical reason, on which a person's aims are not exhaustively concerned with maximizing the satisfaction of her desires, nor even with maximizing her well-being. Instead, practical reason is concerned, on this picture, with the formation and retention of intelligible intentions, policies, and volitional tendencies, and with the execution of these even in the face of obstacles, obstacles which may arise from one's own desires as well as having external causes.

This picture of practical reason is not, I think, a novel one. It is natural to think that our lives are concerned with the execution of our volitions, which have at best an indirect relation to our own well-being.[11] What is relatively novel is the idea that this conception of practical reason is relevant to the puzzle of addictive motivation. It is common to think of people with addictions as capricious and driven by momentary concerns. How then can the puzzle of addiction motivation be addressed by an appeal to this sort of volition-focused conception of our practical lives?

We have already begun to articulate an answer to this question. People with addictions are not, as we have already seen, people who lack self-control, or who are not guided by their volitions. Instead, they are people whose volitions take an atypical form. The puzzle of addiction motivation is then a puzzle of how their volitions may persist even in the face of adverse consequences. But what I have been emphasizing in the foregoing is that this is a puzzle that arises for all of us, in one form or another, insofar as we allow ourselves to be guided by our volitions. This is perhaps a puzzle, on certain conceptions of practical reason, but it is better understood as an aspect of volition and its complicated relationship to well-being. The puzzle of addictive motivation is really a manifestation of this aspect of volition as it shows up in the case of addiction. So understood, the form of a solution to this 'puzzle' begins to suggest itself.

4.6 Volition and Addictive Motivation

Why does the addicted person persist in doing things that she can foresee will lead to suboptimal outcomes for her? Why, for example, does someone persist in drinking alcohol and in revising her prohibitions against alcohol use, even when she recognizes that her alcohol use has led to or will lead to professional and personal losses? First, because she has an atypical tendency to form intentions to use alcohol and to revise policies against using alcohol. That is simply part of what it is to have an addiction to alcohol. But this seems to simply push the question back. Why does she retain this volitional tendency, despite the clear adverse consequence of doing so?

The answer suggested in the previous section is that this aspect of the person addicted to alcohol is an aspect of practical reasoning generally. Most agents, to one degree or another, persist in volitions and volitional tendencies, even when it can be known that these volitions do not maximize one's well-being. In this respect, the difference between addictive motivation and non-addictive motivation is a difference in degree rather than kind.

But what explains the difference in degree? That is, why does the addicted person retain her volitional tendencies in the face of quite severely bad outcomes? For example, people regularly use opiates even when there is a real risk of overdosing and relatively immediate mortality. How then are we to explain someone's persistently forming intentions to use opiates even when she recognizes that opiate use carries a real risk of overdose and death?

Here it is important to appeal to the other aspect of the disability model. The disability model explains the persistence of addictive volitions in the face of bad outcomes not only in terms of volitional diversity but also in terms of the discriminatory structures that are, on the disability model, the primary source of these bad outcomes. Consider opiates. The phenomenon of overdose is not a product of the volitional tendencies of opiate users alone. It is also the product of increasingly sophisticated and concentrated means of the delivery of opiates, along with a medical system that provides inconsistent care to people who are most at risk of overdose. Opium use was widespread in England and the United States in the 19th century, but overdose appears to have been relatively rarer.[12] The phenomenon of overdose is not then a product of volitional tendencies toward opiates themselves, but of the effects that those tendencies have within social structures that are designed to discriminate against and exploit addiction.

Similar phenomena arise for other addictions.[13] The worse consequences of common addictions – major health issues for smoking tobacco, automobile fatalities for alcohol use, rapid bankruptcies from gambling – are not products of volitional diversity itself, but of volitional diversity located within discriminatory and exploitative social conditions.[14] In short, if we want a proper accounting of why addictive use persists even when confronted with severely bad outcomes, we need to take seriously the origins of those outcomes themselves. And those outcomes are typically not due to volitional tendencies themselves, but to volitional tendencies that are embedded within structures that are designed to make the outcomes of those tendencies as bad as they can be. That is what it means for addiction to be the object of discrimination and exploitation.

But can't we still restate the objection? Let us grant that addicted people, confronted with discrimination and exploitation, are subject to especially bad outcomes when they persist in their volitional tendencies. Still, it might be objected, people with addictions, if they have some cognitive sophistication, can recognize this fact about themselves and their environment, and revise their volitions accordingly. Either addicted people lack the cognitive sophistication to recognize these forms of discrimination and exploitation, or they somehow are unconcerned with the severely adverse outcomes that discrimination and exploitation can create. Neither alternative seems plausible.

What then explains the persistence of addictive volitions? Again, the disability model suggests that we should look to the external environment of the addicted person, rather than her internal states, for an explanation. The distinctive malevolence of substances and activities that are designed to exploit addictive motivations is not only that they lead to significant harm but that they are also designed to disguise the harm they cause. For example, a video gambling system may be designed to win a substantial amount of money from a player, while making it appear to her that she is in fact winning money or is likely to do so soon. A substance whose harms are distant and relatively abstract – such as cigarettes – may be accompanied by messaging that makes its apparent rewards far more salient. This is not to say that the harms of addictive patterns of behavior are unrecognizable, but they are deliberately self-effacing, in a way that supports the natural inclination of volitional tendencies to persist.

That then is the solution to the puzzle of addictive motivation, insofar as it is a 'puzzle' at all. Addictive tendencies persist because volitional tendencies persist generally, and they do so even despite great harms because, as part of the discrimination and exploitation to which addicted people are subject, those harms are both amplified and disguised. Indeed, part of what it is for a substance to be 'addictive' on the present account is not for that substance to have some special effect on the will, but for it to be a substance that is interwoven with certain kinds of disadvantage.

One corollary of this kind of view is that the addicted person's motivation can be explained by ordinary mechanisms of motivation, without recourse to finding any defect in the addicted person. Specifically, the disability view rejects the idea, often endorsed by proponents of the disease model, that the addicted person should be understood as compulsive or in any sense unfree. Addicted people, on the disability view, are just as free as anyone else, with respect to their addictive behavior or their behavior more generally. This is an important aspect of the disability view, and it bears considering in some detail.

4.7 Compulsion and Disability

On one picture of addiction, the addicted person is subject to compulsion. Why does someone ingest large amounts of alcohol, for example? There may be many explanations, but if the person in question has an addiction to alcohol, then this explanation, on this picture of addiction, will take a particular form. The addicted person ingests large amounts of alcohol because she is compelled to do so. She literally cannot do anything else. She is not free to do otherwise.

To begin to evaluate this explanation, it will be helpful to make clear what it says. Talk of freedom is notoriously opaque, and so one might rightly wonder whether the appeal to freedom and its absence in this context is meaningful. On one simple picture, freedom should be understood in terms of options (Maier, 2022). An agent is free to do just what she has the option of doing, and so if an agent has exactly one option, then she is not free to do anything else. This claim, if it were true, would plausibly explain the behavior of the addicted person.

But this claim is simply not true. Persons with addictions regularly refrain from using the substances to which they are addicted, either in response to incentives or simply out of a change of mind. The epidemiological data on addiction support this observation: people with addiction gradually over time – often in response to financial and familial pressures – reduce or eliminate their use so that they no longer qualify as addicted. None of these observations is consistent with the theory that the addicted person literally has no option but to use the substance to which she is addicted.

We have already outlined these objections to the compulsion account in some detail. And the disability model, as I have said, rejects this account of addiction. Someone with an addiction has a certain volitional tendency, but she remains free to act contrary to that volitional tendency – just as agents generally remain free to do so. But the disability model adds something further to our understanding of the compulsion account of addiction. It explains why that account, despite its falsehood, has had such lasting appeal.

There is a persistent tendency for disabled people to be understood in terms of lack of abilities or options.[15] A blind person for example is understood, at first approximation, as someone who is deprived of options that non-blind people have, namely the option of perceiving certain kinds of things in her environment through sight. Several authors have argued that this is a poor account of disability.[16] All of us lack some options and have others, and there is no principled way of defining disability in terms of the lack of a particular set of options. A descriptive adequate account of disability requires an appeal to, among other things, the particular forms of discrimination to which disabled people are subject, as I have proposed for the disability model of addiction.

This observation, I believe, is the key to understanding the origin and the persistence of the idea that addiction essentially involves compulsion. Addiction is a disability. And disabilities are often understood in terms of a lack of options. That understanding of disability is incorrect, as I have argued, but it is nonetheless common. The idea that compulsion is characteristic of addiction is, I want to suggest, just an application of this mistaken line of thinking about disability generally to the particular disability that is addiction.

It will be helpful to think through this analogy in some detail. A person who is blind has an atypical sensory system and navigates a world designed for people with a typical sensory system. She therefore confronts a range of obstacles and frustrations that sighted people do not encounter. Her condition is therefore often a disadvantaged one, and people who are not blind often conceptualize that disadvantage in terms of a lack of options. The blind person is disadvantaged, on this line of thinking, due to a lack of options. But this is wrong: the blind person is not especially lacking in options. Her disadvantage is due, in the first place, to discriminatory social conditions.

Something like this line of thinking guides, I believe, a great deal of thinking about addiction. A person who is addicted has an atypical volitional system and encounters a world of acts and incentives designed for people with a typical volitional system. She therefore confronts a range of poor outcomes that people who are not addicted do not confront. Her condition is therefore often a disadvantaged one, and people who are not addicted often conceptualize that disadvantage in terms of a lack of options. On this conception, the addicted person lacks options that the person who is not addicted has. In particular, the addicted person lacks the option of refraining from using the substance to which she is addicted. She is subject to a compulsion. This compulsion drives her to act contrary to her own interests. The addicted person is disadvantaged, on this line of thinking, due to her compulsion, which amounts to a lack of options. But, as I have argued, this too is wrong: the addicted person is not especially lacking in options. Her disadvantage is due, in the first place, to discriminatory and exploitative social conditions.

The idea that addiction essentially involves compulsion, then, does not arise in the first place as a solution to the puzzle of addictive motivation. That is simply one application of this idea. The idea that addiction is defined by compulsion has, by the lights of the disability model, a deeper and more pernicious source. It arises from the fundamentally ableist idea that disability, in this case the disability that is addiction, essentially involves a lack or deprivation of options.

A pernicious aspect of this idea is that, in addition to figuring in the way that addiction is conceptualized and portrayed, it figures also, at times, in the way that addicted people understand themselves. Narratives of addiction are often structured by ideas of unfreedom.[17] One understanding of these narratives – hardly the only one, but one that needs to be acknowledged – is as involving an internalization of an ableist narrative that has been built up around the idea of addiction. This can be an especially pernicious kind of self-stigma, as the belief that one lacks options can be as limiting as the lack of options itself. So, while addiction does not itself involve compulsion, it at times involves the belief that one is subject to compulsion, which can be just as limiting in its effects.

The disability model, then, rejects the idea that addiction involves compulsion. Addicted agents have a plentitude of options, just as almost all agents do. It also, however, explains why the belief that addicted agents are subject to compulsion is so widely held, even among addicted people themselves. It is an application of the ableist myth that disability essentially involves a lack of options. To reject this myth, in the case of addiction, is to reject the idea that addiction involves compulsion.

4.8 Responsibility

The question of the freedom of addicted people, or equivalently of their options, is not confined to debates over compulsion. It also comes up, in philosophical and legal discussions in particular, over questions about responsibility.

These discussions can take any number of forms, but they tend to have a common character. A person with an addiction performs some harmful act. For example, a person with an alcohol addiction drives under the influence of alcohol and strikes a pedestrian, resulting in the pedestrian's death. The question is then asked: how responsible is the addicted person for her behavior? Is she just as responsible as someone who is not addicted to alcohol but who behaved in the same reckless way?[18] Generally, does addiction constitute an exculpating condition for the harms that are done by addicted people?

From the point of view of the disability model, it is curious that these discussions have the prominence that they do. Addicted people are the subjects of widespread discrimination and exploitation, as we have seen. It is an urgent social question to understand and undo the sources of that discrimination and exploitation, and of the disadvantage that it underwrites. From this point of view, it is curious that the harms done not to but by addicted people have been as central as they have been to discussions of addiction and responsibility. This is not to deny that these harms are real and serious. But the emphasis of these discussions is striking.

It is especially striking once we take seriously the analogy between addiction and other disabilities. It is true that people with disabilities sometimes harm other people in a way that may be due in some sense to their disabilities. A blind person may for example inadvertently injure someone when trying to navigate a poorly arranged physical environment.

But the question of whether their disability is an exculpating condition is not the salient legal issue. Rather, the issue is how an environment was arranged to make this injury possible in the first place.

This is the attitude that we should take toward responsibility and addiction, on the disability model. The disability model agrees that the addicted person satisfies a key condition on being responsible: she is free, or has options. If the disability model questions the responsibility of the addicted person, it is not on these grounds. Instead, the disability model denies the very presupposition that guides debates about addiction and responsibility. It denies that individual responsibility is the proper frame for understanding the vast harms that are done to, and sometimes by, addicted people.

A proper accounting of these harms, and how they can be answered, will be developed in what follows. To anticipate, my guiding idea will be that addiction should not be understood primarily in terms of retributive justice, the theory of punishment for wrongs done, as it often is in philosophical discussions. Instead, it should be understood in terms of distributive justice, the theory of the allocation of resources. Once we have a proper accounting of the harms done to addicted people, and how these might be redressed in the theory of distributive justice, we will be better positioned to give an account of the more marginal cases in which addicted people themselves are the agents of harm, and what it would be to arrive at a just outcome in such cases.

4.9 The Question of Recovery

We have now considered in some detail what the disability model has to say about the scope of addiction as well as about the questions about compulsion, freedom, and responsibility that have often occupied the philosophical literature. But there remains a significant aspect of addiction, a sort of subordinate theme in all popular and scientific discussions of addiction, that needs to be addressed. In particular, we need to say what the disability model has to say about this aspect of addiction. This is the question of recovery.

It is difficult to say what the question is without prejudicing this discussion, and even the word 'recovery' may carry presuppositions that some accounts will reject. But it will be helpful to begin with the data. Among people who use a substance addictively at some point in their lives, many will cease to use that substance addictively later in life – indeed, most will do so.[19] Some of these people will give up the use of the substance altogether – this was the phenomenon of abstinence discussed earlier – while others will simply reduce the amount they use. Some will become addicted to some other substance or activity, while others will not. Some will join and identify with a recovery community, such as a twelve-step program, while others will not. When I say that recovery is an aspect of addiction, it is this heterogeneous family of changes that I have in mind.

Despite this variety, there are a couple of real patterns in recovery that bear noting. First, as noted earlier, this is the typical case: most people who use addictively cease to do so later in life. Second, this recovery is typically, in medical terms, spontaneous. That is to say, most people who recover do so without the benefit of any active intervention, such as hospitalization or treatment with medication.

These facts are further evidence, as I have said, against the disease model of addiction. As we noted at the outset, most advocates of this model understand addiction as a chronic disease. But chronic diseases by their very nature do not spontaneously remit, certainly not as the typical case. Recovery from chronic disease, when it is possible at all, typically requires medical intervention, often prolonged and intensive intervention. So this is another way in which addiction does not fit the standard disease model.

But what does the disability model have to say about these facts? For these facts might be posed as a challenge to the disability model as well. Disability is, for many, a temporary condition, such that one has a disability at certain stages of life but not at others. But, it might be objected, people do not in general spontaneously transition out of disabilities. If one has a disability at a certain time then the presumption is that one will continue to have it in the future, in the absence of a significant intervention. This is because both the underlying differences that ground disabilities and the forces of discrimination that define them tend to persist over time. But addiction, as we have said, is not like this. People do tend to, in some sense, recover from addiction. This might suggest that addiction is, at least, quite different from most other disabilities.

The beginning of a response to this argument is to underscore a point already made. This is that, on the disability model, there is a sharp line to be drawn between addiction and use. Someone may have the volitional tendencies involved in addiction, and be subject to discriminatory and exploitative forces, without actually using a substance addictively. Thus, as observed earlier, the disability model gives an account of the phenomenon whereby individuals in recovery communities identify as having an addiction even long after they have ceased to use a given substance addictively. On the disability model, this identification is typically accurate, and, in this sense, recovery is not a process of ceasing to have an addiction but rather of reshaping one's behavior in light of one's persisting addiction.

The simplest case of this will be the individual who chooses to be abstinent and continues to identify as having an addiction, and for that addiction to continue to shape her identity.[20] But this is not the only case. Someone may retain addictive volitions, and continue to use a substance, and yet use it in ways that cease to cause significant harm.[21] Similarly, the discriminatory and exploitative policies that addicted people confront continue to use them long after they have ceased using addictively. These things are true whether or not one continues to identify as having an addiction. In this sense addiction is, as we have said, a historical identity, and not always a chosen one.

In response to the objection from recovery, then, the disability model responds as follows. First, it is true that people with addictions often recover from their addictions, and do so relatively spontaneously. But it does not follow that people often cease to be addicted, nor that they do so spontaneously. To recover from addiction not typically to cease to be addicted, but to develop one's relationship to one's addiction, in a way that recognizes both one's own volitional differences and the reality of a world that persistently discriminates against those differences.

In this sense, the narrative of recovery parallels a process that happens with disability generally, though not always under that name. Part of the process of having a disability involves the recognition, first, that one is disabled and, second, that one is inhabiting a world that is deliberately inhospitable to one's disability. Recognizing these facts, a person with a disability is obliged to modulate her expectations and behavior in light of these conditions. The process of recovery, on the disability model of addiction, is a process of this kind. It is a process of recognizing one's differences and how those differences are discriminated against and exploited, and adjusting one's orientation toward one addiction accordingly. For some people, this process will take the form of voluntary prolonged abstinence, but there are many other possible processes as well, all of which represent varieties of recovery.[22]

4.10 Disability and Change

This chapter has explained how the disability model addresses classic questions in the theory of addiction. These answers are, I have argued, tenable, and in this sense, the disability model articulates a new and compelling theoretical stance on what addiction is and what explains addictive behavior. Yet this is not the primary significance of the account developed thus far. The most important implications of the disability model are not theoretical but practical.

Thus far we have given considerable attention to the discrimination and exploitation to which addicted people are subject. The disability model differs from other models of addiction in that it understands addiction as something that is formed in part by the attitudes and practices that people take toward addiction. Addiction is in this sense a social phenomenon. But the disability model differs from other models of addiction in another way, namely that it emphasizes the contingency of these social conditions. Addiction is not judged negatively because it is inherently defective. Rather, the negative attitudes to which addicted people are subject are unwarranted reactions to a condition that is, in itself, evaluatively neutral. Since these conditions are contingent, they are also changeable. And the disability model suggests ways in which they may be changed.

In this respect, the disability model is importantly unlike other models of addiction. It is in the first place not a medical or even a psychological model of addiction, but a political one. It underscores the conditions that underwrite addiction, asks what it would take for these conditions to be changed, and proposes concrete ways of changing them. This is not to deny the practical implications of other models of addiction. Most prominent models of addiction suggest ways in which our attitudes and practices toward addicted people may change. The disability model, however, proposes that addiction itself is a socially mediated category, and so that changes in our attitudes toward addicted people will be radical in both their scope and their implications.

The subsequent chapters begin to outline what these changes might look like. We begin, in the next chapter, with the most significant development in recent decades in the treatment of addiction in both medicine and public policy. This is the movement toward 'harm reduction.' Many of the interventions that have been made under the name of harm reduction have been significant ones, and ones endorsed by the disability model. Yet harm reduction has, as its name may suggest, traditionally been underwritten by some kind of defect model of addiction. In the next chapter, I articulate what the philosophy of harm reduction might look like once we take seriously the idea that addiction is a disability.

The implications of the disability model extend well beyond medicine and public health. Indeed, a core idea of the disability model is that the proper arenas for addressing addiction are ultimately not hospitals and clinics but courtrooms and legislatures. On the disability model, the issue of addiction is ultimately an issue of justice. So, the consequences of the disability model do not end with questions of medicine and health. Nonetheless, given the medical focus of much recent work on addiction, it is natural for our discussion of those consequences to at least begin with those questions.

Notes

1 The distinction between these two views is intuitively clear, but it can be complicated by certain philosophical theories of disability and disease. For example, the influential theory of Boorse (1975) would treat conditions such as deafness as diseases. If someone held such an expansive view of disease, she might accept many of the arguments made here and nonetheless hold that addiction is a disease. I hold that, first, this is a tendentious view of the scope of disease, and second, even supposing it to be true, it is still the fact that addiction is a disability (whether or not it is in some sense a 'disease') that is of primary significance both for understanding addiction and for making addiction-related policy.

2 Not all addictions are addictions to substance use, but a similar point applies to behavioral addictions: there is the question of demarcating addiction to a behavior (such as gambling or sex) from the simple engagement in that behavior.

3 The disability model then has the implication that, at least as a nominal possibility, the habitual use of tobacco in certain cultures (be they traditional Native American cultures (Godlaski, 2013) or modern industrialized cultures) may not constitute addiction, even though they resemble addictive tobacco use in both their inner motivations and outward behaviors. This is not to deny that habitual tobacco use is harmful, or that tobacco users exhibit the kind of volitional diversity I have been discussing. Rather, it is to point out that whether a certain kind of substance use or behavior constitutes an addiction will depend in part on the attitudes that people take toward that behavior or substance use. This is one implication of the idea that addiction is in some sense a socially determined phenomenon.

4 The disease model has at least some potential to give a better explanation of the goal of abstinence. If one's use of a substance is due to an underlying disease, then it is sensible to aim at something like the total remission of that disease, which may manifest itself as abstinence. This may be one reason why recovery programs that have abstinence as their aim tend to also endorse some version of the disease model.

5 The habitual nature of certain addictions, such as cigarette use, can be striking. These behaviors can strike a casual observer as almost scheduled, and not at all impulsive. Compare the remark of J.L. Austin (Austin, 1956, p. 24): 'We often succumb to temptation with calm and even with finesse.'

6 This is what is standardly known as the requirement of 'completeness.'

7 For an incisive discussion of this phenomenon and its implications, see Pickard (2021).

8 For an early but very useful longitudinal study of relapse and factors that may be protective against relapse, see Vaillant (1988). For a discussion of how the concept of 'relapse' has been understood across a variety of studies, and the difficulties involved in operationalizing this concept, see Moe *et al.* (2022).

9 This conception of addiction may also be developed into the idea that there is such a thing as an 'addictive personality,' an underlying personality trait or type that may be directed at anything whatsoever. While the idea of an addictive personality has great popular appeal, there is limited evidence that there is such a thing, at least if 'personality' is understood in the way in which it typically is in psychology; for one critical discussion, see Griffiths (2017).

10 Suicide, for example, seems to demand a particular kind of explanation. For a compelling articulation of what that explanation might look like, see Joiner (2005).

11 When philosophers propose that there is a connection between psychological states and well-being, they typically propose that well-being is to be understood in terms of the satisfaction of one's desires (Heathwood, 2016). Less commonly defended, but I think more intuitive, is that one's well-being tends to be promoted by the satisfaction of one's intentions (Keller, 2004).

12 When overdoses are reported in this era, they tend to involve intentional overdoses rather than the accidental overdoses that are now widespread.

13 Consider alcohol, which is sometimes thought of as an unchanging addiction but has in fact been conditioned by specific technological and political developments. See the discussion of the 'gin craze' in Warner (2002) for a discussion of how an admixture of social discrimination and new technologies for alcohol delivery gave rise to a new kind of alcohol addiction, with profoundly worse consequences.

14 For a compelling discussion of how these forces play out for the case of tobacco smoking in particular, see Voigt (2010).

15 The distinction between abilities and options (or, as it is sometimes called, between general abilities and specific abilities) is not always marked in the literature on disability, but it is an important distinction in the theory of ability generally. See Maier (2020) for one treatment.

16 For a compelling exposition of these arguments, see Barnes (2016, pp. 16–20).

17 One study finds that addiction narratives are often marked by a kind of biological or genetic determinism about addiction, perhaps due to the influence of the disease model within certain recovery communities (Hammer *et al.*, 2012).

18 This question might, in principle, go in either direction, depending on how we think about responsibility for addiction itself. The addicted person might be less responsible if we see her addiction as a mitigating condition. Or she might be more responsible, if we hold that she is responsible not only for her act but also for the addiction that in some sense led to the act. In what follows, I do not take a stand on the question of whether people with addictions are 'responsible' in some sense for their addictions. I do argue that these questions of responsibility are independent from the questions of justice that will concern us in what follows.

19 One broad study of individuals in the United States finds that, among those who report having a substance use disorder at some point in their life, approximately 75% report no longer having a substance use disorder (Jones *et al.*, 2020).

20 See again Pickard (2021) for a discussion of this kind of phenomenon.

21 The use of nicotine replacement therapy (NRT) by former tobacco users is a clear example of this kind, as do many other examples of 'harm reduction,' which we will consider in detail in the next chapter.

22 The nature of recovery, and the term 'recovery' itself, will come in for further discussion in what follows. In Chapter 7, we will consider the idea of 'recovery capital' and its significance for addiction treatment. In the Conclusion, I will give my own personal reflections on how we should understand the idea of 'recovery,' and how we might improve on it.

Works Cited

Austin, J.L. (1956). A Plea for Excuses: The Presidential Address. *Proceedings of the Aristotelian Society*, 57, 1–30.

Barnes, E. (2016). *The Minority Body: A Theory of Disability*. Oxford University Press.

Boorse, C. (1975). On the Distinction between Disease and Illness. *Philosophy & Public Affairs*, *5*(1), 49–68.

Gentile, D. (2009). Pathological Video-Game Use among Youth Ages 8 to 18: A National Study. *Psychological Science*, *20*(5), 594–602.

Godlaski, T.M. (2013). Holy Smoke: Tobacco Use among Native American Tribes in North America. *Substance Use & Misuse*, *48*(1–2), 1–8.

Griffiths, M.D. (2017). The Myth of 'Addictive Personality.' *Global Journal of Addiction & Rehabilitation Medicine*, *3*(2), 1–3.

Hammer, R.R., Dingel, M.J., Ostergren, J.E., Nowakowski, K.E., & Koenig, B.A. (2012). The Experience of Addiction as Told by the Addicted: Incorporating Biological Understandings into Self-Story. *Culture, Medicine and Psychiatry*, *36*(4), 712–734.

Heathwood, C. (2016). Desire-Fulfillment Theory. In G. Fletcher (Ed.), *The Routledge Handbook of the Philosophy of Well-Being* (pp. 135–147). Routledge.

Joiner, T. (2005). *Why People Die by Suicide*. Harvard University Press.

Jones, C.M., Noonan, R.K., & Compton, W.M. (2020). Prevalence and Correlates of Ever Having a Substance Use Problem and Substance Use Recovery Status among Adults in the United States, 2018. *Drug and Alcohol Dependence*, *214*, 108–169.

Keller, S. (2004). Welfare and the Achievement of Goals. *Philosophical Studies*, *121*, 27–41.

Maier, J.T. (2020). Abilities. In E.N. Zalta (Ed.), *The Stanford Encyclopedia of Philosophy*. Metaphysics Research Lab, Stanford University.

Maier, J.T. (2022). *Options and Agency*. Palgrave Macmillan.

McHugh, R.K., Hearon, B.A., & Otto, M.W. (2010). Cognitive Behavioral Therapy for Substance Use Disorders. *Psychiatric Clinics*, *33*(3), 511–525.

Moe, F.D., Moltu, C., McKay, J.R., Nesvåg, S., & Bjornestad, J. (2022). Is the Relapse Concept in Studies of Substance Use Disorders a 'One Size Fits All' Concept? A Systematic Review of Relapse Operationalisations. *Drug and Alcohol Review*, *41*(4), 743–758.

Pickard, H. (2021). Addiction and the Self. *Noûs*, *55*(4), 737–761.

Vaillant, G.E. (1988). What Can Long-Term Follow-up Teach Us about Relapse and Prevention of Relapse in Addiction? *British Journal of Addiction*, *83*(10), 1147–1157.

Voigt, K. (2010). Smoking and Social Justice. *Public Health Ethics*, *3*(2), 91–106.

Warner, J. (2002). *Craze: Gin and Debauchery in an Age of Reason*. Basic Books.

5

BEYOND HARM REDUCTION

5.1 The Idea of Harm Reduction

Much of the most useful work on addiction in medicine and public health in recent decades has revolved around the idea of harm reduction. Harm reduction is less a specific thesis or treatment than it is a set of policies and strategies guided by a unifying philosophy of how to approach addiction. Beginning in Europe, notably the Netherlands and the United Kingdom, harm reduction approaches began to have significant influence in the United States in the 1990s.

What is harm reduction? An early statement from public health experts in the United States makes the idea clear and bears quoting at length:

> *The principal goal for drug policy should instead be to reduce the harms to society arising from the production, consumption, and control of drugs. Total harm (to users and the rest of society) can be expressed as the product of total use and the average harm per unit of use and thus can be lowered by reducing either component. Attention has been focused on the first; greater attention to the second would be beneficial.*[1]

Before we turn to the specific interventions that have been practiced under the heading of 'harm reduction,' it is worth considering this statement in some detail.

First, as this statement makes clear, the label 'harm reduction' is something of a misnomer, or one that does not fully specify the particular aims of the harm reduction movement. For the idea that drug policy

DOI: 10.4324/9781003410263-6

should be focused on the reduction of harm is, in itself, something that could be widely endorsed by those who endorse strictly medical approaches to addiction. Indeed, many would see it as something of a truism. As one might see the goal of cancer policy as one of reducing the harms associated with cancer, or the goal of HIV policy as reducing the harms associated with HIV, so one might see the goal of drug policy as reducing the harms associated with drugs. That principle will be, at least for many, uncontroversial.

It is the second aspect of harm reduction that is more closely associated with the name. This is not the endorsement of harm reduction per se, but a particular strategy for achieving harm reduction. Instead of attempting to have addicted people reduce the amount of substance they use – which, as the authors note, has been the emphasis of traditional addiction treatment, attention should instead be refocused on reducing the harms associated with use. In this sense, 'harm reduction' strictly denotes, not the reduction of harm generally, but a certain kind of strategy for reducing harm.

Most opponents of harm reduction accept the principle that the aim of drug policy should be the reduction of harm, but either deny that the harm reductionist's preferred strategies are effective means to doing this or argue that they create new and unacceptable harms in other domains. The view suggested by the disability model is almost precisely the opposite. The interventions that have been introduced under the heading of 'harm reduction' are, by and large, good ones. If anything, the disability model recommends extending the scope of these interventions. But these interventions are not best understood as reducing the harms associated with substance use. Nor should the aim of drug policy be taken to be reducing the harms associated with drug use. The disability model proposes an altogether different understanding of the role of drug policy, and how these interventions are ultimately to be justified. The remainder of the discussion in this chapter will elaborate on that understanding.[2]

5.2 The Practice of Harm Reduction

To give some context to these questions, it will be helpful to consider in some detail what harm reduction interventions look like.

Consider sites where users of intravenously injected drugs are provided with new needles and other paraphernalia to use for injection. Such sites are colloquially known as 'needle exchanges,' and in the public health literature are standardly referred to as 'syringe services programs' or SSP's. To return to the distinction made earlier, these sites are not concerned with reducing the quantity of intravenous drugs that are used. Instead, they reduce the harm associated with each use of intravenous drugs. Specifically, by discouraging the reuse of needles, these sites demonstrably reduce the rate of infection with infectious diseases that are spread through the sharing of needles, such as HIV (Hurley *et al.*, 1997).

Sites for the provision of unused needles are cases of what might be called pure harm reduction: they do not aim to do anything but reduce the harms associated with use. Other interventions and strategies that are often taken as instances of harm reduction are somewhat more diffuse in their aims. Consider for example the practice of treating mental health conditions when they occur in conjunction with a substance use disorder. There is a line of thinking on which one must resolve the substance use disorder before proceeding with mental health treatment. A more 'harm reduction' approach to these cases, what are sometimes called co-occurring disorders, is that an intractable substance use disorder is no barrier to receiving treatment for a mental health condition. One may make a person's life better, by treating their mental health condition, regardless of the status of the substance use disorder. Generally, medical and psychological treatment should do what it can to reduce the harm that a person may encounter, even when that person refuses treatment for a substance use disorder. This too is a kind of harm reduction, in a broad sense of that term.

In addition to these specific interventions, whether pure interventions such as sites for the provision of needles or broader interventions such as the provision of care for co-occurring disorders, harm reduction is associated with a certain set of attitudes toward addiction. Most of all, harm reduction strategies are associated with the rejection of stigma around addiction and drug use. In place of these attitudes, advocates of harm reduction advocate an attitude of tolerance and understanding. Indeed, the adoption of such attitudes may itself be understood as an exercise in harm reduction. To take a tolerant attitude toward someone with an addiction may not itself reduce her substance use, but it plausibly will make her life go slightly better than it otherwise would. In this sense, the opposition to stigma is both an inspiration for and a consequence of the harm reductionist stance.

These examples are only a few of the interventions that have been proposed and implemented by the harm reduction movement.[3] They should however give a sense of the specific forms that harm reduction takes, as distinct from the more general philosophy that underwrites harm reduction. This distinction is important because, as I have suggested, the disability model endorses many of these interventions, while expressing more skepticism about the guiding ideas of harm reduction themselves. Let us then consider the grounds of this skepticism.

5.3 The Question of Harm

The harm reduction approach foregrounds the issue of harm in our response to addiction. So, to understand this approach, it is helpful to consider the following question: what kind of harm is involved in addiction, and what is the source of that harm?

As we have already seen, several views of addiction suggest that being addicted itself is a harm, something that in itself makes one's life worse than it would otherwise be. Notably, on the disease model, addiction is in itself a state that makes one worse off and calls for treatment. On other views, addiction is closely associated with harm. For example, on the self-medication model, addiction is a response to an underlying condition or trauma, which will itself be typically a harm.

Therefore, on standard views of addiction, there is a close tie between addiction and harm, such that all or almost all people who have an addiction are subject to harm that is at least closely related to their addiction. If this is one's picture of addiction, then harm reduction will seem a natural stance. If addiction is a harmful state, then the aim of addiction policy, one might reasonably conclude, is to reduce that harm.

But the disability model, as we have already said, rejects many of these presuppositions about addiction and harm. Addiction is not to be understood as a disease, or as a response to a disease or condition. Instead, addiction is grounded in volitional diversity, and volitional diversity is in itself neither good nor bad. The disability model does not deny that there are harms associated with addiction, but it insists that these harms are in some sense external to the addicted person herself. The source of these harms is not the character of the addicted person's will, but rather the discrimination and exploitation to which she is subject.

So, the disability model understands the injunction to reduce harm differently than other models of addiction. For the disability model, since the harms that addicted people face are social and environmental in their origins, harm reduction should mean a focus on improving the social conditions in which addicted people find themselves.

To some degree, the interventions promoted by harm reduction advocates already do precisely that. Consider again sites that provide unused needles. The unavailability of unused needles is itself a clear example of the kind of discriminatory practices to which drug users are subject. It arises, at first approximation, from restrictive paraphernalia laws and the constrained resources of many intravenous drug users. The provision of unused needles effectively counteracts, or at least modulates, the effects of these discriminatory conditions. In this respect, harm reduction is often directed at precisely the kinds of harms that are emphasized by the disability model.

In addition, as we have already seen, harm reduction is not focused only on the effects of discriminatory attitudes, but on those attitudes themselves. The harm reduction movement has generally promoted a tolerant approach toward substance use and addiction, one which has actively combatted stigma and other barriers faced by people with addictions. In this way, too, the aims of the disability model and the aims of the harm reduction movement dovetail with each other.

For all of that, there is nonetheless something problematic, from the point of view of the disability model, about the way that addiction is understood among advocates of harm reduction. To bring out what this is, it is useful to consider what a 'harm reduction' approach to other disabilities might look like. Consider deafness. We could imagine an approach to deafness that went under the heading of harm reduction. It would acknowledge the harms faced by deaf people due to discrimination, both the material effects of discriminatory attitudes and the attitudes themselves. It would work to reduce those harms and to decrease discriminatory attitudes and stigma. It would encourage a tolerant and welcoming attitude toward deaf people.

Such a movement, if it existed, would have generally positive effects for deaf people, and would be consonant with the fact that deafness is a disability. Yet, for all of that, there is something misconceived about the idea of a harm reduction movement focused on deafness. One wants to say, first, that deafness is not in any way a harmful condition, but simply a different one. Second, that while discrimination against deaf people should indeed be combatted, it should be done so under that name rather than in terms of combatting the supposed 'harms' associated with deafness. Third, the idea that deaf people should be treated with tolerance is true but oddly specific – all people should be treated with tolerance, deaf people among them, and the idea that there is a special need to tolerate deaf people in particular has the unwelcome implication that there is some special obstacle to their being tolerated. In short, a harm reduction approach to deafness would get a lot of things right, especially in terms of the actual policies that it would promote, but it seems to put the emphasis in all the wrong places.

I want to say something similar about the harm reduction approach to addiction. Due to social conditions as they actually are, there is significant harm associated with addiction, and it is important to attempt to reduce this harm where possible. Many actual harm reduction efforts have this effect, and in this sense, the interventions promoted by harm reduction are to be welcomed. But the view of addiction and addiction treatment that animates harm reduction is misconceived. This is a theoretical difference, but it has practical differences when we consider the question of how to defend, and extend, programs such as sites providing unused needles. These practical implications will be developed in what follows.

5.4 Harm Reduction and Medicine

How has the harm reduction movement gained so much influence on thinking about addiction, in a relatively short period? One reason is that harm reduction allies well with a view that had already been gaining increasing acceptance and institutional support. This is the idea that addiction is fundamentally a medical problem.

There is a long-standing tradition of understanding addiction as fundamentally a moral or a legal issue. People with addictions are understood as having a moral failing of excessive indulgence in a harmful or simply immoral activity, and the proper question for a just society is how to prevent such activity and how to punish it when it cannot be successfully prevented. On such a model, the primary interventions for responding to addiction will be moral or legal ones, and the appropriate attitudes to take toward addicted people are those taken against immoral actors generally: disapprobation, resentment, and blame.

This kind of attitude toward addiction will be familiar. On the disability model, it still underwrites the way addiction is regarded and treated in society at large. But it is no longer, at least, the dominant mode of understanding addiction in public discourse. It has been replaced in that role, over the last century, by a rather different perspective on addiction. This is the perspective on which addiction is not a moral or legal one but, in the first place, a medical one.

The medical approach to addiction differs in the first place in the interventions that it suggests. Whereas a moral conception of addiction is directed toward correction and punishment, a medical conception of addiction is directed toward the traditional interventions of medicine generally and psychiatry in particular: inpatient care, medication, and psychotherapy. Instead of the essentially punitive attitudes suggested by the moral approach, the medical approach counsels the approach that is appropriate to take toward those who are physically or psychologically ill: tolerance and non-judgmental support.

This medical approach to addiction is closely tied to two ideas that we have already considered. First, it stands in a close relationship to the disease model of addiction. If one adopts a disease model of addiction, then one will typically adopt a medical model of addiction as well, for a medical approach is typically the appropriate response to a disease. I have already argued that we should reject the disease model of addiction. But this is not the only route to a medical approach to addiction. For, second, the medical model stands in a close relationship to the idea that is at issue in this chapter, namely the idea that harm reduction is the appropriate response to addiction.

Whereas the disease model adopts a fundamentally medical diagnosis of addiction, the harm reduction model approach adopts a fundamentally medical treatment of addiction. That is, it advocates the same kind of public health interventions and tolerant attitudes that medicine tends to recommend toward the treatment of illness generally. The harm reduction approach does not assume the disease model, but its effects are often, in practice, much the same.

These effects are, as I have already emphasized, important and valuable ones. Whatever model of addiction one holds, sites for safe injection of intravenous drugs reduce rates of HIV infection, and that is a good thing. Similar arguments can be given for many such harm reduction measures. But the justification for these measures, as I have argued, is fundamentally mistaken, and this mistake has practical consequences. In particular, the harm reduction movement has tended to adopt an overly medical conception of addiction, and this is a conception that we have reason to reject.

It has been difficult to appreciate this point because the effects of harm reduction efforts have been so obviously beneficial and because it is difficult to see in what other way these efforts might be justified. But, in adopting the disability model, we can begin to articulate a different understanding of what justifies interventions such as safe injection sites, one that takes seriously the idea that addiction is a disability.

5.5 The Justification of Harm Reduction

Let us return to the statement of harm reduction that we considered at the outset. It begins with the following claim: *The principal goal for drug policy should instead be to reduce the harms to society arising from the production, consumption, and control of drugs.* This can seem tantamount to a truism. Who could deny that this is the goal of drug policy? The only alternative to it would seem to be an indifference to these harms, or even an active pursuit of such harms, as when drug policy is focused on the punishment of people who use drugs. But such alternatives are clearly implausible, which leads us back to the thought that this simple statement of harm reduction should be undeniable.

But the disability model does deny it, as stated. This is not of course because the disability model counsels indifference to harm, but because its emphasis is quite different, in a few ways. Again, the comparison with other disabilities is instructive. What is the principal goal, for example, of policies related to deafness? Is it reducing the harms to society resulting from deafness? That seems wrong, and it bears considering why exactly it is wrong.

To begin with, the primary object of policies related to deafness should not be society generally, but deaf people specifically. There may well be broader social considerations to policies related to deafness, but deaf people should have priority in the evaluation of these policies: we first consider how these policies will affect deaf people, and only secondarily consider their broader implications for society as a whole.

Even once we have made this correction, the stated policy still seems misconceived. The primary aim of deaf policy should not be one of reducing harm, even when we focus on reducing harm to deaf people in particular. Deaf people have many interests, and reducing the harms to which they are subject is only one of these interests. Like any of us, they may well be willing to tolerate some harms for the sake of other interests. Therefore, at first approximation, the aim of deaf policy should be to protect the rights and interests of deaf people, whatever those interests may be.

This might seem to be a merely notional difference, but in fact, it has quite substantial practical implications. Consider for instance a policy that might increase accommodations afforded to deaf people, but which might have the effect of increasing the discrimination and stigma to which deaf people are subject. It might be, for instance, that the cost of such a policy might produce a popular 'backlash' that results in increases in negative attitudes toward deaf people. It might well be that a policy should be endorsed if our aim is to promote the rights and interests of deaf people, even if it leads to increases in harm to deaf people all things considered. I do not mean to say that this is the only view to take of such a policy, but only to say that it is one viable view and that it is a view that is foreclosed by an exclusive focus on the issue of harm.

I want to suggest that the supposedly truistic remarks that orient the harm reduction approach are similarly mistaken. The aim of drug policy – and of other policies that bear most immediately on addicted people, such as gambling policy – should not be to reduce the harms imposed on society by drug use and other activities associated with drugs (or gambling, or other addictive activities). Instead, such policies should prioritize the interests of addicted people. Furthermore, the aim of policy should not simply be to reduce the harms associated with being addicted but to protect the rights and interests of addicted people, whatever form precisely those take. In short, the idea that drug policy should be oriented around reducing harms to society is mistaken twice over.

This essentially negative claim leaves open at least three positive projects. The first project is to articulate what the proper aim of policy around addictive substances and activities should be, on the disability model. The second is to draw out the broad implications of such an aim for thinking about issues of addiction treatment in particular. The third is to evaluate the specific interventions promoted by harm reduction advocates by the lights of these guidelines. Let us take each of these in turn.

5.6 The Disability Model and Policy

If one adopts the disability model of addiction, how should one understand the aims of addiction-related policy?[4] This is a question that has already been broached by the foregoing discussion, but it will be useful to make our response to it still more clear and explicit.

To begin, the priority in the evaluation of addiction-related policy should be the interests of addicted people. Stated in this way, this principle can seem obvious. After all, many would agree, the priority in the evaluation of (for example) indigenous policy should be the interests of indigenous peoples, and the priority in the evaluation of policy for older adults should be the interests of older adults. By parity of reasoning, our presumption should be that the priority of addiction-related policy should be the interests of addicted people. Yet this principle falls afoul of most thinking about addiction policy.

As we have already seen in one statement of the philosophy of harm reduction, an alternate view is that the priority of addiction policy should be the interests of society as a whole. After all, addiction policy does touch on society as a whole. Any citizen, for example, is affected by the price of cigarettes, whether or not she is addicted to tobacco. The price of cigarettes has ramifications for local taxes, health care costs, and even for the profitability of convenience stores. This is a complicated social calculus that has a bearing on every citizen, whether or not they use cigarettes.

The principle that addicted people should be prioritized in the evaluation of addiction policy agrees with all of this. There are social costs and benefits to any addiction policy, all of which need to be accounted for. It simply insists on giving priority to the interests of addicted people. In evaluating a policy that bears on the use of tobacco, we ought to first ask how it affects the interests of those who are addicted to tobacco, and only subsequently how it affects society as a whole. This principle allows that the interests of society as a whole may, in some cases, trump the interests of addicted people. But it insists that we first consider the interests of addicted people. In this sense, it is not so much a formula as it is a certain kind of decision procedure, one that is in principle compatible with a diverse array of outcomes.[5]

The first recommendation of the disability model for addiction-related policy, then, is that the interests of addicted people be given priority in the evaluation of policies. The second recommendation concerns a specification of what those interests are. As we have seen, on the harm reduction model, the interests of addicted people are construed in terms of harms and benefits, such that an addiction-related policy supports the interests of addicted people just in case it makes addicted people, on average, better off than they would otherwise be. This is a natural way of understanding the interests of addicted people within the broadly medical perspective suggested by the harm reduction approach. But, as we saw in the case of other disabilities, this perspective is somewhat too narrow. A policy may promote the interests of a disabled group (for example, by funding accommodations) even though it may make them slightly worse off overall (for example, by leading to a 'backlash' and increased discrimination). So, the interests of disabled people generally are not to be identified with what makes them better off, all things considered.

A similar point applies to addiction. There may be some policies that make addicted people worse off, overall, and which nonetheless promote the interests of addicted people in the relevant sense. For instance, to vary the example just given, establishing a site providing unused needles in a highly populated area might increase negative attitudes toward people who use intravenous drugs if, for example, it makes more people aware of intravenous drug use in their local area than they might otherwise be. Nonetheless, it is an intervention that promotes the interests of addicted people.

This sort of divergence, between what promotes the average well-being of people with addictions and what promotes the interests of people with addictions, is not at all a rare phenomenon. Instead, it occurs at the very core of much addiction policy. To anticipate a topic that we will consider in much greater detail in what follows, the question of prohibition raises this very dynamic. The prohibition of alcohol, for example, may increase the well-being of people with alcohol use disorders. Yet some will argue that it does not necessarily respect their interests. I do not mean, at this point, to take either side of this dispute, but only to point out that, once we adopt the disability model, such disputes are not to be adjudicated by calculations of well-being alone.

To put this observation in another way, the disability model does not merely ask us to prioritize the interests of people with addictions. It asks us also to understand these interests in terms of the rights of people with addictions. A medical approach to the question of addiction will tend to foreground questions of well-being: how can we most benefit people with addictions, while at the same time not knowingly doing them harm? These are important questions, but they are incomplete as an account of the interests of addicted people. The disability model imposes a different kind of demand on us. It asks us to understand addicted people, not as patients, but as fellow citizens, who have certain rights that must be respected.

The rights of addicted people include negative rights, rights against being treated in certain ways, and positive rights, demands on certain resources.[6] Two core rights are especially salient and are often inscribed into law in jurisdictions that explicitly recognize the rights of people with disabilities. These are, first, a right against being discriminated against and, second, a right to reasonable accommodations. Each of these has clear applications to the case of addiction, and each of these constitutes a new way of thinking about the moral and legal foundations of interventions that have been justified in the name of 'harm reduction.'

5.7 Disability and Discrimination

In the foregoing discussion, we have emphasized that the experience of being disabled is an experience of being the object of discrimination. Indeed, on the present account, this is not merely an accidental fact about disability, but an aspect of the constitution of disability itself. Disability is defined in part by its environmental and social circumstances, and these are, in the first place, circumstances of discrimination.

As I have argued, similar points apply to addiction. People with addictions are subject to systematic discrimination, stigma, and exploitation. Indeed, these phenomena are partly constitutive of addiction. What it is to have an addiction, as opposed to simply exhibiting volitional diversity, is to be the object of discrimination. And these facts ultimately support the thesis that, as I have argued, addiction is itself a kind of disability.

In these arguments, we have tended to treat discrimination as something fixed and immovable, a feature of the environment itself. But while discrimination is a feature of the environment, discrimination is neither fixed nor immovable. Patterns of discrimination can be, and ought to be, changed. Indeed, one of the primary goals of addiction policy is precisely to change them.

If we conceive of addiction policy in terms of minimizing harm, we can go some way toward advocating for the reduction of discrimination. After all, discrimination makes addicted people, and arguably the broader society in which they live, worse off. So, a strategy of harm reduction underwrites the aim of reducing discrimination. Indeed, as already noted earlier, the harm reduction movement has been a leading force in combatting stigma against people with addictions.

Yet on the disability model, the injunction against discrimination has a different, and in a way deeper, justification. The case against discriminating against people with addictions is not that it makes people with addictions worse off, though in many cases it does. The case against discrimination rests rather on the rights of addicted people against discrimination. People with addictions have a disability, and discrimination against people with addictions is a violation of the right of disabled people against discrimination on the basis of disability – regardless of the questions of benefit and harm that are foregrounded in the harm reduction movement.

This conception of the prohibition against discrimination is already operative in countries where there are strong prohibitions against discrimination against disabled people, and where addiction is recognized as a disability. The United States is such a country. Under the Americans with Disabilities Act (ADA), discrimination against individuals with disabilities is a civil rights violation, just as is discrimination on the basis of race or religion. Furthermore, under the ADA, certain major addictions are recognized as disabilities.[7] Therefore, for example, laws that discriminate against people with addictions are violations of the rights of people with addictions and may be struck down on those grounds alone.

The ADA therefore affords quite concrete protections to harm reduction interventions of the sort described earlier. If localities attempt to, for example, exclude such interventions through laws or zoning regulations, they risk falling afoul of the requirements of the ADA.[8] That is, whatever local governments may think about addiction and addiction treatment, they are simply not at liberty to prohibit these kinds of interventions, for people with addictions are a protected class with rights against discrimination.

This legal conception of anti-discrimination represents a fundamental shift in our thinking about the grounds of our treatment of people with addictions. In the harm reduction movement, anti-discrimination is often supported by reasons of beneficence. We feel that we ought to improve the lives of people with addictions, recognize that reducing stigma is one straightforward way of doing so, and conclude we should reduce stigma. This perspective on discrimination is the natural one to take if we are understanding issues from a broadly medical perspective. There is a duty of beneficence toward patients and this, more than anything, is what underwrites the case against stigma and discrimination.

The legal perspective on these issues suggested by the disability model, however, is altogether different. It does not matter whether we feel there is a duty of beneficence toward people with addictions, or indeed whether we are interested in promoting their well-being at all. People with addictions have a right against being discriminated against, a right that obtains whatever our interests or projects may be. In this sense, the prohibition against discrimination is in no way contingent on the project of providing treatment for addiction. The medical and public health community might collectively decide that certain interventions in harm reduction are ineffective and counterproductive. Perhaps some discriminatory practices might lower the incidence of addiction.[9] Such a realization would be, from the point of view of the disability model, irrelevant. Such practices would still be unjust ones, as they violate the rights of addicted people against discrimination, even if (on this supposition) they would promote the well-being of people with addictions overall.

Similarly, the case against discrimination proposed by the disability model is not easily superseded by competing interests. It may at times that considerations of beneficence conflict with anti-discriminatory considerations. To return again to an example that we will be considering at length later, it may be that the prohibition of certain substances or paraphernalia might benefit some class of substance users. Nonetheless, if these prohibitions constitute discrimination – a question to which we will also later return – then this fact will, on the disability model, trump any considerations of beneficence. In short, anti-discrimination and the prohibition of stigma are fundamentally, on the disability view, questions of rights.

5.8 Disability and Accommodation

This then is one broad application of a disability view to questions of policy, The disability view will oppose discrimination and stigma, on the grounds that these violate the rights of people with addictions. In addition to these negative rights, the disability view also underwrites positive rights for people with addictions. In particular, as addiction is a disability, it proposes that people with addictions should be provided with reasonable accommodations.

There are several questions to be asked here: what is an accommodation for a disability, what is it for an accommodation to count as reasonable, and how is the notion of reasonable accommodation to be extended to the case of addiction? Each of these questions is a fraught one, and there is extensive philosophical and legal debate about each of the first two questions. In what follows I will largely focus on the last of these questions. That is, I will assume we have a working understanding of reasonable accommodations for disabilities, by appeal to paradigms such as accessibility ramps or Braille type, and then ask how we might extend these to the disability that is addiction.

If accommodations are understood in this way, what are examples of reasonable accommodations for addiction? As I have already emphasized, the environment that addicted people find themselves in is one that is designed to discriminate against and exploit addictions. To live in most modern industrialized cities is to be frequently confronted with cigarettes, lottery tickets, hard liquor, and, in many places, advertisements for online gambling and cannabis delivery services. These are aspects of the world that actively lead to poor outcomes for addicted people. They are what might be called 'anti-accommodations' for addiction.

A first step in providing accommodations for addicted people may take the form of reducing the power and influence of anti-accommodations. This can take many forms. One example is restrictions on cigarette advertising, and the inclusion of warning labels on cigarette packages.[10] Another is restrictions on the state sponsorship of gambling products, a common practice in the United States. The many anti-accommodations that now exist create many opportunities for straightforward and relatively effective accommodations, where these are nothing but the modulation of anti-accommodations.

What, however, of more positive accommodations for addicted people, which do not merely inhibit discriminatory aspects of the environment but actively intervene on the environment to make it a more hospitable place for people with addictions? It can be difficult to imagine these, as people with addictions do not always confront the kind of tangible impediments that, for example, many people with physical disabilities do. Yet we have seen such examples already, as many of the interventions proposed by the harm reduction movement can be understood in terms of accommodations.

Consider once more, for example, sites that provide individuals who use intravenous drugs with unused needles. These sites effectively make the world somewhat more hospitable for people who are addicted to intravenous drugs. They allow them to continue to use such drugs while not bearing some of the costs associated with such use, such as the risk of contracting infectious diseases. These sites in no way make having an active addiction to intravenous drugs equivalent to not having such an addiction: there are still many disadvantages associated with such an addiction, even when accommodations are in place. But this was never the standard for accommodations generally. Accessibility ramps do not make the world as accessible to people who use wheelchairs as it is to people who do not. Instead, they make the world somewhat more accessible than it would otherwise be. Similarly, sites that dispense unused needles make the world somewhat more hospitable to people with addictions.

Note that, when such sites are understood in this way, as accommodations for disability, the justification for them is quite different. The standard justification for sites that dispense unused needles is that they do a great deal of good for people with addictions and that they do so at a very low cost (Wilson *et al.*, 2015). This justification in terms of cost-benefit analysis is correct so far as it goes, but it is not central to a justification in terms of accommodations.

On the disability model, interventions that count as accommodations are understood in a fundamentally different way. Since these interventions are accommodations for a disability, they are demanded by fundamental considerations of equity. So, cost-benefit reasoning, which has been prominent within the harm reduction movement, is not as central to the disability approach. Indeed, even if the costs of such interventions outweigh their benefits, they may nonetheless be mandated by considerations of accommodation.

This is not to say that there are no limits on how much accommodation may be demanded. Reasonableness imposes some kind of constraint so that not just any intervention that somehow accommodates a person with an addiction is required, whatever the cost. Nonetheless, the disability model suggests that accommodations for people with addictions will often be required, even when their costs outweigh their benefits, so long as the burdens they impose are not unreasonable.[11] This requirement turns on the rights of people with addictions rather than the beneficence of their providers, and turns out to be, in many cases, a more demanding requirement than one that depends on beneficence alone.

5.9 A Disability Model for Interventions

The harm reduction approach has led to vital interventions for people with addictions. As I have argued, however, the philosophy behind the approach itself is in certain ways opposed to the disability approach. It presupposes a broadly medical understanding of addiction, on which interventions to improve the situation of people with addictions are justified in terms of their overall benefits. The disability model, in contrast, is an approach that foregrounds the rights of people with addictions, as opposed to the beneficence of providers and society more generally toward people with addictions.

The foregoing discussion, however, has suggested a way of reconciling harm reduction interventions with the disability approach. These clearly significant interventions may be justified in a different way. The disability model insists on the rights of addicted people, and in particular the rights of addicted people against discrimination and for reasonable accommodation. Therefore, the disability model provides two ways in which interventions may be justified, namely on anti-discriminatory grounds or on grounds of accommodation.

Somewhat more formally, we can apply the following test or rubric to the evaluation of interventions that bear on addiction. We can ask two questions that are relevant to the question of disability and its protection: First, would the failure to provide this intervention constitute discrimination? Second, would the provision of this intervention be a reasonable accommodation?[12]

If the answer to either of these questions is affirmative, then the intervention is justified by the standards of the disability model. Indeed, in many cases, an intervention will be justified by both criteria. In the foregoing, I have been focusing on a central intervention in the management of intravenous drug use, namely the provision of unused needles. To understand the breadth of the disability model, it will be helpful to consider a different example of an intervention that is often promoted under the heading of harm reduction.

Consider, for example, the provision of nicotine replacement therapy for the treatment of tobacco addiction. A best practice in the management of tobacco addiction is to provide ways of administering nicotine (such as through a patch or gum) in a way that does not involve the harmful effects of tobacco. Such therapies are expensive and often difficult to access. Accordingly, one important intervention for people with nicotine addictions is to make such treatments easily available in contexts where it is often not available, such as prisons and emergency shelters, thereby reducing the negative consequences of tobacco addiction.[13] We can now ask: is this kind of intervention demanded by the disability model? It is just in case the answer to one of the questions earlier is affirmative. And, in most cases, this condition is met.

Consider first the question of discrimination. This will depend heavily on context. The mere failure to provide recommended treatments in under-resourced settings is not invariably discriminatory. But in many cases, it is. Some correctional facilities, for instance, will offer medications to inmates but will deny nicotine replacement therapy on the hypothesis that it promotes or 'enables' addiction. Such differential denial of treatment is patently discriminatory. Therefore, the failure to provide this intervention will sometimes be discriminatory and, when it is, the intervention will be mandated by the disability model.

Consider then the question of accommodation. Here the answer is more general. In any context, the provision of nicotine replacement therapy is an accommodation for people with tobacco addictions. It prevents the negative cognitive consequences of nicotine withdrawal, while at the same time reducing the significant health disadvantages of tobacco consumption (Apelberg et al., 2010). It thereby goes some ways toward establishing health equity between people with tobacco addictions and those who do not have tobacco addictions. The disability model therefore clearly recommends the provision of nicotine replacement therapy and indeed recommends that it be provided freely wherever this can be reasonably done. Context is also relevant here. It may be that there are some cases – such as settings where only basic medical care is available – where the demand to provide nicotine replacement therapy is an unreasonable one, but these are comparatively rare, at least in modern industrialized countries.

In short, the provision of nicotine replacement therapy is generally mandated by the disability model: in some cases, it is discriminatory not to provide it, and, in most cases, it is a reasonable accommodation to provide it. This then is a clear application of the disability model for interventions, and another case in which its recommendations are substantially the same as those of the harm reduction approach.

This example supports the general proposal already made, namely that the disability model can endorse the specific interventions advocated by harm reduction proponents without accepting the philosophical grounds of harm reduction itself. I have also suggested the disability model has two further, independent, advantages. First, it gives these interventions a distinct, and more secure, justification. Second, it suggests ways of extending interventions beyond what has been conceived by the harm reduction model. I close by considering each of these differences and their significance.

5.10 Justifying Interventions

As I have argued, the disability model justifies interventions in a fundamentally different way from the way that they are justified by the harm reduction approach. They are not justified solely in terms of the benefits that they provide for addicted people – though these interventions do in fact do that – but in terms of the rights of addicted people to these interventions. The points emphasized in the model just sketched help to articulate what these rights are. People with addictions have a right against discrimination and a right to reasonable accommodation. Making interventions such as nicotine replacement therapy freely available to people with tobacco addictions is an example of an intervention that, at least in some cases, is demanded by both of these rights.

I have also emphasized the relative stringency of the justifications provided by the disability model. The harm reduction approach has its basis in a medical model that seeks to deliver maximum benefits to patients, ideally at a relatively low cost. The disability model, in contrast, is relatively insensitive to cost-benefit calculations. Its primary concern is securing the rights of addicted people, so long as that can be done at a reasonable cost. And, since the rights in question are fundamental ones, the threshold of what costs count as reasonable will be set accordingly high.

To understand the approach to justification taken by the disability model, it may be helpful to contrast the broadly medical approach of the harm reduction approach with the broadly legal or political approach taken by the disability model. As the disability model conceives of matters, addicted people are in the first place citizens, and a central concern of addiction policy should be to respect and advance their interests. This is the sort of consideration that should be addressed, in the first place, within the ordinary political process, where the interests of minority groups are brought to bear on the organization of social institutions. When this process fails, and the rights of people with addictions are infringed upon, they may reasonably avail themselves of the legal process, so that the appropriate protection of their rights may be enforced. On the disability model, this is the proper way of thinking about the formation of addiction policy, which is fundamentally a policy oriented around the protection of certain rights.

The opinions of medical experts are not irrelevant to this process. The judgment that nicotine replacement therapy is an appropriate intervention for tobacco addiction, for example, rests largely on medical research and judgment. The role of medical opinion within the disability model, however, is largely evidential rather than authoritative. That is, the disability model does not hold that certain interventions are warranted in virtue of being medical 'best practices' for the treatment of addiction. Rather, the disability model insists on the right of addicted people to reasonable accommodation and looks to medical opinion for information about what form those accommodations may best take.

The disability model and the harm reduction approach therefore justify similar interventions in different ways. For the harm reduction approach, these interventions are fundamentally underwritten by considerations of beneficence, and they are guided by a broadly medical perspective on addiction. On the disability model, on the other hand, justification begins with a recognition that addicted people are fellow citizens and that interventions are required to satisfy their rights against discrimination and rights to reasonable accommodation. One consequence of this difference is a difference in the arenas that each of these approaches looks to when interventions are under threat. The harm reduction approach appeals to the judgment of physicians and public health experts, while the disability model will appeal to legislators and, where appropriate, to the courts. For the justification for these interventions is ultimately, on the disability model, not medical but legal.

5.11 Extending Interventions

There is a further difference between the harm reduction approach and the disability model. In addition to justifying interventions in a more fundamental and rights-oriented way, the disability model also has a broader conception of what interventions for addiction might look like. On harm reduction approaches, interventions tend to be tied closely to the use of substances, and in particular to medical interventions that can reduce the harm associated with the use of individual substances. This, recall, was the focus of the harm reduction philosophy that we discussed at the outset, namely reducing 'average harm per unit of use.'

Such interventions are, on the disability model, important. But they do not exhaust the range of interventions that may be demanded. Recall that on the present view addiction is defined in part by widespread and systematic patterns of discrimination and exploitation. As the disability model sees interventions as, in part, a way of responding to discrimination and exploitation, any of these is potentially a target for an intervention. The kinds of harms that have been central to the harm reduction movement – such as the high incidence of HIV infection among users of intravenous drugs (Mathers et al., 2008) – are an example of this, but only one example. Other examples of discrimination and exploitation of people with addiction are perhaps less blatant but at the same time more widespread and insidious.

Consider housing. Housing represents a basic or 'primary' good, something that most people want, regardless of their more specific goals in life.[14] Yet housing is consistently difficult for people with addictions to secure. This difficulty has several sources. In part, it is due to individual-level discrimination: a majority of people think, for example, that it is appropriate for a landlord to refuse to accept a person with a drug addiction as a tenant.[15] It is due also to more systematic forms of discrimination, such as zoning laws prohibiting housing for people newly in recovery from certain neighborhoods. Finally, it is due to still more fundamental forms of discrimination, especially the forms of disadvantage that lead housing to be unaffordable for people with addictions.

On the disability model, one role for interventions is precisely to combat these forms of discrimination and inequality. For example, striking down discriminatory zoning laws may well be mandated as an intervention under the disability model. Similarly, the provision of housing vouchers in expensive real estate markets may well be a reasonable accommodation for people with addictions. Indeed, there is a case to be made that in jurisdictions where the rights of people with addictions are legally protected – including the United States since the passage of the Americans with Disabilities Act – these kinds of interventions are legally required.[16]

This kind of intervention goes well beyond what has traditionally fallen under the scope of harm reduction. Making it easier for addicted people to access housing does reduce the harm associated with addiction, namely the myriad harms associated with lack of adequate housing. But it is not focused on reducing the 'average harm per unit of use,' as on traditional harm reduction approaches. Nor, more fundamentally, is ensuring access to housing sensibly framed in terms of reducing harm at all. Rather, the primary aim of such interventions is to secure the rights of people with addictions. That does tend to reduce the harms they experience, but that is not the primary object of these interventions, nor their primary justification.

Once we think of interventions in this broader way, we begin to understand a further reason for hesitation about the project of harm reduction, even as we endorse its interventions and their effects. The criticism is that harm reduction is too limited in its aims. Harm reduction asks us to pursue a society where stigma against people with addictions is reduced or eliminated, and where people can use substances without experiencing the litany of harms associated with them. These are worthwhile goals. But if these are the central demands that are being made on behalf of people with addictions, then we are asking too little.

In general, an oppressed or disadvantaged group might ask that the effects of discrimination and exploitation be modulated and that they might be able to pursue their life projects without experiencing active deprivation. These are reasonable things to ask. But it would be unfortunate if the demands of such a group ended there. What such a group can reasonably ask is nothing less than full equality under the law and full equity in access to resources. The last criticism of harm reduction, if conceived of as a full approach to the treatment of addiction, is that it asks for less than this.

The disability model, on the other hand, is more ambitious in its aims. It demands that interventions for addicted people properly address the rights of those people, in particular that they counteract discrimination and provide reasonable accommodation. Given the scope of discrimination against people with addictions, and how inaccessible society often is to them, these interventions often demand significantly more than has been considered within the ambit of harm reduction. They demand nothing less than large-scale social change.

In this sense, on the disability model, the questions rightly broached by harm reduction are not, in the end, questions of medicine or public health. They are ultimately political questions, about how to respect the rights of individuals in a society and how to ensure the equitable distribution of basic goods. In short, they are questions of justice. Addiction is, on the disability model, fundamentally an issue of justice. Accordingly, this discussion of policy will conclude later, in Chapter 7, with a consideration of questions of justice.

Before we turn to the general question of justice, there is one particular kind of policy that deserves special consideration, and which has already come in for discussion in the foregoing. In many jurisdictions, substances or activities that are considered addictive are often prohibited under law, though the scope and the force of these prohibitions vary widely. As the scope and force of these prohibitions varies widely, so too do the forms of opposition to them. The harm reduction movement has generally rejected policies of prohibition, and indeed a harm reduction approach is sometimes simply taken to be synonymous with the rejection of prohibition (Tammi & Hurme, 2007). As I have argued in this chapter, the disability model generally endorses the interventions, though not necessarily the philosophy, of harm reduction. What then does the disability model have to say about prohibition?

The answer to this question turns out to be complex. The disability model prioritizes the rights and interests of people with addictions and gives priority to their concerns in the evaluation of addiction policy. Policies of prohibition, however, affect the interests of addicted people in complicated ways, which depend in part on the scope and force of these policies but also on the nature of addictive motivation itself. The disability model therefore does not issue any clear pronouncements about prohibition in general, though it does offer more specific judgments about particular forms of prohibition and, more importantly, a framework for addressing issues of prohibition, one which puts the interests of addicted people first. This is a perspective that is, I think, generally missing from contemporary debates about prohibition. The next chapter, Chapter 6, is devoted to developing and defending this perspective.

Notes

1 Quoted in Marlatt (1996, pp. 779–780).
2 The project of this chapter, which is to articulate a broadly philosophical ground of the interventions labeled as 'harm reduction,' is a relatively unexplored one, even outside the disability perspective advocated here. Dea (2020) notes the relative paucity of philosophical literature on harm reduction. King (2020) criticizes Utilitarian defenses of harm reduction, as will I, but advocates a defense of harm reduction founded on the virtue of 'compassion,' which is quite different from the kind of defense that, I will argue, is suggested by the disability view.
3 Other examples include the wide distribution of overdose prevention medications such as Naloxone, medications for opioid use disorders such as Suboxone, safe smoking supplies such as pipettes for users of inhaled drugs, and drug

safety measures such as Fentanyl testing kits. Nor does harm reduction need to be restricted to the case of 'illicit' drugs such as opiates. The development and distribution of nicotine replacement therapy (such as nicotine gums and lozenges) is a form of harm reduction for tobacco use disorder.

4 At first approximation, policy is 'addiction-related' just when it concerns the regulation of some substance or activity that is a typical object of addiction in a given society. In this sense drug and alcohol policy will usually be addiction-related, as will gambling policy; so too, at least relative to certain societies, will be policies concerning video games and pornography.

5 While this procedure is compatible with a broad range of outcomes, it still imposes substantive restrictions on what kinds of policies are permissible. As I will shortly argue, this decision procedure in fact has concrete and often anti-majoritarian implications for policy.

6 I am working here with an intuitive notion of rights, one which has at least two key elements. First, as noted in the text, individuals may have positive as well as negative rights. Second, as is central to the argument of this chapter, considerations of rights may sometimes trump considerations of welfare, in the sense that a policy that makes people better off may nonetheless be rejected on the grounds that it violates the rights of some individual or class of individuals. Beyond those requirements, I take my view here to be non-committal on theories of rights of the kind surveyed in Wenar (2023).

7 More precisely, alcohol addiction is recognized as a disability, and drug addiction is recognized as an addiction so long as the person in question does not 'currently' the drug in question (Henderson, 1991).

8 The scope and limits of these protections are not fully determined and are currently being litigated in the courts. See Maier (2023) for one discussion of some recent efforts to enforce the rights of people with addictions against discrimination.

9 For example, anti-smoking campaigns have the result of reducing smoking rates at the cost of increasing stigma against people who smoke or who have diseases associated with smoking (Riley *et al.*, 2017). While such campaigns are not in themselves discriminatory, they succeed by way of promoting negative attitudes against a minority that is already subject to widespread discrimination and stigma. Accordingly, these are the kinds of campaigns that, on the disability model, ought to at least be reconsidered.

10 Data on these particular forms of restrictions, however, is mixed. One meta-analysis suggests that cigarette advertising bans have no significant effect on use (Capella *et al.*, 2008), while experimental evidence on warning labels is modest at best (Shadel *et al.*, 2019). These data should not lead us to give up on reducing the influence of anti-accommodations, although they should encourage us to consider more radical measures, as I will do in the next chapter.

11 So, costs are relevant for the disability approach, but they arise at a different point in the calculus. If an accommodation is extraordinarily costly then it may be, for that reason, not a reasonable one. In fact, the accommodations for addiction that are under consideration here are rarely so costly as to exceed the threshold of reasonableness.

12 I include here as well the case of providing an accommodation 'negatively,' that is by somehow restricting what I have called an anti-accommodation.

13 The distribution of nicotine replacement therapies among disadvantaged populations is a challenging but vital intervention. For one recent attempt to do this in shelters in San Francisco, see Hartman-Filson *et al.* (2022).

14 I am here appealing to John Rawls's notion of a 'primary good' (Rawls, 1971), something that we will have reason to consider in more detail, in the context of addiction, in Chapter 7.

15 This is one of the findings in the aforementioned (Barry *et al.*, 2014).

16 On the use of the ADA to strike down zoning restrictions, see Fletes *et al.* (2022). On the use of the ADA to address housing issues for people with addictions more broadly, see Adams (2022).

Works Cited

Adams, H. (2022). A Public Health Approach to Addiction Starts at Home. *Harvard Law Review*, 391–417.

Apelberg, B.J., Onicescu, G., Avila-Tang, E., & Samet, J.M. (2010). Estimating the Risks and Benefits of Nicotine Replacement Therapy for Smoking Cessation in the United States. *American Journal of Public Health*, *100*(2), 341–348.

Barry, C.L., McGinty, E.E., Pescosolido, B., & Goldman, H.H. (2014). Stigma, Discrimination, Treatment Effectiveness and Policy Support: Comparing Public Views about Drug Addiction with Mental Illness. *Psychiatric Services*, *65*(10), 1269–1272.

Capella, M.L., Taylor, C.R., & Webster, C. (2008). The Effect of Cigarette Advertising Bans on Consumption: A Meta-Analysis. *Journal of Advertising*, *37*(2), 7–18.

Dea, S. (2020). Toward a Philosophy of Harm Reduction. *Health Care Analysis: Journal of Health Philosophy and Policy*, *28*(4), 302–313.

Fletes, A., Reyes, M.K.D., Messinger, J., Blake, V., & Beletsky, L. (2022). Advancing Harm Reduction Services in the United States: The Untapped Role of the Americans with Disabilities Act. *Yale Journal of Health Policy, Law, and Ethics*, 61–89.

Hartman-Filson, M., Chen, J., Lee, P., Phan, M., Apollonio, D.E., Kroon, L., Donald, F., & Vijayaraghavan, M. (2022). A Community-Based Tobacco Cessation Program for Individuals Experiencing Homelessness. *Addictive Behaviors*, *129*, 1072–1082.

Henderson, R.J.J. (1991). Addiction as Disability: The Protection of Alcoholics and Drug Addicts under the Americans with Disabilities Act of 1990. *Vanderbilt Law Review*, *44*, 713–740.

Hurley, S.F., Jolley, D.J., & Kaldor, J.M. (1997). Effectiveness of Needle-Exchange Programmes for Prevention of HIV Infection. *The Lancet*, *349*, 1797–1800.

King, N.B. (2020). Harm Reduction: A Misnomer. *Health Care Analysis: Journal of Health Philosophy and Policy*, *28*(4), 324–334.

Maier, J.T. (2023). How Treating Addiction as a Disability Could Transform Treatment. *Slate*. February 1, 2023.

Marlatt, G.A. (1996). Harm Reduction: Come as You Are. *Addictive Behaviors*, *21*(6), 779–788.

Mathers, B.M., Degenhardt, L., Phillips, B., Wiessing, L., Hickman, M., Strathdee, S.A., Wodak, A., Panda, S., Tyndall, M., Toufik, A., & Mattick, R.P. (2008). Global Epidemiology of Injecting Drug Use and HIV among People Who Inject Drugs: A Systematic Review. *The Lancet*, *372*, 1733–1745.

Rawls, J. (1971). *A Theory of Justice*. Belknap Press.

Riley, K.E., Ulrich, M.R., Hamann, H.A., & Ostroff, J.S. (2017). Decreasing Smoking but Increasing Stigma? Anti-tobacco Campaigns, Public Health, and Cancer Care. *AMA Journal of Ethics*, *19*(5), 475–485.

Shadel, W.G., Martino, S.C., Setodji, C.M., Dunbar, M., Scharf, D., & Creswell, K.G. (2019). Do Graphic Health Warning Labels on Cigarette Packages Deter Purchases at Point-of-Sale? An Experiment with Adult Smokers. *Health Education Research*, *34*(3), 321–331.

Tammi, T., & Hurme, T. (2007). How the Harm Reduction Movement Contrasts Itself against Punitive Prohibition. *The International Journal on Drug Policy*, *18*(2), 84–87.

Wenar, L. (2023). Rights. In E.N. Zalta & U. Nodelman (Eds.), *The Stanford Encyclopedia of Philosophy*. Metaphysics Research Lab, Stanford University.

Wilson, D.P., Donald, B., Shattock, A.J., Wilson, D., & Fraser-Hurt, N. (2015). The Cost-Effectiveness of Harm Reduction. *International Journal of Drug Policy*, *26*, 5–11.

6

THE PROBLEM OF PROHIBITION

6.1 Policy and Prohibition

In the previous chapter, we approached questions of addiction policy from the point of view of the disability model. We took seriously the idea that the primary aim of addiction policy is to protect the rights and interests of addicted people. Since people with addictions are people with disabilities, this means that people with addictions should be protected from discrimination and entitled to reasonable accommodations, as are disabled people generally. We found that, from this perspective, many of the interventions pursued under the name of harm reduction are supported by the disability model. Indeed, the disability model gives these a more inviolable, rights-based, justification, and suggests ways of extending these interventions beyond what has been accomplished by advocates of harm reduction.

In this discussion, we have considered how the circumstances of addicted people might be changed. But we have taken as fixed a basic fact about the circumstances of addicted people: this is that addicted people inhabit a world in which the substances to which they are addicted are, to some degree, available. The availability of addictive substances, of course, varies widely.[1] Some substances are legally available at a relatively affordable cost, such as alcohol and tobacco in many contemporary societies.[2] Some substances are available only on illegal markets and are subject to severe legal penalties, including prolonged imprisonment. And many substances fall somewhere between these two poles.

We have been treating these facts as fixed but, of course, they can be changed. Availability of substances under the law varies widely from place

DOI: 10.4324/9781003410263-7

to place and has varied widely over time. Confronting our contemporary society and laws, we can ask: what is the correct level of availability for any given addictive substance, and how is that level to be enforced? Many individuals or organizations have advocated answers to that question.[3] The aim of this chapter will be to evaluate those answers and then to articulate a general framework for thinking about how to answer this question, one which is grounded in the disability model, and which has not previously been central to the discussion of those questions.

The discussion will revolve around the question of prohibition, by which I mean laws against the manufacture, sale, or use of a given substance. In the United States, this term is associated especially with the prohibition of alcohol in the early 20th century, a policy that is widely considered to have been a failure.[4] Indeed, the term 'prohibition' itself is an epithet in certain contexts, where it represents a regressive approach to be contrasted with the more progressive approach represented by 'harm reduction' (Tammi & Hurme, 2007). As I argued in the previous chapter, the disability model yields a qualified endorsement of the program of harm reduction, if not of its underlying philosophy. What then does it have to say about the program of prohibition?

The deliverances of the disability model on this question are, in fact, equivocal. The question of whether a given substance is to be prohibited will depend heavily on questions about how society is already organized with respect to the use of that substance. Often there will be a disconnect between what ideally ought to be the case and what ought to be the case relative to certain contingent but intransigent facts about social organization and social attitudes. But in many cases, I will argue, there is an argument that prohibition is the policy that best respects the interests of people with addictions.

This may seem surprising. As noted earlier, the rhetoric of prohibition is often associated with policies that oppose the interests of addicted people. Furthermore, there is a familiar dialectic, which we will explore further later, between rights-based approaches that take a liberal view of substance use, and welfare-based approaches that take a more restrictive view. Since the disability model is emphatically one that foregrounds the rights of people with addictions, there can be an impression that it should therefore take a liberal and non-restrictive view on substance use.

But this impression is mistaken. There is a rights-based argument for prohibition. This argument does not always apply, the interests of addicted people may tell in favor of restriction on certain classes of substances. Such restrictions will often be at odds with the interests of people who use, but are not addicted, to the substances in question. But, again, the disability model is distinguished by the priority that it puts on the interests of addicted people. And in some cases, prohibition is the policy that best serves those interests.

6.2 Varieties of Restriction

The discussion thus far has focused on the stark question of whether substances should be prohibited, or whether they should not be. But there are a variety of restrictions on substances that might be considered, and several gradations that views on this issue might take.

To begin with, there is the question of what substance or activity is in question. As noted earlier, substances like alcohol and tobacco are legal and relatively affordable in most contemporary societies. Other substances are almost universally prohibited. These include, for example, heroin, cocaine, and many psychedelic drugs. Other drugs occupy a more complicated intermediate status: cannabis, for example, is prohibited in some places but not in others.

One task of a theoretical approach to addiction policy is to try to make sense of these various restrictions. Many have argued, for example, that the asymmetrical treatment of alcohol and cannabis in many jurisdictions is not sensible, as, it is argued, that alcohol is the more harmful of these substances while cannabis is the more heavily restricted. An approach to addiction policy cannot be expected to deliver a clear answer to the restriction of any given substance, but it may give guidelines for thinking about these questions of differential restriction. The disability model, I will suggest in what follows, does in fact provide a way of thinking about such questions.

In addition to variety in the substances or activities that are restricted, there is also variety in the nature of the restriction itself. Thus far we have been speaking generally of prohibition, but there are distinctions to be made within prohibition. As prohibition is associated with the imposition of criminal sanctions, there will be varieties of prohibition insofar as there are differences in what kinds of sanctions are imposed, and for what reasons. One distinction that will be important in what follows is between laws that impose penalties on the manufacture or sale of substances, or *production prohibition*, and those that impose penalties on the purchase or use of substances, or *consumption prohibition*.

Prohibition is often contrasted with legalization, but there are important intermediary steps between the two. Especially prominent in recent decades has been the movement toward decriminalization of substances. While prohibition involves the imposition of criminal sanctions, the advocate of decriminalization will advocate the imposition of sanctions that are not criminal, such as civil sanctions or fines. Decriminalization is itself a broad movement. On a narrow understanding, it typically involves removing criminal sanctions against those who use, but do not manufacture or sell, the substance in question. So understood, it is compatible with what we are understanding as production prohibition. Indeed, depending on how decriminalization is understood, in many cases there will be scarcely any substantive difference between production prohibition on the one hand and decriminalization on the other.

There is one more approach to substance regulation that bears mention. This is the imposition of significant financial costs on a given substance trade. This may take the form of the imposition of civil fines, as in certain decriminalization regimes. More commonly, it will take the form of significant taxes on the sale of a given substance, such as tobacco in many countries today (Hiilamo & Glantz, 2022). Such taxes typically have a dual purpose: to raise revenue for the state and to discourage the use of the substance in question. They do so by discouraging the manufacture of the substance in question and, more immediately, by imposing high fixed costs on users of the substance in question. Such taxes are not strictly restrictions on use, but as they loom large in the history and contemporary practice of substance restriction, they will come in for discussion here.

Another task of a theoretical approach to addiction policy is to sort out these kinds of restrictions. Is prohibition ever called for, and, if it is, is production or consumption prohibition the more just kind of prohibition? When, if ever, is decriminalization called for, and what is the material difference between prohibition on the one hand and decriminalization on the other? Is the imposition of taxes on given substances a sensible policy, and what are the legitimate aims of such taxation? These are questions that an account of addiction policy ought to answer.

The disability model provides answers to each of these questions. It articulates a general approach to thinking about restrictions on substances, one that does not mandate any particular kind of restriction though it is, as I have indicated, sympathetic to certain forms of prohibition. This approach is distinguished less by any policy than it is by its priorities: it gives, as I have said, priority to the interests of people with addictions. To see what exactly this means, it will be helpful to distinguish the approach of the disability model from two more common approaches to substance restrictions: these are a liberal view on substance use and, on the other hand, a more restrictive view. I will focus on these views as they apply to cases that remain contentious in many contemporary societies, namely 'illicit' drugs such as cannabis. These views are worth considering on their own terms and to understand why the disability model is different from each of them.

6.3 The Liberal View

The liberal view on substance use takes many forms.[5] In its simplest form, it holds that there should be no laws whatsoever prohibiting the manufacture, sale, or use of drugs such as cannabis, cocaine, and heroin, at least not for adequately informed adults.[6] As we have indicated, this is roughly the position that is taken, in many jurisdictions, on alcohol. The liberal view holds that this asymmetrical treatment of alcohol is puzzling. It proposes to resolve the puzzle by treating other drugs as alcohol is commonly treated. All such drugs should be open for sale on the market, with provisions for the protection of minors and perhaps with moderate consumption taxes and restrictions on advertising, again as is the case for alcohol.

What is the argument for this view? Perhaps the strongest argument for this view is that it is our default view for substances generally. An adult can buy alcohol freely in many jurisdictions. An adult can buy milk, doughnuts, or chewing gum freely in almost every jurisdiction.[7] The liberal view simply represents our view of substances generally, extended to the case of drugs such as cannabis. If the liberal view is false, there must be some special argument why this extension is illegitimate.

We will consider the most common such arguments, in favor of a restrictive view, later. But whatever arguments are given, the advocate of the liberal review has a simple rejoinder to them. The issue is not merely that people in fact can purchase and use milk, doughnuts, and chewing gum. It is that they have a right to do so. Our default view of substances is that people should have the right to engage with them, or not engage with them, however they like. The advocate of restrictions is proposing to restrict that right in certain quite general ways. She therefore not only owes us an argument about why reducing the use of a given substance would be desirable but also why it is appropriate to restrict the right of people to use that substance.

This consideration is especially salient when we consider the people most immediately affected by such restrictions: the people who use the substance whose restriction is being proposed. Substance restrictions are especially onerous, it would seem, for those who use the substances in question. Arguably, these are especially onerous for people who are addicted to the use of those substances. If, for example, one held the view that an addiction compels a person to use the substances to which she is addicted, policies such as consumption prohibition would seem to put the addicted person in an especially unjust double bind: she cannot refrain from using the substance (due to her compulsion), on the one hand, and she faces criminal penalties if she uses the substance (due to the consumption prohibition), on the other.

I have explained, in Chapter 4, my reasons for rejecting the idea that addiction typically involves compulsion. Nonetheless, an important question remains to be answered. On the disability model of addiction, addiction still does involve a special relationship to the substance to which one is addicted, even if it is not a compulsive one. Policies of prohibition therefore have a disproportionate impact on people with addictions. Can such policies be justified, considering that impact? This is a question that we will consider shortly. If we cannot give an adequate answer to this question, that will naturally draw us back to the liberal view of these matters.

6.4 The Restrictive View

The restrictive view, in contrast, holds that there should be laws prohibiting the manufacture, sale, or use of drugs such as cannabis. Something like the restrictive view represents the status quo in many contemporary societies. Some advocates of the restrictive view may even push for a more extensive version of this view. For example, noting the very asymmetrical treatment of alcohol that was emphasized by the liberal view, the advocate of the restrictive view might propose that the asymmetry be resolved in the opposite way and that prohibitions ought to be imposed on alcohol as well.

What is the argument for the restrictive view? The simplest argument is an argument from welfare. The use of the drugs under consideration is associated with bad outcomes, laws prohibiting those drugs reduce the frequency of such use, and therefore laws prohibiting those drugs should be associated with a decrease in bad outcomes. This line of reasoning is underwritten by the principle that raising the cost of an activity reduces the incidence of that activity, conjoined with the observation that the use of drugs such as cannabis does tend to lead to bad outcomes, in society as it is actually structured.[8]

This simple connection between restriction and welfare, however, is subject to a number of important qualifications. The first is one that we have already emphasized. The bad outcomes associated with the use of certain drugs are not inherent facts about those drugs. Rather, they are the product of contingent social circumstances, ones that involve systematic discrimination and exploitation of people who use those circumstances. Even granting that restrictive policies do reduce the incidence of bad outcomes, this is a curious strategy for reducing them. It would make more sense to address the social circumstances themselves.

This concern is exacerbated by a second point, which is that restrictive policies themselves add to the bad outcomes to which people who use substances are subject. This is especially so when restriction takes the form of consumption prohibition. And it is especially so when these prohibitions intersect with the machinations of the carceral state, as they often have in the United States and elsewhere. When this is so, restrictive policies will themselves be the source of bad outcomes, often implemented in racist and otherwise discriminatory ways. Even if these bad outcomes are in some sense outweighed by the bad outcomes prevented by restrictive policies, they still need to be counted as considerations against restriction.

Let us say however that we have made this calculation to our satisfaction. We grant that there are considerable harms done by restrictive policies, to a group that is already subject to widespread discrimination and exploitation. Nonetheless, we argue, this harm is considerably less than the vast harms that, we claim, are prevented by restrictive policies. The benefits are worth the cost. Even then, and even granting the empirical claims about benefits and costs, the advocate of restrictions faces a remaining, more fundamental, objection.

The objection is that, even if the reduction of use has good effects, it is not acceptable for the state to restrict the rights of individuals simply because doing so would have, on balance, good benefits. Any such restriction must have a considerable weight of evidence behind it, such that the benefits of restriction far exceed those of the more liberal default, if such a restriction is to be justified. Opponents of restriction will argue that this is simply not a threshold that restrictive policies can meet.

This objection is a powerful one. Nonetheless, it is one that a principled advocate of restrictions might well be willing to accept. She may respond either that the benefits of restriction (or the harms of non-restriction) are indeed so vast as to justify these restrictions, or she might deny that the threshold set by the liberal is indeed a reasonable one. Perhaps some slight benefit to all is indeed worth some limitations of rights. This is a familiar debate, one that in some sense goes beyond the specific case of addictive substances, and touches on foundational issues in political theory generally.

There is another rights-based objection to restrictive approaches, however, that I think has received insufficient attention. This is that restrictive approaches are objectionable not merely because they infringe on the rights of people generally, but because they infringe on the rights of addicted people in particular. According to this approach, even if one accepts that some curtailment of rights is warranted when it leads to an overall improvement of welfare, there is something especially objectionable about curtailing the rights of the very people most impacted by addiction policy. This is especially so if, as indicated earlier, one holds a view on which addicted people are compelled to use the substances to which they are addicted. Even if one denies this – as the disability view does – one may still object to constraining the rights of a vulnerable class of people on the grounds of some greater benefit.

What is most objectionable about traditional restrictive views is that they do not adequately consider the rights and interests of addicted people. Liberal views take more seriously the rights of addicted people, but only in virtue of taking seriously the rights of people generally. What is wanted to move beyond the traditional dialectic in this area is to articulate a view that puts the rights and interests of addicted people first. The disability model allows us to do that. And, as I indicated earlier, it ultimately guides us toward a new version of a restrictive view, one arrived at via a very different route.

6.5 The Priority of Addiction

Thus far I have indicated that the disability model favors an approach to substance policy that gives priority to the rights and interests of addicted people. What exactly does this mean, and what is the argument in its favor?

Begin with the first question: what does it mean to put the rights and interests of addicted people first? This can sound like an appealing and even anodyne view, something like saying that educational policy should put the interests of children first. But, in fact, it is a view with quite specific and, to some, unwelcome implications, and it is helpful to focus on what these are. When we put the rights and interests of addicted people first, we necessarily consider the rights and interests of other people only second-arily, and we should be clear about this aspect of the view.

We have already given one example of this in the previous chapter. Harm reduction advocates have worked to establish sites where intra-venous drug users have access to unused needles. These sites are often opposed by local municipalities, as they are used only by a relatively small minority of citizens, often citizens without significant political influence, and arguably impose costs on the community as a whole. A vote on such sites might well tell in favor of closing them.[9] One thing that is meant by putting the interests of addicted people first is that this vote is trumped by the interests of addicted people. If these sites are reasonable accommoda-tions for people with addictions – as I have argued in the previous chapter that they are – then they should be maintained even if there is significant and indeed overwhelming public sentiment against them. In this sense, giving priority to the rights and interests of addicted people has real and often anti-majoritarian consequences.

This is a case in which giving priority to addicted people is aligned with the policies generally endorsed by public health approaches as well as broadly progressive approaches to substance use. But, in other cases, a priority approach may conflict with such tendencies. Consider concerns about the effects of prohibitionary substance policies on substance users who are not addicted. Many people who use substances are not, in fact, addicted to those substances. Some have argued that prohibitionary policies on drugs have the effect of subjecting these occasional or 'recreational' users to severe criminal penalties, even though their use is relatively modest. This seems to be unjust. It seems to penalize occasional users for the behavior of people with addictions, whose use is often more than occasional.[10]

This is a line of thought that encourages greater tolerance of substance use, and arguably a further consideration against restrictive policies. But if we want to put addicted people first in our approach to substance policy, it is a line of thought that we should reject. The interests of people who use substances occasionally are of secondary importance in the determination of substance policy. The key question is whether a given policy advances the rights and interests of addicted people. Taking this perspective will often align with a progressive approach to substance policy, as it does in the case of the provision of unused syringes. But, at other times, this perspective will align with harsher attitudes toward substance use. In particular, it involves not prioritizing the interests of people who use substances occasionally, even when those people are subject to genuine injustice.[11] In this sense putting the interests of addicted people first is not at all anodyne, but involves making substantive and at times unpopular choices in substance policy.

These then are some examples of the material effects of putting addicted people first. Let us spell out, more specifically, what exactly is involved in putting addicted people first in policy decisions. As I will understand it, this involves committing ourselves to a certain decision procedure in the evaluation of substance policies. In particular, there are three questions to be asked about any such policy. The first two questions are questions about the rights of addicted people. The third question is a question about the interests or welfare of addicted people.

The first question is the following: does this policy violate or constrain the rights of addicted people with respect to the substances to which they are addicted? If it does, then the policy is subject to an extremely high standard. The policy is acceptable only if it can be expected to make addicted people far better off than they would otherwise be, where the threshold of what counts as 'far better' is to be determined, at least in part, by the perspective of addicted people themselves. That is to say, only when policies that substantially improve the welfare of addicted people, by the lights of addicted people themselves, is the restriction of the rights of addicted people ever acceptable.

The second question is: does this policy secure or advance the rights of addicted people? Whereas the first question seeks to rule out policies, the second question seeks to endorse them. The rights of addicted people require certain interventions, and the second question asks whether such requirements are at issue. It will be most clearly applicable in the case of reasonable accommodations. For example, a policy mandating that sites for the provision of unused needles be established in certain neighborhoods may well elicit an affirmative answer to the second question and, if it does, this approach to policy would mandate that it be enacted. The qualification here is that such policies should be enacted unless they pose unreasonable costs.[12] So, while the first test forbids the violation of addicted people's rights unless doing so makes them far better off than they would otherwise be (by the lights of addicted people themselves), the second question mandates the protection of addicted people's rights unless the cost of doing so is unreasonable (by the lights of society as a whole).

I have emphasized that this approach to substance policy gives priority to the rights and interests of addicted people. Between the two of these, it is rights that are prioritized. The first two questions to be asked, when we approach substance policy in this way, are questions about the rights of addicted people. Responding to these questions goes some way toward yielding a determinate approach to substance policy. It is only when these questions are settled that we turn to the interests of addicted people.

These interests are addressed by the third question: does the policy make addicted people better off than they would otherwise be? If the answer to this question is affirmative and the policy is neutral with respect to the rights of addicted people, then the policy should generally be accepted. If the answer to this question is negative and the policy is neutral with respect to the rights of addicted people, then the policy should generally be rejected. The exceptions will be cases, if there are any, where the impact on the interests of non-addicted people (positive or negative) is so vast, and the impact on the interests of addicted people is so slight, that the former plausibly trump the latter. In most actual cases, this will not happen, and it is the interests of addicted people alone that will decide. This is because, as we have already said, it addicted people whose interests are most closely tied to the outcomes of substance policy.

Asking these three questions will settle most questions that might be asked about substance policy. That, then, is a specific implementation of the idea of giving priority to addicted people. This is far from an anodyne platitude. It is a decision procedure with implications that are determinate and, in some ways, as we will shortly see, unexpected.

6.6 The Defense of Priority

That is what it means, on the present approach, to put addicted people first. What, however, is the argument for this decision procedure? What justification is there for approaching policy in this way?

The justification for this approach lies in the disability model of addiction. Once we recognize that addiction is a disability, we should realize that certain people are differentially affected by substance policy, namely the people who are addicted to the substance in question. This is not simply because they use the substance in question more frequently, or are especially likely to face sanctions for use, though these things may be true. It is because their addiction itself is partly a function of social forces of discrimination and exploitation, forces which substance policy can reasonably be expected to redress. So long as this is the situation that addicted people confront, addicted people should have priority in the evaluation of substance policy.

This approach to priority is not unique to the case of addiction. It makes sense in many cases where a class of individuals is both differentially impacted by a certain kind of policy and where that group is itself subject to systematic discrimination. This will be the case for many disabilities, for racial groups that have been subject to historical discrimination and disadvantage, and for many sexual and gender minorities. Priority for these groups in the determination of policy is often the most just strategy. The priority I am suggesting that we give to the rights and interests in setting substance policy is an application of this general approach to justice.

Some might advocate for a more limited approach to priority. We might accept the disability model, for example, and grant that the rights and interests of people who are addicted to intravenous drug use should be given priority in decisions about sites for the provision of unused needles. But the priority approach demands something more than this. Consider, for example, alcohol policy. Alcohol policy in a given jurisdiction has vast political and economic effects. Many people use alcohol, but only a minority of those people have an alcohol addiction.[13] One might ask whether it makes sense to prioritize the interests of people with alcohol addictions in this way when the interests of so many people are at stake.

But this is precisely what the priority approach demands that we do. Indeed, it is in just such cases that this approach is especially appropriate. When a substance is known mainly in the context of addiction, as many intravenous drugs are, the prioritization of addiction can seem uncontentious. But when a given substance or activity is part of the fabric of everyday life for people, it is natural to overlook the rights and interests of addicted people. So it is particularly in such cases that the prioritization of addicted people's rights and interests needs to be demanded. As the argument for priority rests on the rights of a certain disadvantaged class of people, it is not trumped simply because a substantial majority is immediately affected by policy changes, as is the case for alcohol and a handful of other substances and activities. The case for priority is no less compelling in these cases.

The disability model, then, requires us to prioritize the rights and interests of a certain class of people when it comes to policy decisions. To some extent, we have become accustomed to this kind of prioritization when it comes to, for example, physical disabilities. For example, many of us recognize that automobile parking in public streets and private parking lots ought to be organized in a certain way, by giving preferential access to those who are disabled, even when the majority might prefer some different form of organization. The disability model asks us to extend this kind of prioritization to the case of addiction. Ultimately, the defense of this prioritization is the disability model itself: addiction is a disability, the rights and interests of people with disabilities should be prioritized in certain contexts, and so the rights and interests of people with addictions should be prioritized in certain contexts, in particular, as I have proposed here, in the context of substance policy.

6.7 The Extent of Accommodation

With that general approach to substance policy in place, let us turn to the practical question of what kinds of policies are recommended when we prioritize the rights and interests of addicted people. In the previous chapter, we identified two core policy aims supported by the disability model: preventing discrimination and providing accommodation. When we seek to prioritize the rights and interests of people with disabilities, these aims are plausibly what should come first. The prevention of discrimination is a vital but relatively circumscribed aim. If we want to think more expansively about policies that might prioritize addicted people, it is accommodation that is the most central, and ultimately the most expansive, notion.[14]

Begin with accommodations that are clearly supported by the disability model. The most straightforward of these are those that have already been defended under the aegis of harm reduction, such as sites for the distribution of unused needles for people addicted to intravenous drug use, or the medical provision of nicotine replacement therapy for people with tobacco addictions. As I argued in the last chapter, the disability model allows us to extend these accommodations beyond what falls within the rubric of harm reduction as traditionally understood. For example, a disability model underwrites an argument for housing assistance for people with addictions, both as a reasonable accommodation and in light of the widespread discrimination to which addicted people are subject. The disability model therefore suggests a more expansive conception of accommodations, one which is underwritten not by considerations of beneficence but rather as a proper acknowledgement of the rights of addicted people.

We can, on reflection, expand the notion of accommodation still further. In the previous chapter, I introduced the idea of anti-accommodations. These are items or activities that are specifically designed to exploit the volitional tendencies of people with addictions. Certain recent technological products, such as the profusion of online gambling apps or the availability of cannabis delivery services, provide perhaps the clearest form of anti-accommodations. But more entrenched developments – which were themselves technological innovations – are also plausible examples of anti-accommodations. 'Scratch tickets,' which are now a familiar and state-sponsored presence in many jurisdictions in the United States, are a kind of anti-accommodation for people with gambling addictions. Cigarettes, a fixture of life in the last century, may be thought of as an anti-accommodation for people with tobacco addictions, especially relative to the older forms of tobacco delivery that cigarettes supplanted.

In the previous chapter, I also briefly introduced the idea that accommodations for addicted people might take the form of restrictions on anti-accommodations. For example, a jurisdiction that was serious about protecting the rights and interests of people with gambling addictions might at the very least stop the state sponsorship of scratch tickets; it might, more ambitiously, restrict the availability of technologies such as gambling apps. A jurisdiction might impose restrictions on the sales or advertisement of cigarettes; it might even prohibit altogether kinds of cigarettes that are held to be especially exploitative, as the United States banned flavored cigarettes with the aim of reducing cigarette use by adolescents (Rossheim *et al.*, 2020).

If anti-accommodations indeed make the world more inaccessible for people with addictions, then it makes sense that a program of accommodation might lead to their restriction. But in another way, this is puzzling. After all, many people with gambling addictions might prefer that scratch tickets be readily available, or that they can download and use gambling apps on their phones; indeed, they prefer this very strongly. In the same way, many people with tobacco addictions might prefer unfettered access to cigarettes. But we are now proposing that, in light of the rights and interests of addicted people, we ought to sometimes consider restricting gambling technologies or cigarettes, on the grounds that these are anti-accommodations. But how, one might reasonably ask, can a policy program that purports to be defending the rights and interests of addicted people lead us to policy choices that many addicted people would forcefully reject?

This is a profound question, and much of the remaining discussion will be devoted to answering it. I want to begin to approach it by distinguishing two ways in which it might be answered. The first is in some ways the standard response to this question that has been given, in one guise or another, by most proponents of restrictions on the rights and interests of addicted people. The second is the rather different response that I will defend here.

6.8 Restriction and Interests

Begin with the first response. The first response, at its core, holds that the restrictions on addicted people are justified because they are *in the best interests* of addicted people. A restriction on gambling apps and scratch tickets is in the best interests of people with gambling addictions. Their preference for these items does not trump this fact. Indeed, it is evidence of the very tendency that these restrictions aim to curtail. Similarly, restrictions on flavored cigarettes are in the best interests of people with tobacco addictions, and their opposition to such restrictions is simply confirmation of this fact.

This response, it must be admitted, has considerable power. It is empirically true that bad outcomes related to gambling addictions occur less frequently when gambling technologies are restricted (Sulkunen *et al.*, 2021). It is plausibly also true that the increase in tobacco-related restrictions in many developed countries and the significant decrease in addictive tobacco use (and tobacco-related poor health outcomes) are related, although it can be challenging to demonstrate causal relationships here.[15] The empirical support for the first response is real, and its implications for the well-being of addicted people are significant.

Nonetheless, these considerations are ultimately not sufficient, for the simple reason that it is not, in general, justified to restrict the rights of people for their own well-being. We all recognize exemptions to this general policy, such as driving restrictions and other limits imposed for the sake of public safety. We also recognize that there are certain people who, for one reason or another, may have their rights restricted. Young children, for example, are plausibly one such group. If, however, an adult wants to download a gambling app and use it to wager her savings on football games, or if an adult wants to smoke a menthol cigarette, these are not generally the kinds of things that she may be restricted from doing for her own good, even if she would be better off were she subject to such restrictions. This is just the fundamental objection to restrictive policies that we considered earlier, now deployed as an objection against restricting the rights of addicted people in particular.

There is a distinct restriction strategy that focuses even more narrowly on addicted people. This response, which might in some ways seem more principled, would restrict only the behavior of addicted people. We might, for example, allow people to purchase scratch tickets or menthol cigarettes only if they can demonstrate that they do not have a gambling or a tobacco addiction, respectively. This would be a pure case of restricting the behavior of addicted people for the sake of the interests of addicted people.

There are several objections one might make against such a proposal. There are obvious difficulties with implementation, such as finding some way of determining who counts as addicted. More fundamentally, there is an objection from discrimination: this kind of proposal is facially discriminatory, as it explicitly treats addicted people differently from people who are not addicted. It is not acceptable, as we emphasized in the previous chapter, to discriminate against people with addictions. This discrimination is no more acceptable when it is supposedly in their best interests.

We have been considering proposals that restrict the rights of addicted people for the sake of the benefit of addicted people. Such proposals do, to their credit, prioritize the interests of addicted people, and they plausibly would make a real impact on their well-being. We have found, however, that such proposals restrict the rights of addicted people in objectionable ways. When such restrictions apply to everyone, addicted and non-addicted alike, they nonetheless restrict the rights of addicted people, namely their rights to engage in their preferred behavior, be it gambling, tobacco use, or other such activities. When such restrictions apply only to people with addictions, they restrict the rights of addicted people to engage in those activities, and they also violate the rights of addicted people against discrimination.

Recall the question we posed earlier: how can a policy program that purports to defend the rights and interests of addicted people lead us to policy choices that many addicted people would forcefully reject? We have found that a traditional response to this question, one that prioritizes the interests of addicted people, does not succeed. I indicated, however, that there is also a second way of answering this question. Let us now consider that answer.

6.9 Restriction and Rights

If considerations about the interests of addicted people do not justify restrictions on their behavior, might considerations about their rights instead justify such restrictions? This can seem paradoxical: how could restrictions on the rights of a group be justified by the demand to protect the rights of that same group? But in fact, this is not paradoxical at all and rather emerges naturally from what we have already said about the place of addiction in contemporary societies.

An addicted person, as we have already said, is subject to widespread discrimination and exploitation. The proper role of the state is to intervene in ways that allow the person to have the same access to basic goods as a person who does not have an addiction. We have already seen how accommodations – from nicotine replacement therapy to housing assist-ance – might advance that aim. What bears emphasis here is that these are rights-based, rather than interest-based, interventions. What justifies making nicotine replacement therapy accessible to people with tobacco addictions is not that it is expected to make them better off, though that is likely true. It is rather that, in a world full of cigarettes and other technologies designed to exploit people with tobacco addictions, nicotine replacement therapy helps to secure their access to primary goods such as health and longevity, and they have a right to such access.

As we have seen, this defense makes such measures immune to a certain kind of challenge: even if measures such as nicotine replacement therapy turn out to fare poorly on a cost-benefit analysis, they may still be justified, so long as their costs are reasonable. For such interventions are justified not on the grounds of welfare, but rather in terms of rights. We can now note that this defense protects these measures against a different kind of challenge as well. Let us say that some intervention restricts certain rights. If the intervention were justified on the grounds of the benefit that it yields, then it would be subject to an objection that we have considered at several junctures in this discussion, namely that it is inappropriate to restrict some people's rights to benefit other people or even to benefit those people themselves. If, however, the intervention is justified in terms of rights, then this objection may be answered in a new way. It may be justified to restrict certain people's rights to protect other people's rights. It may even be justified to restrict certain people's rights to protect the rights of those people themselves.

Consider, from that perspective, restrictions on anti-accommodations. One way of making basic goods accessible to people with tobacco addictions is to accommodate their addiction by making nicotine replace-ment therapy easily available to them. Another way of doing so is by restricting anti-accommodations for tobacco addictions. These are tech-nologies and interventions that aim to exploit tobacco addiction, such as cigarettes with flavored tobacco. A restriction on such products is a limitation of the rights of people generally, including people with tobacco addictions. It may be justified, however, because, all things considered, it best protects the rights of people with tobacco addictions.

When is it acceptable to restrict the rights of individuals to protect their rights? I do not propose to develop a general answer to this question.[16] The point here is that there is a plausible route from the idea of accommodations for addiction, through the idea of anti-accommodations, to the imposition of some restrictions on the behavior of people to use certain kinds of addictive substances. These restrictions apply to addicted and non-addicted people alike – this is mandated by considerations of anti-discrimination, as was argued earlier – though their force will be felt especially by people with addictions. So too, however, will be the accommodation and access that such restrictions make possible.

We have developed this argument with respect to quite specific kinds of restrictions, such as restrictions on flavored tobacco. One can see how the line of argument developed here might extend to other restrictions on anti-accommodations, such as restrictions on online gambling apps or scratch tickets. Once, however, we have appreciated the point that restrictions may be justified on the grounds that they protect the rights of addicted people, we can ask how far this kind of justification extends. How should general questions in substance policy – questions concerning prohibition, decriminalization, and taxation – be understood from a perspective that is oriented around the rights of addicted people? The subsequent discussion develops answers to these questions.

6.10 On Prohibition

I have suggested that, if we accept the disability model, we should sometimes be willing to endorse certain forms of prohibition. For example, on the present approach, it is sensible to prohibit some forms of anti-accommodation, such as online gambling apps or flavored tobacco. This raises a couple of questions. First, what kinds of prohibition are supported by a rights-based approach to substance policy? Second, what kinds of substances or activities may be legitimately prohibited?[17]

As to the first question, it is helpful to recall a distinction that we introduced earlier. This is the distinction between production prohibition, which forbids the manufacture or sale of the prohibited substance, and consumption prohibition, which forbids the purchase or use of that substance. As most addictive substances constitute a market, which demands both the supply and demand of that substance, both forms of prohibition will tend to dramatically curtail the exchange of the prohibited substance. But the impacts of their associated punishments will be significantly different. Production prohibition will tend to impact those who produce and market the substances in question, which will tend to be larger enterprises. Consumption prohibition will tend to impact those who actually use the substances, who will tend to be individuals.

If we come to prohibition from a concern with the rights of addicted people, we will favor production prohibition. Prohibition that focuses on those who use the substances in question will often fall on people who are addicted, which is one reason why those who have advocated for the interests of people with addictions – such as advocates of harm reduction – have been so strongly opposed to prohibition. This same consideration applies when we turn to a focus on the rights of people with addictions. It applies, however, primarily to consumption prohibition, which will tend to involve severe violations of the rights of people with addictions, through incarceration and similar penalties. Production prohibition does involve some indirect restriction on the rights of addicted people – by effectively limiting their access to substances that they may prefer to use – but its impact is significantly less.[18] And, as I have argued, appropriately targeted forms of prohibition will tend to significantly enhance the rights of addicted people, by increasing their access to basic goods of life. So, a rights-based approach to substance policy, when it favors prohibition, will generally favor production prohibition.

I did not explicitly note this point in our earlier discussion of anti-accommodations, but we can reconsider that discussion with this distinction in mind. If we want to prohibit, for example, flavored tobacco, there are a couple of ways in which we might do so. We might subject those who use or purchase flavored tobacco to fines or even criminal sanctions. Alternatively, we might impose fines or criminal sanctions on corporations that manufacture or sell flavored tobacco. It is the latter policy, which is a form of production prohibition that a rights-based approach favors, for this is an approach that enhances the rights of people with tobacco addictions while restricting those rights as minimally as is feasible.

Now consider the second question. What kind of substances may in principle be prohibited by a rights-based approach? In principle, the answer is that any kind of substance may be prohibited. Some arguments turn essentially on qualities of the prohibited substances. For example, certain arguments for prohibiting substances such as heroin while not prohibiting substances such as alcohol turn on claims about the harms done, respectively, by these substances. Whatever the merits of such an argument, the rights-based argument for prohibition is not of this kind. As it is concerned exclusively with what best supports the rights of addicted people, it is not in principle limited to any given substance.

One might be concerned that prohibiting entire classes of substances might be objectionable from the point of view of rights. We have considered prohibited flavored tobacco, or online gambling apps. But such restrictions leave open other modes of consumption for those who are addicted to tobacco, or gambling. But what of a prohibition of tobacco altogether, or gambling altogether? These blanket kinds of prohibitions – which are the kinds that have traditionally figured as the most contentious forms of prohibition – seem to constitute sweeping restrictions on the rights of addicted people. Can they be justified?

They can. A ban on flavored tobacco and other forms of exploitation gives a person with a tobacco addiction better access to the primary goods of life. Even more so, arguably, does a ban on tobacco products altogether. The point is not the familiar one that people with tobacco addictions would be better off in a world without tobacco, though that is plausibly true. It is instead that accommodation of people with tobacco addictions demands that tobacco be prohibited for everyone, whether or not they have an addiction.

This argument does not always hold. It must be shown that allowing the sale and production of tobacco will actually lead to discrimination and exploitation of people with tobacco addictions, that the prohibition of tobacco is an effective means of preventing this discrimination and exploitation, and that doing this is more significant, from the point of view of rights, than the restrictions that are being imposed. In practice, this will tend to demand that this prohibition take certain forms. Production prohibition, as we have already said, will be far more defensible than any form of consumption prohibition. And prohibition will be far more defensible if it is supplanted with sensible forms of accommodation, such as access to nicotine replacement therapy. But, if conditions like these can be met, then there is a rights-based argument for the prohibition of tobacco generally.

This conclusion may be welcome, as many jurisdictions are already moving closer to a total prohibition on tobacco (McCall, 2022). But a rights-based approach is not restricted to the case of tobacco. It applies also to substances and activities that are, unlike tobacco, conventionally held to be acceptable. Gambling, which was discussed earlier, is one such example. Many people gamble occasionally for entertainment, so the prospect of a prohibition on gambling for the sake of those people who have a gambling addiction will tend to be unpopular. But it should now be clear why, whatever its popularity may be, a rights-based approach may nonetheless support just such a prohibition.

The implications of such an approach can be still more unpopular, from the point of view of contemporary sentiment. Consider alcohol. Alcohol is widely used in many contemporary societies, and, among those who use alcohol, those who have alcohol addictions are significantly outnumbered by those who do not.[19] Accordingly, the question of whether to prohibit alcohol scarcely arises, and if anything in many municipalities the tendency has been to increase the availability and ease of access to alcohol.[20] The sweeping form of production prohibition on alcohol that was implemented in the 20th-century United States is widely seen as a historical calamity.[21]

Yet a rights-based approach to substance policy encourages us to reconsider a production prohibition of alcohol. When it comes to the restriction of alcohol, the interests of most people who consume alcohol are, on the present approach, to be given relatively little weight. Rather, the rights of people with alcohol addiction are to be prioritized in arriving at a sensible alcohol policy. For the very reasons already given, this approach may well support a production prohibition on alcohol. This is one policy that most participants in contemporary substance debates hold to have been a mistake. But a rights-based approach yields a new foundation for this supposedly outmoded approach to alcohol.[22]

6.11 On Moderate Restrictions

As noted earlier, there are a variety of options in substance policy that fall somewhere between prohibition and legalization. I have argued that a rights-based approach will sometimes, though not always, support the prohibition of substances. What should a rights-based approach say about these more moderate forms of restriction, which are more restrictive in some way than legalization, but which fall short of prohibition?

Consider the various policies that might be called 'decriminalization.' There are at least two kinds of policies that might be put under this label. First, there is the policy of eliminating criminal penalties on the possession or use of a substance while at the same time enforcing criminal penalties on the sale and manufacture of that substance. This form of decriminalization converges with what I described, earlier, as production prohibition, and a rights-based approach will tend to look favorably on it for the reasons I have already indicated. Indeed, as I noted earlier, decriminalization in this sense can be understood as production prohibition under another name.

Sometimes, however, decriminalization implies more robust forms of tolerance for substance production. This is arguably the case for many contemporary regimes of decriminalization for, for example, cannabis. A world where individuals are not subject to criminal sanctions for cannabis use but have cannabis readily available in convenient and accessible forms is not a world in which the rights of people with cannabis addictions are necessarily being protected. Their right against unjust imprisonment is indeed protected, and that marks an important advance in justice, but in other ways, people with cannabis addictions remain, under such an arrangement, the subjects of exploitation in a fundamentally discriminatory social order, one which does not properly protect the rights of addicted people.

A rights-based approach therefore turns a somewhat skeptical eye on proposals of 'decriminalization.' When such proposals eliminate criminal penalties but leave systems of discrimination and exploitation in place, their impact on the rights of addicted people is real but also limited. Only when coupled with production probation do these strategies of decriminalization secure truly radical advances in the social situation of people with addictions.

What about still less restrictive measures, such as taxes on the purchase of addictive substances, such as cigarettes or alcohol? Such taxes have the effect of decreasing both production and consumption, and in this sense are clearly in the best interests of people with addictions. At the same time, these taxes, by their very nature, fall disproportionately on people with addictions. In this way, these taxes are, in practice, discriminatory. What is more, these taxes tend to be paid disproportionately by a relatively small group of consumers, who typically have incomes lower than the general population (Conlon *et al.*, 2022). These taxes – sometimes known by the stigmatized name of 'sin taxes' – are therefore regressive as well as discriminatory.

Moderate forms of restriction – including more permissive forms of decriminalization and selective taxation of addictive substances – do not in fact support the rights of people with addictions. These kinds of interventions are often supported by considerations of beneficence, since they do make people with addictions, on balance, better off. Yet, from the point of view of rights, they either leave significant threats to the rights of addicted people unchanged, as in the case of some forms of decriminalization, or they actively infringe on the rights of addicted people, as in the case of discriminatory taxation. Moderate restrictions often strike an unhappy compromise: they neither leave addicted people alone nor do they dismantle the structures of discrimination and exploitation that sustain addiction. When it does favor restrictions, a rights-based approach will tend to favor the more radical approach of production prohibition.

6.12 The Contingency of Prohibition

I have at several points emphasized that the question of whether prohibition (specifically, production prohibition) is justified will depend on specific questions about what is prohibited. It will depend partly on the substance in question: it might make sense to prohibit tobacco, for example, but not to prohibit certain hallucinogens.[23] But it will depend more broadly on the kind of society in which a given substance might be used. Certain forms of social arrangement lend themselves to structures of discrimination and exploitation of preferences, such that, if someone has a volitional tendency toward a certain substance or activity, there are strong incentives to profit off that tendency as much as one can. In such societies – what might be called, for lack of a better word, capitalist societies – the discrimination and exploitation of addiction will be especially pronounced. In such societies, the case for prohibition will tend to be stronger.[24]

There may be other forms of social arrangement where substance use is treated differently. In such societies, it may well be that people can indulge their volitional tendencies without significant risk of discrimination or exploitation. In these societies, if such there be, it may well be that a rights-based approach supports a strong argument against prohibition. In this way, the case for prohibition will depend in significant part on the particular political circumstances in which it might be imposed. This is to be expected, as our concern is with the rights of addicted people, which are in large part a product of social conditions.

In this sense, thinking seriously about substance policy, as it affects people with addictions, naturally draws our attention to larger questions. I have argued that substance policy ought to give priority to the rights of addicted people. But the predicament of addicted people is connected to many political realities beyond just substance policy. Ultimately, it is connected to nothing less than the political structure of society itself. In this respect, the question of addiction and its accommodation is fundamentally a question for the theory of justice. Therefore, the next and last chapter turns to questions of justice.

Notes

1 By an 'addictive substance' I mean only a substance that is typically the object of addiction. I do not presume that some substances are inherently addictive, independent of the environment in which their use occurs. Indeed, that presumption is contrary to the spirit of the broadly social or environmental view of addiction that I have been developing. Note also here that the reference to substances is not intended to exclude behavioral addictions, such as addiction to gambling or sexual behavior, and what I say in this chapter about restrictions on substances applies to the objects of behavioral addictions (such as gambling apps, gaming machines, and possibly even pornography) as well.

2 While tobacco remains relatively inexpensive in many parts of the world, a number of developed countries are moving toward high levels of taxation on tobacco and on cigarettes in particular. The attitude of the disability model toward these sorts of taxation penalties is generally skeptical since these policies tend to simply multiply the disadvantage to which people with addictions are subject. Taxation of this kind is generally inferior to a simpler policy that I will argue we ought to consider more seriously, namely a total prohibition on the manufacture and sale of the substances that are currently taxed.

3 The literature on this topic is, accordingly, substantial. One helpful introduction to these debates and the larger philosophical issues that they raise is Husak & de Marneffe (2005).

4 For a useful corrective to contemporary understandings of this policy, one which locates it within a broader global movement, see Schrad (2021).

5 I am using the term 'liberal' here in something like its classical sense, where it denotes a priority on the protection of individual rights and liberties.

6 Some opponents of such prohibitions nonetheless think there should be prohibitions against the free use of 'prescription' drugs such as blood pressure medications or psychiatric medications, which typically require a prescription from a physician in many countries. For an argument for extending the liberal case to these drugs as well, see Flanigan (2017).

7 These allowances are not universal. Singapore, for example, has long banned the import and sale of chewing gum. Arguably, there are benefits (in terms of cleanliness and perhaps public health) to banning chewing gum. Nonetheless, to many, such a ban feels like an unreasonable incursion into private activities. So, according to many liberals, is a ban on cannabis unreasonable.

8 This argument is fundamentally an empirical one, and the actual evidence for it is unclear. At this point in the argument, I want to grant the empirical premise, and consider problems for this argument that arise even when it is granted. I will return to empirical questions in detail later. A separate concern, pointed out to me by Jessica Flanigan, is that the plausibility of this argument will depend in part on how we understand welfare. If our notion of welfare is one that prioritizes health measures and life expectancy, then this argument may seem plausible. If, however, we focus on considerations such as recreation and life satisfaction, this argument may seem less plausible.

9 On local opposition to such programs and the roots of that opposition, see Tempalski *et al.* (2007)

10 Hart (2021) develops a powerful argument for this line of thought, emphasizing the severe consequences of this approach to drugs on historically disadvantaged communities. The argument of the present approach is that, while Hart's position is scientifically and politically compelling in many ways, it does not take sufficiently seriously the priority of addiction.

11 These injustices, of course, still matter, and drug policy should as much as possible be rid of long-standing inequities, for example in disparate sentencing guidelines for the distribution of similar substances, disparities that are grounded in racist or otherwise objectionable presuppositions. The argument here is simply that, when it comes to drug policy, injustices against people with addictions should take priority.

12 This is the same criterion of 'reasonableness' that figured in the account of accommodations developed in Chapter 5.

13 The 2021 National Survey on Drug Use and Health (SAMSHA, 2021) reports that 78.3% of American adults drank alcohol at some point in their lives, while only 10.6% met criteria for alcohol use disorder in the last year.

14 On another understanding, the demands of anti-discrimination and of accommodation are not so distinct after all. See Brown (2021) for an argument that the failure to provide reasonable accommodations should itself be understood as discrimination.

15 For a comprehensive recent survey of this data and some of the difficulties involved in establishing causality, see DeCicca *et al.* (2022).

16 For a general philosophical defense of the restriction of rights or autonomy, see Conly (2012). The specific implementation at issue here, namely restricting the

rights of individuals in order to protect them from exploitation, may seem to be an objectionable one, even among those who are sympathetic to some restrictions on rights. One possible analogy, suggested by Jessica Flanigan, is found in debates on the ethics of sweatshops. Some argue that people in developing countries should be prohibited from taking employment in sweat-shops on the grounds that such employment would be exploitative, even when they would prefer such employment to their other alternatives (Kates, 2019). I think the argument in the text is in at least one way stronger than the argument against sweatshop contracts, insofar as it appeals to the special significance of disability in justifying such restrictions. Nonetheless, there is a parallel, and in some way a precedent, for these arguments in the previous literature on markets and exploitation.

17 In addition to these broadly political questions, there are empirical issues that any complete defense of prohibition needs to address. Specifically, prohibition is well-known to lead to 'black markets,' which lead to widespread harms that tend to fall especially hard on people who are already disadvantaged (Naylor, 2004). I want to leave open the possibility that, although prohibition is theoretically justified, the effects of 'black markets' are so harmful that we should not in fact enact prohibition. The disability approach only insists on a procedure for deciding this question: in weighing the advantages of prohibition against the harms of black markets, it is the rights and interests of addicted people that should be given priority.

18 Production prohibition may affect people with addictions in another way, namely when they themselves are involved in the production and sale of substances. This risk is a real one, as the lines between minor distributors and habitual users can blur in the case of the illegal drug trade. A well-designed policy of production prohibition will err on the side of a permissive attitude toward these inevitable borderline cases between production and consumption.

19 As noted earlier, the most recent survey of American adolescents and adults (SAMSHA, 2021) indicates that the number of people who have used alcohol significantly outnumbers the number of people who have had an alcohol use disorder.

20 There is, for example, the emergence of services for the online purchase and delivery of alcohol, which remain largely unregulated in many jurisdictions (Colbert et al., 2021).

21 Although see again Schrad (2021) for a revisionary understanding of this policy, one which locates it within an appropriately international perspective.

22 What would a 'new Prohibition' look like? At first approximation, it might involve the prohibition on the manufacture and sale of especially harmful alcohol products, namely spirits, with the penalties for sale and distribution falling squarely on those who are responsible for their manufacture and sale. It might also include a prohibition on novel alcohol drinks such as 'alcopops' and other heavily marketed products (Mart, 2011). Such a policy would not constitute a total ban on alcohol, and it certainly would not mean an end to alcohol use or alcohol addiction, but it would constitute a turning back of the most sophisticated and damaging forms of alcohol production and distribution, under the penalty of criminal sanction.

23 The current situation in most countries is, of course, precisely the reverse of this. There are a number of reasons for this, foremost among them is that these restrictions involve a degree of path-dependence: once an addictive substance such as tobacco is treated as legal, there are strong pressures against its prohibition, while a substance that is novel either because it is newly invented

(such as LSD) or newly introduced to a given culture (such as psilocybin) will tend to be regarded as having a more tenuous claim to legality.

24 The partly contingent and empirical nature of these arguments also implies that what is known as 'comparative policy analysis,' namely the empirical study of policy outcomes, will be crucial to arriving at the best view of policy. For a recent survey of comparative policy analyses for drug and alcohol policy, and the challenges that they face, see Ritter *et al.* (2016).

Works Cited

Brown, J.M. (2021). What Makes Disability Discrimination Wrong? *Law and Philosophy*, *40*(1), 1–31.

Colbert, S., Wilkinson, C., Thornton, L., Feng, X., & Richmond, R. (2021). Online Alcohol Sales and Home Delivery: An International Policy Review and Systematic Literature Review. *Health Policy*, *125*(9), 1222–1237.

Conlon, C., Rao, N., & Wang, Y. (2022). Who Pays Sin Taxes? Understanding the Overlapping Burdens of Corrective Taxes. *The Review of Economics and Statistics*, 1–27. Advance online publication. https://doi.org/10.1162/rest_a_01235

Conly, S. (2012). *Against Autonomy: Justifying Coercive Paternalism*. Cambridge University Press.

DeCicca, P., Kenkel, D.S., & Lovenheim, M.F. (2022). The Economics of Tobacco Regulation: A Comprehensive Review. *Journal of Economic Literature*, *60*(3), 883–970.

Flanigan, J. (2017). *Pharmaceutical Freedom: Why Patients Have a Right to Self-Medicate*. Oxford University Press.

Hart, C. (2021). *Drug Use for Grown-Ups: Chasing Liberty in the Land of Fear*. Penguin.

Hiilamo, H., & Glantz, S. (2022). Global Implementation of Tobacco Demand Reduction Measures Specified in Framework Convention on Tobacco Control. *Nicotine & Tobacco Research*, *24*(4), 503–510.

Husak, D., & de Marneffe, P. (2005). *The Legalization of Drugs (For and Against)*. Cambridge University Press.

Kates, M. (2019). Sweatshops, Exploitation, and the Case for a Fair Wage. *Journal of Political Philosophy*, *27*(1), 26–47.

Mart, S.M. (2011). Alcohol Marketing in the 21st Century: New Methods, Old Problems. *Substance Use & Misuse*, *46*(7), 889–892.

McCall, C. (2022). A Smoke-Free Generation: New Zealand's Tobacco Ban. *The Lancet*, *399*(10339), 1930–1931.

Naylor, R.T. (2004). *Wages of Crime: Black Markets, Illegal Finance, and the Underworld Economy*. Cornell University Press.

Ritter, A., Livingston, M., Chalmers, J., Berends, L., & Reuter, P. (2016). Comparative Policy Analysis for Alcohol and Drugs: Current State of the Field. *International Journal of Drug Policy*, *31*, 39–50.

Rossheim, M.E., Livingston, M.D., Krall, J.R., Barnett, T.E., Thombs, D.L., McDonald, K.K., & Gimm, G.W. (2020). Cigarette Use before and after the 2009 Flavored Cigarette Ban. *Journal of Adolescent Health*, *67*(3), 432–437.

SAMSHA. (2021). *National Survey of Drug Use and Health*. Substance Abuse and Mental Health Services Administration.

Schrad, M.L. (2021). *Smashing the Liquor Machine: A Global History of Prohibition.* Oxford University Press.

Sulkunen, P., Babor, T.F., Cisneros Örnberg, J., Egerer, M., Hellman, M., Livingstone, C., Marionneau, V., Nikkinen, J., Orford, J., Room, R., & Rossow, I. (2021). Setting Limits: Gambling, Science and Public Policy—Summary of Results. *Addiction, 116*(1), 32–40.

Tammi, T., & Hurme, T. (2007). How the Harm Reduction Movement Contrasts Itself against Punitive Prohibition. *The International Journal on Drug Policy, 18*(2), 84–87.

Tempalski, B., Friedman, R., Keem, M., Cooper, H., & Friedman, S.R. (2007). NIMBY Localism and National Inequitable Exclusion Alliances: The Case of Syringe Exchange Programs in the United States. *Geoforum, 38*(6), 1250–1263.

7

ADDICTION AND THE DEMANDS OF JUSTICE

7.1 The Political Conception of Addiction

One way of understanding the story of addiction in modern societies is in terms of its relationship to two institutional forces: medicine and the law. The story of addiction up until the last century is largely, though not entirely, a legal one, where addiction is understood in the first place in terms of transgression and punishment, either of addictive use itself or of the behaviors associated with it. Over the previous century, however, the story of addiction has increasingly been a medical one. This medical narrative of addiction is one that has been rehearsed, and questioned, in the previous chapters.

To some extent, this dialectic between law and medicine is not unique to addiction. It is, to a greater or lesser extent, the story of many marginalized groups. As medicine and law represent the central instruments of power in most modern societies, groups that are understood as threatening or problematic will be managed by law, medicine, or both. In particular, this has been the experience of disabled people in many places and times. And, as I have argued, the treatment of addicted people in modern societies is in many ways a special case of the treatment of disabled people generally.

Law and medicine, however, do not exhaust our options. In the previous chapter, we have begun to see an alternative to the conception of the addicted person as criminal and the conception of the addicted person as patient. We have begun to articulate a third conception of addiction, which is the conception of the addicted person as citizen, with certain rights to be

DOI: 10.4324/9781003410263-8

protected and interests to be advanced. The dialectic between the legal view of addiction and the medical view of addiction finds its synthesis in a political conception of addiction.

The political conception of addiction is not entirely separate from previous conceptions of addiction. As we have already seen, it makes significant use of the law. It is largely not the criminal law that is relevant for this approach to addiction, however, but employment law and other laws codifying protections for disabled people. It also grants an important role to medicine. Many of the accommodations discussed in the previous chapter, such as the provision of unused needles or nicotine replacement therapy, are medical interventions, and a political approach to addiction is altogether compatible with acknowledging their vital importance. The political conception of addiction, then, does not deny the importance of law or medicine in the social response to addiction. It does, however, deny the authority of either the law or medicine in determining the proper shape of that response. That is to be determined, on a political conception, by addicted people themselves.

As I have indicated, this political approach to addiction is already implicit in the approach to questions of substance policy articulated in the previous chapter. Indeed, it is already implicit in the disability view of addiction itself. The idea that disability is fundamentally a political category is a familiar one within the disability rights movement (Siebers, 2008). In this way, the political conception of addiction is a natural corollary of the disability view.

What does it mean to endorse a political conception of addiction? In part, it is simply to foreground certain questions of policy in one's approach to addiction. Sometimes, these policies will align with ones already embraced by other conceptions of addiction, such as some of the harm reduction interventions already advocated by medical approaches to addiction. Sometimes these policies may be more unique to a political conception, such as the rights-based argument for prohibition advanced in the previous chapter. In either case, however, endorsing the political conception is sometimes simply a matter of doing politics: that is, the principled advocacy of particular social policies.

Endorsing a political conception of addiction can also mean something more than this, however. It may mean articulating a sense of how addiction is to be addressed within the basic institutions of a society. So understood, addiction is not simply an issue for politics, but an issue for political philosophy. What bearing does addiction have on our most basic views about the proper organization of society and the state? It is this kind of question that this chapter aims to answer.

7.2 Two Kinds of Justice

One way of making such questions more precise is by framing them in terms of justice. One fundamental question in political philosophy is the question of what kinds of social arrangements are most just. So, if we want to articulate the foundations of a political conception of addiction, we can ask: how should addiction be treated within the theory of justice?

There are at least two kinds of justice that should be distinguished here. There have been extensive discussions of addiction as a problem in what is sometimes called 'retributive justice.' These are questions, in the first place, about punishment. To what degree should someone with an alcohol addiction be punished if she injures someone through driving while intoxicated? Is her addiction a mitigating factor? Or does it perhaps call for even more severe punishment?

These questions are not unimportant but, as we have already said, their prominence within discussions of addiction is misplaced. Earlier I argued that the centrality of questions of moral responsibility and blame in discussions of addiction is puzzling. A focus on questions of retributive justice simply transposes these questions from the moral to the political domain. The idea that such questions should be central to a discussion of a politics of addiction rests on a view of addictive behavior as inherently problematic or objectionable, one that I have argued at length that we ought to reject.

One response to this point is to simply take addiction outside the realm of justice altogether. This is the response made by medical view of addiction. There is, however, an alternative. Questions of justice need not be exhausted by questions of retributive justice. We might instead see questions about addiction as primarily concerned with a different species of justice. In particular, I want to suggest, the most central questions in the politics of addiction are questions of distributive justice.

What does it mean to say that these questions are questions of distributive justice? It means, first, that these are not primarily questions of retributive justice. The political questions bearing on the punishment of addicted people are real but comparatively limited in their scope. What affects all people who are addicted, as well as many people who are not addicted, is the question of how addiction bears on the just distribution of goods in a given society.

To some extent, the idea that addiction policy must address itself to questions of distributive justice is not a novel one. Consider, for example, health care. Any society faces the choice of what level of health care it wishes to provide to its citizens, and at what cost. Insofar as people with addictions are especially in need of medical services – something that is plausible even when we reject an overly medical view of addiction itself – they tend to be disproportionately affected by such policies. In this way, any serious reckoning with fundamental questions of distribution in a given society, such as the distribution of health care, will need to reckon with the prevalence and nature of addiction in that society. To be seriously engaged with questions of distribution, then, is already to be engaged with the issue of addiction.

Addiction is connected to questions of distribution in other ways as well. One of the fundamental questions in distributive justice is what the basic liberties of individuals are, and to what degree those liberties may be constrained in response to some greater good. This is a question that, as noted in the previous chapter, is unavoidable in questions of substance policy. In this sense, both questions of the distribution of goods (such as health care) and of the restriction of liberties (such as liberties to purchase and consume addictive substances) inevitably present themselves in thinking about the proper social response to addiction.

But I want to suggest that addiction is a problem of distributive justice in a still more fundamental way as well. In the previous chapter, I began to articulate a view of substance policy on which addicted people are granted a certain kind of priority. On a properly political view of addiction, this priority does not simply bear on the determination of substance policy. Rather, addicted people as a class require a special kind of acknowledgment. In determining the basic distribution of goods in a society, we cannot abstract away from the fact that some people are addicted, and some are not.[1] This is the sense in which addiction is an issue for distributive justice in its very foundations. The next few sections spell out this perspective on distributive justice and the implications of taking this perspective.[2]

7.3 Disability and Distributive Justice

Why does addiction have this special place in the theory of distributive justice? In the first place because it is a disability. There are particular features of addiction that pose special issues for the theory of justice, but it will be helpful to begin by considering the issues that disability generally requires us to address.

What is the problem posed by disability for theories of distributive justice? One way of approaching this problem is by thinking about what gets distributed when we are concerned with questions of distributive justice. A just society is one in which goods are justly distributed. But what, exactly, are the goods in question? Music is a good for many people, but some people are indifferent to it. Animal meat is a good for many people, but some people are actively opposed to it. Deciding what we are to distribute would seem to depend on responding to individual differences in value in a way that seems nearly impossible to aptly capture in all its variation.

John Rawls, the leading philosopher of distributive justice in the last century, resolves this problem in an elegant way. The goods to be distributed, says Rawls, are primary goods, which are goods that anyone is presumed to want, whatever her plans in life. These include, notably, liberties and opportunities, as well as income and wealth (Rawls, 1971, pp. 54–55). The just distribution of goods, for Rawls, will in the first place a just distribution of these primary goods.

Taking primary goods to be the objects of justice, we can then ask: what distribution of these primary goods is just? Different theories of justice will yield different answers to this question. Some philosophers hold that only an egalitarian distribution is justice: everyone should receive the same amount of primary goods. Other philosophers modify their egalitarianism in certain ways. One such philosopher is Rawls himself, who proposes that inequality in the distribution of primary goods is justified only if it is to the benefit of those who are least well off.[3]

Whichever of these theories one endorses, there is a simple objection to these theories initially presented with great force by the philosopher and economist Amartya Sen (Sen, 1980). As Sen points out, the problem is brought out especially forcefully by the problem of disability. Imagine two people, one of whom has a disability and one of whom does not. An egalitarian distribution of primary goods will give the disabled person and the non-disabled person the same amount of primary goods. A Rawlsian approach might allow some inequality in distribution, but only insofar as it benefits those who receive the least.

Sen objects that both approaches are mistaken: the disabled person has a demand to a greater share of resources, but her demand is not captured by the broadly structural or economic inequalities that are allowed for by Rawls. It is grounded, rather, in a constitutional difference between the disabled and non-disabled person, one which any theory of justice which is supposed to apply to beings like us needs to acknowledge.

What lesson should we draw from this point? Sen proposes that we should reject the idea that the object of distributive justice should be thought of in terms of primary goods. I will consider this proposal in detail shortly. Before coming to that, however, it bears thinking more carefully about the role of disability within the theory of distributive justice, for Rawls himself has a response to these kinds of concerns, although not necessarily one that makes his treatment of disability any more appealing.

Rawls endorses a broadly contractual understanding of distributive justice, on which the principles of justice are those that would be chosen by parties contracting to the principles that will govern a given society, where they are unaware of the particular position that they will occupy in that society. In the 'original position' people choose behind a 'veil of ignorance,' where they are unaware of their gender, their race, and their particular preferences and affinities (Rawls, 1971, pp. 118–122).

They do know, however, that they are not disabled, or at least that they do not have certain long-term forms of disability. Such disabilities, Rawls suggests, might prevent someone from being a fully cooperative participant in a given society.[4] But the original position is open only to those who can participate in this way. The needs of those who cannot – including children and non-human animals, in addition to the permanently disabled – are to be deferred to a later, 'legislative,' stage, where the welfare of those who cannot contribute may be addressed (Rawls, 1971, pp. 174–175). If this is right, then Sen's objection does not quite get a grip against Rawls, at least not in a straightforward way. The concerns of the disabled do not tell against a given theory of justice, for the disabled, or at least certain disabled people, are not parties to the principles of justice in the first place.

It should be clear that this is a view of disability sharply at odds with the one that has been advanced here. However precisely we should think about the theory of justice, the disabled should be participants from the very beginning. In particular, people with addictions – even addictions that are life-long and limiting – should be full parties to the determination of justice. Therefore, to answer Sen's objection, it will not do to simply exclude the disabled (including addicted people) from foundational deliberations. Instead, we want a conception of distributive justice that is responsive to Sen's concerns, and to the needs of the disabled more generally.

7.4 The Capability Approach

The most prominent attempt to do this is proposed by Sen himself, and subsequently developed by the philosopher Martha Nussbaum (Nussbaum, 2013) among others. Sen's objection arose when we thought of the basic objects of distributive justice as primary goods such as liberty and wealth. The capability approach suggests that we should think of the basic objects of distributive justice differently. We should think of them, specifically, as capabilities.

What is a capability? At first approximation, a capability is a real opportunity or power to do something. Consider the freedom of movement between two countries. Certain legislation may establish legal freedom of movement between those two countries. But this freedom is in a certain sense formal. If someone has the legal freedom to move between two countries, but cannot afford transportation from one to the other, then in a certain sense she does not really have the freedom to move between countries. She lacks, we may say, the capability to move from one to the other. The capability approach takes this kind of real freedom to be the basic object of distributive justice (Robeyns & Byskov, 2023).

If we conceive of the object of distributive justice in this way, then we have a response to Sen's initial concern. If we think in terms of primary goods, the distribution of equal degrees of primary goods to a disabled and a non-disabled person might nonetheless leave the disabled person worse off. We can now understand this distributive situation differently. What is appropriate in this situation is an even distribution of capabilities to the two individuals. And this might well mean a greater distribution of primary goods – that is, goods such as income and wealth – to the disabled person. This is not because the disabled person deserves a greater share of goods, but because an equitable distribution of the real goods of distributive justice – namely, capabilities – may require an uneven distribution of the kinds of primary goods that Rawls takes to be central.

In addition to responding to the particular puzzle raised by Sen, the capability approach aspires to address the broader limitations of Rawls's approach to distributive justice. As noted earlier, Rawls suggests that those who have certain kinds of prolonged disability are to be excluded from fundamental deliberations about justice in the first place. The capability approach allows us to articulate a broader conception of what these deliberations might look like (Stark, 2007). Once we understand the objects of distribution to be capabilities, we can imagine people who are ignorant of their initial situation, including those with a spectrum of possible disabilities, collaborating to decide on an environment and social institutions that ensure real equity of capability for everyone.

There is extensive debate about the proper form of the capability approach, and whether it is the best way of understanding disability within the theory of distributive justice.[5] I want to grant, for the moment, that the capability approach does indeed give an adequate account of how to think about justice and the objects of distribution, for a wide range of disabilities. But I want to step back and consider a different question. Does the capability approach – or indeed any extant approach to distributive justice – give an adequate account of how to think about the relationship between distributive justice and the specific disability of addiction?

7.5 Addiction and Distributive Justice

The topic of addiction is scarcely addressed within the extensive literature on distributive justice. The term does not appear in Rawls's *A Theory of*

Justice. In one way, this is understandable. If we conceive of addiction as a disease, or endorse some other defect model, there is no particular reason why it should be addressed within the theory of justice. I have argued, however, that these conceptions are mistaken, and that we should understand addiction as a disability, and thus that addiction needs to be addressed within an account of distributive justice, just as disabilities generally must be.

Addiction, I will argue, poses special problems for an account of distributive justice. To think about these problems, it is helpful to consider a variation on the case introduced earlier by Sen. Consider two people. One of them has an addiction, while one of them does not. On the present account, people may have addictions without necessarily actively using the substance in question, but it will be helpful to consider the case where the addicted person is actively using the substance or activity to which she is addicted. All else being equal, what would a fair distribution of goods to these two individuals look like?

A preliminary response is to deny that all else is equal. Some will point out that an addicted person is in some sense the source of her own predicament. If she needs more resources than someone who is not addicted, that is due to her own actions. And, we might suggest, the purpose of distributive justice is to ensure fairness by counteracting natural disadvantages, such as differences in intelligence or height.[6] If people act in ways that generate disadvantage, then it is not the purpose of distributive justice to redress these.

This objection, however, is mistaken in a couple of ways. First, it is not in general true that distributive justice does not address differences due to an individual's own actions. If a person is disabled due to her reckless driving, she is not thereby outside the scope of distributive justice. Questions of distribution do not, in general, hang on the etiology of the inequalities that they are intended to address. Second, it is not in general true that the disadvantages that addicted people encounter are due to their own actions, at least not exclusively so. Rather, as I have emphasized throughout the foregoing discussion, the inequalities that addicted people encounter are due to social forces of discrimination and exploitation. And these are precisely the kind of forces that a fair distribution can be expected to correct.

We can then ask what a fair distribution between an addicted person and a non-addicted person might look like. We might begin by focusing, like Rawls, on the distribution of primary goods. A fair distribution might be one in which an addicted person has as much by way of primary goods such as wealth and income as a non-addicted person. But this approach is subject to two objections. The first is simply a variation on Sen's objection.

Due to the disadvantages to which addicted people are subject, an addicted person might require a greater share of primary goods than a non-addicted person. In this sense, an even distribution of primary goods might be unfair to people with addictions.

There is a second objection, however, that is distinctive to addiction. An increase in the primary goods available to a person with an addiction, particularly one who is actively using the substance or activity to which she is addicted, might paradoxically make that person worse off than she would otherwise be. If someone has a tendency toward using a substance or activity of a certain kind, and it is costly to use that substance, then basic economic principles imply that an increase in her wealth or income will tend to increase her consumption. The relationships here are far from straightforward, and many hold that prolonged economic hardship is itself a source of addictive behavior (Glei & Weinstein, 2019). Nonetheless, an account of distributive justice raises an issue that is simply not present in the case of other disabilities, namely that an increased provision of primary goods may make the addicted person worse off than she would otherwise be.

Even more so in the case of disability generally, then, there is a case against conceiving of primary goods as the objects of justice. Once we take seriously the idea that addiction is a disability, we are faced with further reasons for reconceiving the objects of distributive justice.

7.6 Addiction and the Capability Approach

The problems just raised arise from taking addiction to be a disability and taking primary goods to be the primary objects of distributive justice. Let us consider how things look when we revise the second of these claims and conceive of the objects of distributive justice differently. Specifically, how should we think about distribution and addiction when the objects of distributive justice are conceived of as capabilities?

If our goal is for people with addictions to have equality of capabilities, then we may need to give a greater share of certain goods to people with addictions. For example, since addiction can have significant health consequences, ensuring equal capabilities for people with addictions might require a greater degree of medical funding and other health resources. This responds to the first concern raised earlier, namely that an equal distribution of primary goods might not provide addicted people with sufficient resources. This concern, like Sen's original objection, may be addressed by a turn to capabilities as the objects of justice.

In another way, however, equality of capabilities may not address all the objections that are raised by the problem of addiction. The guiding idea of the capability approach is that we want to equalize people's real starting points but then allow for differences based on the choices that they make. But when we are concerned with a disability connected to the faculty of choice itself, this distinction is not always a straightforward one to make. Two people may have equal capabilities, at least in the sense traditionally adopted within the capability approach, and yet one may be in a worse predicament than the other if one has an addiction and one does not.

Consider, for example, the predicament of two people with equal capabilities, one of whom has a gambling addiction, in a world where there are extensive 'anti-accommodations' such as scratch tickets and online gambling apps. We can imagine that each of these has equal real access to a satisfactory quality of life. It is foreseeable, however, that the person with a gambling addiction is much less likely to achieve this satisfactory quality of life. The prevalence of anti-accommodations makes it a likely possibility that the person with the gambling addiction will end up in a suboptimal situation. In this sense, the person with a gambling addiction is not really in a position equal to the person without a gambling addiction, despite their equality of capability. So, in cases of addiction, equality of capability is not equality after all.

There are at least three responses that one might make to this objection. The first two attempt to preserve the capability approach in the face of this objection, while the third of these asks us to envisage a new kind of approach.

The first response is the simplest. It holds that, so long as we have equality of capability, the person with a gambling addiction and the person who does not have a gambling addiction are equally well off. The capability approach was never intended to guarantee equality of outcomes. If a person with a gambling addiction ends up worse off, that is due to her gambling addiction, not to social conditions, at least not to the kinds of social conditions that the capability approach is intended to address. These kinds of human proclivities simply fall outside the scope of distributive justice.

This response is a variation on one we have already considered: that individuals with addictions are in some sense responsible for the bad outcomes they encounter, and that these are not the kinds of bad outcomes that the theory of justice is intended to redress. This response is not unreasonable relative to many theories of addiction. But I have now argued, at length, against those theories of addiction, and against the perspective that they purportedly support. Addiction is not something that can be understood wholly apolitically, but is partly defined by its relationships to systems of discrimination and exploitation. Addiction is a disability, and if an account of distributive justice can be expected to address disabilities such as blindness and deafness – as advocates of the capability approach accept that it can – then it must address addiction as well. The first response simply rejects the task that, I have argued, addiction presents for a theory of distributive justice.

The second response is more responsive to the question of addiction. We should not accept the claim that the person with a gambling addiction and the person without one have the same capabilities after all. We might say that environmental circumstances, such as anti-accommodations, are capability-undermining. Establishing true equality of capability may require an asymmetrical treatment of people with addictions and people who do not have addictions after all. We simply need to avail ourselves of a more expansive notion of capability, one that recognizes that environmental circumstances may indeed threaten capabilities for some people but not for others.

To address this response, we need to consider in more detail the question of what, exactly, a capability is supposed to be. We have said that capabilities involve the real freedom to perform certain acts, without thereby guaranteeing or even rendering probable any particular outcome. Someone may have the capability to find stable housing or to become a doctor, without necessarily availing herself of either capability. This essentially modal aspect of capabilities is what allows them to preserve Rawls's idea that what distributive justice does is to put individuals in place to execute their plans of life, without taking a view on the advisability of any given plan that an individual might have.

With that understanding of capability in place, we can ask: what capabilities, precisely, are lacking in a person with a gambling addiction situated in an environment with anti-accommodations such as scratch tickets? These might be, for example the capabilities for pursuing various goods such as work and relationships. Yet it is unclear how precisely the existence of anti-accommodations undermines those capabilities. One way of putting this unclarity is as follows. In a world where those anti-accommodations are absent, the person in question would have these capabilities. How does the addition of these elements to her environment deprive her of capabilities that she would otherwise have?

I do not want to suggest that this question is unanswerable. After all, a theme of the foregoing discussion has been that addiction is to a great degree an environmental phenomenon and that various facts about an addicted person will depend in part on facts about the environment in which she is situated. The point here is rather one about the capability approach itself. On the capability approach, as standardly developed, capabilities are not the sort of thing that can be diminished by addition. That is, the enrichment of a person's environment will increase or leave unchanged her capabilities, and will not diminish them, at least as long as it does not literally prevent her from carrying out certain acts.[7] Yet one of the distinctive aspects of addiction is that enrichment of the environment may leave a person, in a certain respect, worse off. This is a fact that standard developments of the capability approach have difficulty capturing.

In a way, this objection to the capability approach is simply a version of our earlier objection to Rawls's approach to distributive justice. The objection there was that addiction had a somewhat paradoxical character with respect to the traditional objects of distributive justice. If someone has an addiction, then an increase in her primary goods – in particular, her wealth – might make her, in a certain respect, worse off. The present point suggests that, even when shift our account of the primary objects of distributive justice, a similar issue arises. The addition to someone's environment of certain features, in particular those that we have characterized as anti-accommodations, may make that person worse off, even though it involves no diminishment of her capabilities. Again, we are seeing that, with respect to addiction, an expansion in apparent resources is not always for the best.

This brings us to the third response, which is to acknowledge that, in light of considerations about addiction, there is more to equality than equality of capabilities.[8] This is in effect to make the same response to the capability approach, in light of addiction, that the advocate of the capability approach urges us to make to the traditional Rawlsian approach, in light of disability. It is not to deny the significance of capability, or for that matter of primary goods, to the distributive situation of people with addictions. But it recognizes that, in light of the special issues posed by the disability that is addiction, we need to expand our understanding of the objects of distributive justice.

7.7 Addiction and Recovery Capital

What might this expansion look like? What are the goods that outrun primary goods and capabilities, and which adequate provision for addiction demands? I do not want to attempt a definitive enumeration of these goods, any more than we should attempt to give a definitive enumeration of primary goods or capabilities. Instead, I want to introduce a framework for thinking about these goods, one which can at least organize our thinking about what a proper distributive response to addiction might look like.

The framework that is particularly useful is the idea of recovery capital. Initially introduced by the social worker William Cloud and the sociologist Robert Granfield, the notion of recovery capital is supposed to capture a familiar and fundamental idea: that people recover from addictions in virtue of access to personal and social resources. These resources may be as formal as medical insurance or as diffuse as networks of social connections. The idea of recovery capital has the advantage of uniting this array of resources under a single heading. Recovery capital, write Cloud and Granfield, 'is the sum total of one's resources that can be brought to bear on the initiation and maintenance of substance misuse cessation.' (Cloud & Granfield, 2008, p. 1972).

The notion of recovery capital is meant to make rigorous certain ideas that are common in clinical discussions of addiction, such as the notion of 'protective factors.' It is often claimed, for example, that a strong spiritual life is a 'protective factor' for people in treatment for addictions. This leaves unclear precisely who is being protected, and from what, and in what manner. The notion of recovery capital is meant to reorient this framing of addiction treatment away from ideas of 'protection' and toward a more autonomous understanding of recovery, on which individuals have certain resources of which they may avail themselves, as they see fit. In this sense, it already has a kinship with the kinds of ideas – such as primary goods and capabilities – that traditionally figure in theories of distributive justice.

At the same time, the kinds of goods that are counted as recovery capital are in an important way circumscribed, relative to the kind of highly general resources represented by primary goods or capabilities. Unlike the idea of capital itself, recovery capital is not an all-purpose good that might be invested in any end whatsoever. Rather, it is restricted to those goods that might be good for the purpose of recovery. An immediate consequence is that recovery capital is not subject to the objection that we brought against Rawls's account of primary goods. Since recovery capital does not consist of fungible resources such as wealth, it is not the sort of resource such that a greater amount of it might make someone with an addiction, paradoxically, worse off. As recovery capital involves only those goods that are useful from the point of recovery, it is not subject to objections from the fact that many useful goods may, in some circumstances, make the addicted person worse off than she might otherwise be.

Yet, for the very reason that it escapes this objection, the recovery capital approach may seem to be subject to a different kind of objection. It was the inherent generality of primary goods that subjected them to the objection that they might make an addicted person worse off. Yet it is precisely the same generality of primary goods (or of capabilities) that allows them to maintain a liberal indifference toward individuals' plans of life. Primary goods and capabilities are good for a person, whatever her values might be. But recovery capital appears not to be like this. As its name suggests, recovery capital is directed toward recovery. 'Recovery' is understood in different ways, but it is generally understood as prolonged abstinence from the substance or activity to which one is addicted, along with the reestablishment of the kinds of personal and professional relationships that are often diminished by addictive substance use or other addictive activity.

This aspect of recovery capital may appear to make it a poor fit, from the point of view of addiction and distributive justice. For the idea of recovery capital appears to build a quite specific goal into the nature of the good itself, a goal that many people with addictions will not share. This appears to violate the idea that the objects of distributive justice should be neutral with respect to the particular goals of individuals.

There are a couple of ways in which this objection might be met. One is to broaden our understanding of 'recovery.' In Chapter 4, I sketched a conception of recovery somewhat more consonant with the disability view. On this view, the core idea in recovery was not abstinence, but rather the idea of recognizing one's differences and how those differences are discriminated against, and adjusting one's behavior and aims accordingly. This is a process that might lead to abstinence, but it might lead to many other ways of being as well. On this broader understanding of recovery, the notion of recovery capital becomes less monolithic in the values and norms that it seems to imply.

A second way to respond to this objection is to think through the concrete items that are taken to be recovery capital and to think through the nature of these goods, and whether they are subject to the kinds of objections just raised. I will argue that, so understood, they are not. That is, even if we remain skeptical of the notion of recovery, we should still support those goods that go under the name 'recovery capital.' Indeed, I eventually want to suggest, the idea of recovery capital is simply an alternative way of approaching an idea that is already central to the disability model, namely the idea of accommodation itself.

7.8 Understanding Recovery Capital

Cloud and Granfield distinguish four kinds of recovery capital: social capital, market or 'physical' capital, human capital, and cultural capital. Social capital involves the benefits as well as the responsibilities involved in belonging to a social group, be it a family, a church, or some more loosely defined community. Market capital includes capital as traditionally conceived, including wealth and income – in this respect, it comes closest to Rawlsian primary goods a point to which we will return. Human capital consists of 'natural' resources such as physical qualities as well as acquired resources such as educational credentials – it is all that capital that, at first approximation, resides in the individual herself. Finally, cultural capital involves those resources that inhere in one's membership in a given group, one which may be relatively privileged or relatively disenfranchised.

The first thing to note about these resources is that they look very much like the constituents of a good life, on a broad construal of that notion. Most of us wish to have social connections, adequate financial resources, adequate individual endowments, and some degree of relative status. We might reasonably ask: what in these resources is particular to the idea of recovery?

The proper answer to this question is that what makes recovery capital specifically connected to recovery is not the kinds of resources that it involves, but the distinctive purposes to which it tends to be directed. Consider market capital. The specific examples Cloud and Granfield provide of this category involve adequate health insurance and employment that allows for extended medical leave (Cloud & Granfield, 2008, pp. 1973–1974). For market capital, and the varieties of capital more generally, what is important is not the form of capital per se but the uses to which it can be put in providing assistance to people with addictions.

This aspect of recovery capital helps to explain why it is not subject to the kind of objection that we brought against Rawls's account of primary goods. There is no presumption, in recognizing that market capital is needed for recovery, that one is in all cases better off with more financial resources. As we have already observed, an excess of financial resources can in certain cases lead to worse outcomes. But the idea of recovery capital already anticipates this idea. Financial resources are important just insofar as they are actually beneficial to people with addictions. Typically, this will involve ensuring that resources are adequate rather than that they are maximized as much as possible. This is why certain basic and non-fungible goods – such as health insurance and leave from work – are most central to the market component of recovery capital.

This response, which appeals to the limited nature of recovery capital, may seem to invite another objection raised earlier, namely that recovery capital involves too strong a presupposition of what an individual might want, at least when 'recovery' is construed narrowly. What if, for example, someone with an addiction does not want 'recovery,' where this is understood as demanding prolonged abstinence from the substance or activity to which one is addicted? If recovery capital cannot be put to use in advancing other ends, then it may be objected that it demands of its recipients an embrace of a way of life that they may not themselves endorse.

But, when we consider the kinds of resources that in fact constitute recovery capital, this objection loses a great deal of its force. Social connections, financial and individual resources, and status are indeed useful if one's goal is prolonged abstinence from the use of a given substance. But they are also useful if one's goal is continued use while retaining adequate medical and social support. When considered from this point of view, the role of recovery capital begins to converge with that of the kind of harm reduction approaches that we considered earlier. In short, there is a wide range of behaviors and ways of life for people with addictions that may be supported by the sensible provision of recovery capital.[9]

More broadly, we can say that the language of 'recovery capital' is inessential to the theoretical picture that Cloud and Granfield, and those influenced by them, have developed. As we have just seen, the core interest of this model lies in the specific resources and interventions that are captured under the heading of recovery capital rather than with the particular way in which we label them. In fact, the points just made motivate a certain kind of reframing of the idea of recovery capital, one that makes clear its role in a theory of distributive justice and its connections with the core ideas of the disability model.

7.9 From Recovery Capital to Accommodation

What is a different way of framing recovery capital? I believe the disability model suggests such a framing. In particular, we can understand recovery capital in terms of accommodations. More specifically, almost all the resources identified by Cloud and Granfield as kinds of recovery capital would count, on the disability model, as kinds of accommodation.

Consider, for example, social capital. Social connections are supportive of people with addictions, whether they are supportive of abstinence or safe use. Notably, large-scale studies indicate that, in the United States, drug overdose rates are inversely correlated with the existence of social capital in a region (Zoorob & Salemi, 2017). Accordingly, the development and support of social connections can be seen as a key accommodation for people with addictions.[10]

Similar observations apply to financial capital, such as health insurance, or individual capital, such as education.[11] The case of cultural capital is interestingly different. In the foregoing, we have emphasized the significance of discrimination and how much it shapes and hinders the efforts of people with addictions. There are some direct ways in which discrimination might be addressed, for example through anti-discrimination legislation. The idea of cultural capital suggests another way. One way of addressing discrimination against people with addictions may be by raising the relative status of people with addictions, or at least by acknowledging having an addiction as a valid and socially supported identity.[12] In this respect, the idea of cultural capital can be thought of as a specific kind of accommodation for addiction, one specifically addressed toward supporting what is undermined by discrimination against people with addictions.

Thus, most or all of the resources traditionally understood as recovery capital can be understood, instead, as accommodations. This has the advantage of divorcing recovering capital from any particular conception of what people with addictions should have as their goals. If someone's goal is extended abstinence, then these accommodations will be useful for her. If someone's goal is continued use, then these accommodations will be useful for her as well, and will reduce the negative side-effects of use, in this way constituting a kind of harm reduction. These accommodations support a person with addictions, whatever her aims with respect to her addiction might be.

In addition, understanding these resources as accommodations makes clear the moral argument for why a just society should provide these resources to people with addictions. Recovery capital can be seen through a lens of beneficence, as a kind of good that may be provided to people with addictions, when possible, but which is not in any sense obligatory to provide. Accommodations, as I have emphasized, are different. Accommodations are something that a just society is obliged to provide, so long as they are reasonable. They are demanded by the requirements of justice.

The resources typically classified as recovery capital, then, are also accommodations, and thinking of them as accommodations is a better way of understanding them. First, it divorces these resources from any tendentious account of what kinds of goals people with addictions are supposed to have. Second, it illuminates a connection between these resources and the requirements of justice, a connection that I will describe at great length in what follows.

Before coming to that, it will be helpful to consider another question. All or almost all instances of recovery capital, I have argued, are accommodations. Does the converse hold? That is, are all the accommodations that we have considered in the foregoing also instances of recovery capital, so that the idea of accommodation and the idea of recovery capital end up collapsing into one another?

This is not quite the case. Consider the interventions defended by advocates of harm reduction, such as the provision of unused syringes, or nicotine replacement therapy. These are, as I have argued, accommodations. But these are not typically understood as kinds of recovery capital. While recovery capital need not be constitutively connected to a goal of prolonged abstinence, as I argued earlier, it tends to at least be neutral with respect to substance use. In contrast, accommodations such as the provision of unused syringes have the effect of facilitating substance use (while reducing the harms associated with its use). So, these kinds of interventions are instances of accommodations that do not count as recovery capital.

What then is the relationship between recovery capital and accommodation? I want to suggest that recovery capital may be thought of as the most general kind of accommodation. Certain accommodations are useful only to those who are addicted to a particular kind of substance or activity, or who have particular goals concerning their addiction. For example, the provision of unused needles is useful only to those who want to use intravenously injected drugs. But some accommodations are useful to anyone with an addiction, whatever the substance or activity to which they are addicted, and whether their goal is abstinence, safe use, or something else. It is these accommodations that are classed together as recovery capital.

This understanding of recovery capital in terms of accommodations echoes Rawls's account of primary goods. Recovery capital has the kind of neutrality and plan-independence that tends to characterize primary goods. This brings us back to the questions with which we began. Once we are thinking within a framework of accommodations, how should we think about addressing addiction within the framework of distributive justice? What does justice demand that we distribute to people with addictions, and how does the present framework answer the objections that we brought against the answers to this question given in terms of primary goods, or in terms of capabilities? Let us now consider those questions.

7.10 Accommodation and Distribution

Let us return to the distributive predicament with which we began. Consider two people, one of whom has an addiction, and one who does not. For simplicity, let us imagine that neither person has any other disabilities. What is the proper distribution of resources to these two individuals? And by what principles should arrive at an account of this distribution?

Some answers we have considered, and rejected, earlier. One response is to deny that this is the proper way of thinking about the treatment of addiction within the theory of distributive justice. Addiction policy is an important question for any society, but it is something to be decided at some later stage of the process – in what Rawls would call the 'legislative' stage. When we consider fundamental questions of distribution, we should focus on people without addictions, or at least adopt the working assumption that the parties to the deliberative process do not have addictions. Addiction may be dealt with after fundamental issues of distribution are decided.

I indicated earlier that the present approach rejects this stance, which was Rawls's own, both for disability generally and for addiction in particular. It is worth dwelling on the case for this with respect to addiction. Recall that on the present view, once we abstract away from discrimination and exploitation, that characteristic that underlies addiction is a certain kind of volitional diversity. People with addictions have atypical patterns of intention and policy revision. But this is just to say that these patterns are different from those that are typical in a given population, not that they are in any respect worse. Everyone has a distinctive volitional style, so by its nature, a consideration of basic questions of distribution must take into account the fact that people have different volitional styles.[13] From this point of view, the present proposal is not advocating for the inclusion of some group that requires some independent argument in its favor. Rather, the present proposal simply acknowledges the full range of volitional diversity and rejects an arbitrary restriction on that range.

Once we have included people with addictions in the distributive situation, we face the problem described earlier. Should people with addictions receive a different distribution of resources and, if so, what should that difference look like? It can reasonably be expected that people with addictions will be subject to disadvantage, so it is reasonable to think that, if anything, they will deserve a greater measure of resources.[14] But we have already encountered problems with the standard ways of implementing this idea. If we think of distribution in terms of primary goods, and we propose that people with addictions receive a greater distribution of primary goods, then we run up against the seeming paradox that receiving a greater measure of primary goods – and, in particular, income and wealth – may make people with addictions worse off. Even if we shift to an understanding of distributive justice in terms of capabilities – perhaps in light of recognizing that addiction is a disability – the problem of distribution is not solved. The distinctive dynamics of addiction allow for cases in which someone may be strictly worse off than another person even though they are equal in terms of capabilities.

The framework of recovery capital suggests a way out of this kind of problem. If someone has an addiction, then an adequate distribution will allocate to that person a measure of recovery capital. As indicated earlier, the essentially limited and non-fungible aspect of recovery capital is what answers the problem that we raised against thinking of distribution for people with addictions solely in terms of primary goods. Similarly, the focus on specific goods that support people with addictions even in environments that may be unfavorable to them responds to the objection that we brought against thinking of distribution for people with addictions solely in terms of capabilities, at least if capabilities are understood as they traditionally have been in work on distributive justice.[15] By attending to the specific questions that arise for people with addictions, the recovery capital approach addresses the shortcomings of approaches, such as the primary goods approach and the capability approach, that abstract away from these concerns.

We can still ask: accepting that recovery capital should be allocated to people with addictions, just how much recovery capital should be allocated to a given person? The answer is that she should be allocated just so much recovery capital to ensure equality with people who do not have addictions.[16] In this sense, as stated, recovery capital is not a replacement for the framework of primary goods and capabilities. It is not being proposed as the single object of distributive justice. Rather, on the approach suggested here, there should be a degree of pluralism to the objects of distributive justice. In particular, once we recognize the significance of addiction for distributive justice, we should include recovery capital in the scope of resources considered for distribution.[17]

What justifies this asymmetry in distribution, such that the addicted person receives a family of goods (recovery capital) that the non-addicted person does not receive? First, that all individuals are entitled to a just distribution of resources, and that what this means for people with addictions is a certain measure of recovery capital. Second, that people with addictions are people with disabilities, that people with disabilities are entitled to accommodations, and that recovery capital is the most basic and general kind of accommodation for people with addictions. These two arguments – one from general principles of distributive justice, and one from the specific thesis that addiction is a disability – are simply two approaches that converge on a single practical upshot, namely that people with addictions deserve an adequate allocation of recovery capital, where an allocation is adequate just when it redresses any inequalities between people with addictions and people who do not have addictions. This, on the view developed in the foregoing, is simply what justice demands.

7.11 Toward a Politics of Addiction

The questions discussed in this chapter are generally not taken up in philosophical discussions of addiction. Addiction is not generally seen as an issue for political philosophy or, when it is, discussions generally focus on the specific questions of substance policy that we discussed earlier. The idea that people with addictions constitute a class, with specific interests and rights that need to be addressed, is a novel one. Accordingly, most discussions of the politics of addiction are too limited in their scope.

As I indicated at the outset of this chapter, however, a political conception of addiction follows naturally from the disability model. The idea that disability generally is a fundamentally political category – as opposed to, for instance, a medical one – is foundational for the disability rights movement. The present approach simply extends this political conception to the disability that is addiction.

The questions of distributive justice discussed here are foundational to developing a politics of addiction. They are, however, just a beginning. The route to a genuine politics of addiction is a long one, and it will proceed largely outside of the ken of the specifically philosophical questions addressed here. I want to make, however, a few suggestions about what a politics of addiction might look like, and how we might move toward a more political understanding of addiction.

The first area for progress is legal. In the United States, the Americans with Disabilities Act (ADA) has protected at least some people with addictions since its enactment in 1994. Attorneys are just beginning, however, to test the scope and potential impact of these protections. The ADA has the potential to redress significant forms of discrimination and disadvantage for people with addictions, and in this sense to be a practical implementation of some of the political principles elucidated in this chapter. The legal situation in other countries is different, and not always as inclusive of addictions.[18] It may well be that what is required in these countries is not just legal but also legislative work, so that people with addictions receive the same protections in these countries that they do, at least in the letter of the law, in the United States under the ADA.

This legal and legislative process should be one in which people with addictions should be centrally involved. This brings us to a second area for progress, which is the integration of people with addictions into the political work that needs to be done, at every level of that work. 'Nothing about us without us' is a slogan of the disability rights movement, indicating that policies that impact a group should always be informed by the perspectives of people within that group (Charlton, 1998). This is a principle that, I suggest, should be brought to bear on addiction policy as well. Adopting the disability model encourages a shift to institutions and organizations that are led by and for people with addictions, one on which outside experts play an important, but decidedly secondary, role.

This brings us to a third and final area for progress, which concerns the collective identity of addicted people themselves. The disability rights movement has encouraged the significance of identifying oneself as disabled and the role that disabled people as a class have to play in the determination of policy. This is an identity that, I have suggested, encompassed addicted people as well. But there remains a further and complementary step, which is for addicted people to identify as a distinct class themselves, a class that is included within disability, but which has distinctive characteristics of its own.

This is something that has not happened, even in communities that tend to be supportive of the rights and interests of people with addictions. Insofar as people identify as people with addictions, it is often at an individual level, and often in the context of a particular narrative of their own recovery. This way of identifying is important, but it leaves more political needs unmet. In the United States, there is no major national organization that advocates for the needs and interests of addicted people, led by addicted people themselves, in the way that, for example, the National Association of the Deaf advocates for the interests of deaf people.[19] The issues posed by addiction are, ultimately, political ones, and progress on political issues demands collective action. In this way, the next stage in our response to addiction will depend on the forms of organization that addicted people elect for themselves.

Notes

1 This is to say, in the terms of (Rawls, 1971), that one cannot abstract away from disability in the 'original position.' I will consider Rawls's own treatment of disability and objections to it in greater detail later.

2 Another important attempt to conceive of psychological kinds within the framework of distributive justice is Jerome Wakefield's work on 'psychological justice.' Wakefield proposes that the aim of psychological justice is the following: *to treat normal, nondisordered human variation that happens not to match our society's demands and needs and therefore reduces the individual's opportunity for social participation, contribution, and fulfillment ... equipping individuals with a fair complement of the psychological features that our society demands* (Wakefield, 2013, p. 133) This has some points of contact with the view of addiction and distributive justice to be developed here, but with a crucial difference: I hold that the primary aim of justice should not be equipping atypical individuals with more typical psychological features, but rather modifying society itself to accommodate psychological, and more specifically volitional, diversity.

3 This is the second clause of Rawls's second principle of justice, or what is called the 'Difference Principle.' See Rawls (1971, pp. 65–70) for a detailed discussion of this principle and its implications for distribution.

4 This is suggested, for example, in Rawls (1993), where he writes that in the original position 'no one suffers from unusual needs that are especially difficult to fulfill, for example, unusual and costly medical requirements' (Rawls, 1993, p. 18).

5 For a helpful overview of some of these topics, see Wasserman (1998). For an important recent treatment, see Begon (2023).

6 Rawls himself advocates a broader conception of the natural lottery than this, one which extends well beyond genetic endowment, and which may be another reason for being skeptical of this argument from responsibility: *There is no more reason to permit the distribution of income and wealth to be settled by the distribution of natural assets than by historical and social fortune. Furthermore, the principle of fair opportunity can be only imperfectly carried out, at least as long as some form of the family exists. The extent to which natural capacities develop and reach fruition is affected by all kinds of social conditions and class attitudes. Even the willingness to make an effort, to try, and so to be deserving in the ordinary sense is itself dependent upon happy family and social circumstances. It is impossible in practice to secure equal chances of achievement and culture for those similarly endowed, and therefore we may want to adopt a principle which recognizes this fact and also mitigates the arbitrary effects of the natural lottery itself.* (Rawls, 1971, p. 64).

7 For example, the introduction of physical obstacles into the environment might limit someone's capabilities, especially for people who are physically disabled. But in most other cases the enrichment of the environment will leave people's capabilities, at worst, unchanged.

8 Depending on how broadly we construe capabilities, the second and the third responses may not be so distinct from each other. Should we say that there is more to equality than equality of capabilities, or that in order to give a proper account of equality of capability we need to construe capabilities more broadly than is standardly done? To a certain degree this is just a question of phrasing. I think it makes more sense to retain a clear and well-defined notion of capability, which is why I advocate the third response, but one might make similar points in different terms, and so understand this instead as a version of the second response.

9 This is not to say that any goal whatsoever is to be supported. Perhaps goals involving radical degrees of harm, to oneself or others, may not be the sort of enterprises that call for recovery capital. The point of recovery capital is to support a range of activities for people with addictions, including some substance use, which may not necessarily correspond with standard conceptions of what recovery might look like, but this range is not unlimited.

10 Note that, like other forms of recovery capital, what is to be provided is the resources to form social connections rather than social connections themselves. For example, resources might go to support clubs and other forms of free association among people who identify as having addictions.

11 As noted earlier, financial capital is not an unalloyed good; at some point, the unlimited provision of financial capital may itself be harmful. For this reason, the non-fungible character of goods such as health insurance is an important aspect of the kind of financial capital emphasized by the recovery capital modal.

12 See Pickard (2021) for an important discussion of this relationship between addiction and self-identity.

13 This tolerance of volitional variation is already suggested by Rawls himself, as when he writes: *Since each person is free to plan his life as he pleases (so long as his intentions are consistent with the principles of justice), unanimity concerning the standards of rationality is not required. All the theory of justice assumes is that, in the thin account of the good, the evident criteria of rational choice are sufficient to explain the preference for the primary goods, and that such variations as exist in conceptions of rationality do not affect the principles of justice adopted in the original position* (Rawls, 1971, p. 392).

14 This disadvantage is reasonable to expect for it tends to follow from the fact that the volitional tendencies of people with addictions are minority ones and that the majority has incentives to exploit the minority when they can. In deciding on a just distribution, we are not planning for an ideal society, but for one in which people's basic psychologies and tendencies remain roughly as they actually are.

15 Alternatively, as noted earlier, we might widen our notion of a capability if we want to address the distributive questions posed by addiction while retaining the broad outlines of a capability approach to distributive justice.

16 This answer supposes there is such an amount. If there is not, then the task for distribution of recovery capital should be to ensure that people with addictions are brought as close to equality as can reasonably be done.

17 There is also space here to reconsider a more unified approach to the objects of distributive justice. Once we have developed an account of distributive justice for people with addictions that focuses on recovery capital, we might ask whether this notion might itself be widened to accommodate other distributive questions. In this way, the recovery capital approach might ultimately not simply be an approach to distribution and addiction, but an approach to distributive justice more broadly, on equal footing with the primary goods approach and the capability approach.

18 The United Kingdom, for example, explicitly excludes people with addictions from disability protections; see Flacks (2012) for context and discussion.

19 Alcoholics Anonymous is perhaps the closest candidate for such an organization, one which has done vast good and which has long been organized and operated by people who identify as being addicted to alcohol (Gross, 2010). It also, however, deliberately disavows the kind of political ambitions that, I suggest, some organization representative of people with addictions will ultimately need to embrace.

Works Cited

Begon, J. (2023). *Disability through the Lens of Justice*. Oxford University Press.

Charlton, J. (1998). *Nothing about Us without Us: Disability Oppression and Empowerment*. University of California Press.

Cloud, W., & Granfield, R. (2008). Conceptualizing Recovery Capital: Expansion of a Theoretical Construct. *Substance Use & Misuse, 43*(12–13), 1971–1986.

Flacks, S. (2012). Deviant Disabilities: The Exclusion of Drug and Alcohol Addiction from the Equality Act 2010. *Social & Legal Studies, 21*(3), 395–412.

Glei, D.A., & Weinstein, M. (2019). Drug and Alcohol Abuse: The Role of Economic Insecurity. *American Journal of Health Behavior, 43*(4), 838–853.

Gross, M. (2010). Alcoholics Anonymous: Still Sober after 75 Years. *American Journal of Public Health, 100*(12), 2361–2363.

Nussbaum, M.C. (2013). *Creating Capabilities: The Human Development Approach*. Harvard University Press.

Pickard, H. (2021). Addiction and the Self. *Noûs, 55*(4), 737–761.

Rawls, J. (1971). *A Theory of Justice*. Belknap Press.

Rawls, J. (1993). *Political Liberalism*. Columbia University Press.

Robeyns, I., & Byskov, M.F. (2023). The Capability Approach. In E.N. Zalta & U. Nodelman (Eds.), *The Stanford Encyclopedia of Philosophy. Metaphysics Research Lab*. Stanford University.

Sen, A. (1980). *Equality of What?* Cambridge University Press.

Siebers, T. (2008). *Disability Theory.* University of Michigan Press.

Silvers, A., Wasserman, D.T., & Mahowald, M.B. (1998). *Disability, Difference, Discrimination: Perspectives on Justice in Bioethics and Public Policy.* Rowman & Littlefield.

Stark, C.A. (2007). How to Include the Severely Disabled in a Contractarian Theory of Justice. *Journal of Political Philosophy, 15*(2), 127–145.

Wakefield, J.C. (2013). DSM-5 and Clinical Social Work: Mental Disorder and Psychological Justice as Goals of Clinical Intervention. *Clinical Social Work Journal, 41*, 131–138.

Zoorob, M.J., & Salemi, J.L. (2017). Bowling Alone, Dying Together: The Role of Social Capital in Mitigating the Drug Overdose Epidemic in the United States. *Drug and Alcohol Dependence, 173*, 1–9.

CONCLUSION

The view of addiction that I have developed in the foregoing is one that, if I have been successful, should stand on its own. I have said, as clearly as I can, what the case is for thinking addiction is a disability, and what kind of disability exactly is involved in addiction. I have also explained the practical implications of this view, some of which are already being practiced and some of which remain to be tried. There is doubtless more to be said about all these issues. But the reader should at this point have a decent sense of what the disability view of addiction is and what it implies.

There is a further question, however, of whether any given reader in fact believes or accepts the disability view. None of the considerations I have given earlier are, I think, absolutely decisive. There may be areas where consensus is reasonable to expect, but addiction is not at this point among them. The topic of addiction is vexed enough, and the arguments that bear on it are diverse enough, that it is reasonable to expect some measure of disagreement about addiction. The disability view, then, is one which many people will, on consideration, reject. This is a general dialectical feature of views of addiction, at least at this point in the ongoing evolution of our understanding, and it is a feature that any appropriately modest proponent of an account of addiction should be willing to accept.

There is however an additional distinctive aspect of the disability view that puts it in a more complicated dialectical position than most other views of addiction. While it is true that everyone must decide individually whether to accept the disability view, the decisions of some people carry, by the lights of the disability view itself, a special weight. In particular, as I have said, the decision of people with addictions themselves carries special

DOI: 10.4324/9781003410263-9

weight. Since disability is to some degree a self-selecting category, such that the question of whether one is disabled hinges in part on the question of whether one identifies as disabled, the validity of the disability view will depend in part on whether a critical mass of people with addictions judge, on reflection, the disability view to be correct.

I indicated at the outset that the conditions for adequate reflection have not yet generally been met. The view that addiction is a disability is sufficiently novel, at least to most people, that we are not yet in a position to decide whether it is, on consideration, true. Yet, if someone has made it to this point in the book, then she plausibly may have reached a point where she has reflected enough. And she can ask herself, if she identifies as an addicted person: does this view describe me?

If enough people with addictions answer this question affirmatively, this should make us more confident in the disability view. Conversely, we should consider what would follow if most people with addictions, having asked themselves this question, answer negatively. If that were the case, then I think we should be willing to at least consider revising or altogether abandoning the disability view. In this sense, the disability view is beholden, in the end, to the testimony and judgment of those whom it purports to describe.

This brings us, finally, to my own story. I have a history of addiction, and it informs, inevitably, how I myself see the disability view. I do not claim that my experience, such as it is, gives me any privileged insight or advantage in understanding addiction. But I do claim that the fact that I accept my own view, as an addicted person, has a special weight. If nothing else, the demand for deference is met in at least one case. I can look at the disability view and say: yes, that is me, that is how it was, and how it still is.

In the course of working on this book, I have often felt uncertain about how much of my own history to share. What are the expectations for disclosure, for someone working on the topic of addiction? A cursory reading of recent work on addiction might suggest the expectations are relatively high. There are a significant number of excellent memoirs about addiction. Tellingly, even non-fiction works that propose theoretical accounts of addiction are interwoven with accounts of the author's own experience with addiction.[1] There seems to be a kind of presumption in favor of disclosure, at least when one aims to say something new or provocative about addiction.

On the one hand, this presumption is understandable. Addiction is a topic that affects many people in profound ways, and it seems fair to ask someone who purports to make a claim about addiction whether she herself has been so affected. On the other hand, this presumption can seem curious. We do not ask cardiologists to disclose their history of heart disease, nor do we ask experts on religious history to disclose their personal religious beliefs. Indeed, in both cases, an over-reliance on personal experience can seem intellectually unwise. So, while there does seem to be some such presumption in favor of disclosure, the case for it seems decidedly mixed, and to depend in part on how we are understanding addiction.

At this point, it is instructive to appeal to the understanding suggested by the disability view. Once we think of addiction as a disability, how should we think about disclosure? The first implication of the disability view is that there should be no presumption or expectation of disclosure. The question of whether a given person has a disability is up to that person to disclose, and we should resist any presumption or expectation for her to make that disclosure in any given way. This principle is a legal one under the ADA, which generally prohibits, for example, employers from asking job candidates about their disability status. But we may also think of it, more broadly, as a social or moral one, according to which disclosure is left altogether to the preferences of the person whose disclosure it is to make.

Reflection on the disability view, however, also suggests another aspect of disclosure. For many disabilities, the choice between disclosure and non-disclosure is not always an option, at least relative to many contexts. It will often be clear in many physical environments whether a certain person is blind or not, especially as physical environments are typically structured to serve the interests of sighted people. In this sense, the decision to disclose one's disability is not always a decision over which a disabled person has full control. In many cases, the disclosure is effectively forced by the discriminatory environment itself.

Addiction, however, is not this kind of disability, at least not typically. One can be addicted and yet have most or all people in one's environment be unaware of it. This can include casual acquaintances, but it can also include one's professional colleagues and even one's most intimate relationships. Addiction can in this sense be an 'invisible' disability. This is especially so when the primary object of one's addiction is a substance, like alcohol, whose use is socially permissible, or even socially encouraged.

Reflection on this asymmetry is part of what has led me to be more open, in contexts like these, about my own addiction history. I have stressed throughout the analogies between addiction and more commonly recognized disabilities. But one important difference is that addiction is often, as I have said, invisible. In thinking about the burdens of discrimination and exploitation, it is hard to disregard how these burdens fall on those who do not have the option of hiding their disability, as I typically do. Disclosure is, in this way, a form of solidarity. I do not say that this is mandatory or even advisable for anyone else with an addiction – I have emphasized that people with addictions have a basic right to privacy and should not be expected to disclose anything – but simply that these are some of the considerations that have moved me.

Another consideration, as I have said, is deference. Among the weightiest objections that might be brought against the disability view is that people with addictions find it implausible or inaccurate to their own experience. I have tried to acknowledge the force of this kind of consideration, but I also want to underscore that I, on reflection, do not see it this way. On the contrary, this view fits well with my own experience of addiction and helps to articulate what it means, to me, to be a person with an addiction.[2] This reaction is not at all decisive, but it is, at least, one piece of evidence in favor of the disability view.

These are the sorts of considerations that lead me to mention that I have a history of alcohol addiction, or alcohol use disorder. I was fortunate to avoid a number of the severe outcomes faced by many people with alcohol addictions, notably gradual or sudden death. Overall, however, my main recollection of my alcohol use is one of struggle. Many things were harder when I was actively using alcohol than they are now: writing, maintaining connections with family and friends, and even making doctor's and dentist's appointments. But none of these things was impossible. Nor, now that I am not using alcohol, do I find any of these things effortless. Rather, speaking now just for myself, life's challenges felt more challenging when I was actively addicted to alcohol.

This is precisely what we should expect on the disability view. If someone is blind, she is not incapable of pursuing her projects, or the various benefits and responsibilities of everyday life. But she will often find these more challenging than do people who are not blind. This is in large part because society is generally structured with an indifference to the needs of people who are not sighted. Accordingly, life as a blind person will be more challenging than life as a person who is not blind.

That is at least part of what is going on, I want to say, in cases of addiction, including my own. Addiction is not a defective state whether the defect is understood morally or medically. Rather, it is a state of difference, specifically of a difference that is systematically discriminated against and exploited. Accordingly, life with an addiction will be much more difficult than it needs to be.

There are many ways in which someone can respond to this difficulty. In my case, I gradually came to abstain completely from the use of alcohol. I have not used alcohol in over six years, at the time of this writing. For several reasons, I choose not to disclose how precisely I came to be abstinent, or the supports that I use in my continued abstinence. This too is a set of considerations that will vary from person to person, and that each person will resolve in her own way.

While I have been abstinent for several years, I still identify as having an addiction. This too is a decision that each person with an addiction must make on their own. Many people with a history of addiction would not count themselves as currently addicted. Indeed, many clinicians would not regard me as meeting the criteria for any kind of substance use disorder, as five years is one standard threshold for full remission (Worley, 2017). I think of myself, however, as still having an addiction. And, if we accept the disability view, as I do, this is an identity where a person's own decision carries considerable, and typically, decisive, weight. Finally, since I accept the disability view, I therefore think of myself as a person with this disability, namely the disability that is addiction.

As I have emphasized at length, my own view is not decisive, nor is that of any individual addicted person. After all, there are many people with an experience of addiction and they disagree widely with one another, as their own views are often idiosyncratic and sometimes, I would hazard, simply false. There are limits to deference. Nonetheless, I do think that a threshold for the acceptability of the disability view is that a critical mass of people with addictions, on reflection, accept it. I myself accept it, but that is not sufficient. At best, my attitude toward the view is a case study in how someone may accept the disability view reflectively and also use it to frame their own experience and identity. In this respect, I have found the disability view useful. Whether other people with addictions will so find it is a question that remains to be answered.

There is an understanding of disability, and specifically physical disability, that is sometimes called the 'tragedy' model. On this model, a physical disability is an extremely bad outcome that befalls a person, and the appropriate response to that outcome is beneficence: in the emotional mode, pity, and, in the practical mode, charity. If a person has a physical disability, her life is in virtue of that fact suboptimal, and the appropriate response of the people around her is to remedy that fact, insofar as they can.

This view is naturally extended to addiction too. If someone is a promising athlete who does not follow through on their initial promise due to developing an opiate addiction, this is a tragedy. Or, if someone who has traditionally performed well academically finds herself failing out of college due to alcohol use, that is a tragedy. Addiction is a tragedy that, regrettably but inevitably, befalls certain people while sparing others.

We should reject the tragedy model of addiction. Addiction is not a tragedy, but a different way in which the will might be structured, one which is systematically discriminated against and exploited. There are many ways in which an addicted individual may respond to this fact, and one common response is abstinence from the substance or activity to which one is addicted.

This is not how prolonged abstinence is commonly understood. There is a tendency to think of abstinence in terms of success and to think that sustained abstinence, and the social goods that often accompany it, as a kind of achievement, or a triumph over a tragedy. But there is no triumph here, for there was no tragedy to begin with. Abstinence is simply one kind of adaptive response to recognizing a disconnect between the structure of one's will, on the one hand, and the ways in which society happens to be structured, on the other.

This brings us, again, to the question of recovery. In the last chapter, I suggested that we should reconceive what is normally referred to as 'recovery capital' in terms more amenable to the disability view. There I suggested that we should understand recovery capital, instead, in terms of accommodation. But that proposal leaves unresolved a fundamental question, which I broached in Chapter 4 but which bears revisiting now. What should do the work of the idea of 'recovery' itself, once we have accepted the disability view?

There is, as I suggested in the earlier discussion, no simple answer to this question. The natural history of addiction is heterogeneous, and the phenomena that tend to be described as 'recovery' are diverse in their forms. Sometimes this denotes a gradual process, and sometimes a sudden one. Sometimes 'recovery' denotes complete abstinence from use, as in my case, and sometimes it involves instead a return to typical or moderate use. There are countless ways this process may go, and this is an area where the demands of deference are especially strong. Ultimately it is up to addicted people themselves to decide what, if anything, will take the place of recovery.

Speaking from my case, perhaps the most important aspect of what is left out in the idea of 'recovery' is its focus on the individual. Recovery is something that happens to an individual and essentially involves a change that happens in that individual. Speaking for myself – that is, appealing both to my own experience and to the disability view of addiction – this seems to be too narrow an understanding of what addiction involves. Often, what goes under the name 'recovery' is less a matter of changing oneself than it is of recognizing certain facts, not always pleasing facts, about one's relationship to the world that one inhabits, and learning how one can adjust one's choices in light of those facts.

To describe the ways in which the world should adjust itself to people with addictions, I have used the language of accommodation. To describe the ways in which individuals with addiction should adjust themselves to the world as they find it, we might speak instead of reconciliation. By reconciliation, I mean a process by which one acknowledges the idiosyncrasies of one's own will, and the idiosyncrasies of the world as one finds it, and tries to bring these into closer agreement, insofar as one can. It may be that much of what goes under the name of recovery, of people with addictions becoming better or becoming well, is better understood in terms of reconciliation.

Throughout this discussion I have insisted on the boundary between the disability view, a certain model of what addiction is, and my personal experience with addiction, which I have outlined briefly earlier. At this point in the discussion, the boundary between these becomes less sharp. The reconciliation model is a certain conception of one form that the natural history of addiction might take, a form that is often called recovery. But is informed just as much by own experience and judgment as it is by the letter of the disability view, and it should be understood in that spirit.

It is left to the reader, then, to decide what might stand in for the language of recovery. This is a task that has already been set for anyone with an addiction, at least anyone who might identify as being 'in recovery' without thereby thinking of herself as being or having in any way been, flawed or defective. The disability view, which articulates an account of what addiction is, offers one foundation for elaborating such an account, an account of what comes after recovery. But we can expect that this account will differ from person to person, and that the forms that it may take will be various.

Notes

1 Some important books in this genre include Marc Lewis, *Memoirs of an Addicted Brain* (Lewis, 2012), Gabor Maté, *In The Realm of Hungry Ghosts* (Maté, 2011), and Maia Szalavitz, *Unbroken Brain* (Szalavitz, 2016).
2 In describing my own experience, at least in this context, I prefer to use the same person-centered language that I have used throughout this book. This may be a good point to add a personal note on terminology. I do not like being described as an 'addict' – the term feels, speaking just for myself, stigmatizing and insulting. Other people with addictions feel differently and are of course free to choose for themselves which label feels most suitable. But is a distinctly uncomfortable feeling to read or participate in academic discussions that freely use this term, as many still do. I recognize there are arguments for embracing this kind of language, but I think it worthwhile to register the shudder I feel whenever I hear myself described in this way.

Works Cited

Lewis, M. (2012). *Memoirs of an Addicted Brain*. PublicAffairs.
Maté, G. (2011). *In the Realm of Hungry Ghosts*. North Atlantic Books.
Szalavitz, M. (2016). *Unbroken Brain: A Revolutionary New Way of Understanding Addiction*. St. Martin's.
Worley, J. (2017). Recovery in Substance Use Disorders: What to Know to Inform Practice. *Issues in Mental Health Nursing*, *38*(1), 80–91.

INDEX